Instant Vortex Air Fryer Oven Cookbook

600 Affordable and Delicious Air Fryer Oven Recipes for Cooking Easier, Faster, And More Enjoyable for You and Your Family!

Dianh Braden

Marye Soudar

Table of contents

Introduction

Air Fryer Ovens are making a new buzz in the food tech market, these appliances have practically brought all the kitchen gadgets, that we routinely use, in a single unit. An Air fryer oven has a peculiar electric oven built with a heating mechanism so dynamic that it can Air fry the food, roast it, bake it, dehydrate it, and toast it. Ever since Air fryer ovens became widely popular among professionals, several tech giants have stepped and launched a variety of Air Fryer ovens equipped state of the art technology. Instant Vortex Air fryer oven has become a new highlight in this regard, as it is built with adjustable working space and multifunctioning cooking modes. Similarly, Cosori is another good name in the market that has yet again impressed its customers with an amazing multipurpose Air fryer oven. Like any other electric oven, these Air fryer ovens are also controlled by a user-friendly control panel. By using their button and rotating dials, the users can easily switch between the cooking modes, and change the temperature and time settings as required. Here in this cookbook, the major focus is to give all its readers a huge collection of recipes that can be easily cooked in an Air fryer oven.

Chapter 1: Breakfast & Brunch Recipes

Eggs in Avocado Cups

Preparation Time: 10 minutes; Cooking Time: 10 minutes; Servings: 2

Ingredients:

- 1 avocado, halved and pitted
- 2 large eggs
- Salt and ground black pepper, as required
- 2 cooked bacon slices, crumbled

Method:

1. Carefully, scoop out about 2 teaspoons of flesh from each avocado half.
2. Crack 1 egg in each avocado half and sprinkle with salt and black pepper.
3. Press "Power Button" of Air Fry Oven and turn the dial to select the "Air Roast" mode.
4. Press the Time button and again turn the dial to set the cooking time to 10 minutes.
5. Now push the Temp button and rotate the dial to set the temperature at 375 degrees F.
6. Press "Start/Pause" button to start.
7. When the unit beeps to show that it is preheated, open the lid and line the "Sheet Pan" with a lightly, grease piece of foil.
8. Arrange avocado halves into the "Sheet Pan" and insert in the oven.
9. Top each avocado half with bacon pieces and serve.

Nutritional Information per Serving:

Calories 300; Total Fat 26.6 g; Saturated Fat 6.4 g; Cholesterol 190 mg; Sodium 229 mg

Cinnamon French Toasts

Preparation Time: 10 minutes; Cooking Time: 5 minutes; Servings: 2

Ingredients:

- 2 eggs
- ¼ cup whole milk
- 3 tablespoons sugar
- 2 teaspoons olive oil
- 1/8 teaspoon vanilla extract
- 1/8 teaspoon ground cinnamon
- 4 bread slices

Method:

1. In a large bowl, mix together all the ingredients except bread slices.
2. Coat the bread slices with egg mixture evenly.
3. Press "Power Button" of Air Fry Oven and turn the dial to select the "Air Fry" mode.
4. Press the Time button and again turn the dial to set the cooking time to 6 minutes.
5. Now push the Temp button and rotate the dial to set the temperature at 390 degrees F.
6. Press "Start/Pause" button to start.
7. When the unit beeps to show that it is preheated, open the lid and lightly, grease the sheet pan.
8. Arrange the bread slices into "Air Fry Basket" and insert in the oven.
9. Flip the bread slices once halfway through.
10. Serve warm.

Nutritional Information per Serving:

Calories 238; Total Fat 10.6 g; Saturated Fat 2.7 g; Cholesterol 167 mg; Sodium 122 mg

Sweet Spiced Toasts

Preparation Time: 10 minutes; Cooking Time: 5 minutes; Servings: 3

Ingredients:

- ¼ cup sugar
- ½ teaspoon ground cinnamon
- 1/8 teaspoon ground cloves
- 1/8 teaspoon ground ginger
- ½ teaspoons vanilla extract
- ¼ cup salted butter, softened

- 6 bread slices

Method:
1. In a bowl, add the sugar, vanilla, cinnamon, pepper, and butter. Mix until smooth.
2. Spread the butter mixture evenly over each bread slice.
3. Press "Power Button" of Air Fry Oven and turn the dial to select the "Air Fry" mode.
4. Press the Time button and again turn the dial to set the cooking time to 4 minutes.
5. Now push the Temp button and rotate the dial to set the temperature at 400 degrees F.
6. Press "Start/Pause" button to start.
7. When the unit beeps to show that it is preheated, open the lid and lightly, grease the sheet pan.
8. Arrange the bread slices into "Air Fry Basket" buttered-side up and insert in the oven.
9. Serve warm.

Nutritional Information per Serving:
Calories 250; Total Fat 16 g; Saturated Fat 9.9 g; Cholesterol 41 mg; Sodium 232 mg

Savory French Toast

Preparation Time: 10 minutes; Cooking Time: 5 minutes; Servings: 2
Ingredients:
- ¼ cup chickpea flour
- 3 tablespoons onion, finely chopped
- 2 teaspoons green chili, seeded and finely chopped
- ½ teaspoon red chili powder
- ¼ teaspoon ground turmeric
- ¼ teaspoon ground cumin
- Salt, to taste
- Water, as needed
- 4 bread slices

Method:
1. Add all the ingredients except bread slices in a large bowl and mix until a thick mixture form.
2. With a spoon, spread the mixture over both sides of each bread slice.
3. Arrange the bread slices into the lightly greased the sheet pan.
4. Press "Power Button" of Air Fry Oven and turn the dial to select the "Air Fry" mode.
5. Press the Time button and again turn the dial to set the cooking time to 5 minutes.
6. Now push the Temp button and rotate the dial to set the temperature at 390 degrees F.
7. Press "Start/Pause" button to start.
8. When the unit beeps to show that it is preheated, open the lid and lightly, grease sheet pan.
9. Arrange the bread slices into "Air Fry Basket" and insert in the oven.
10. Flip the bread slices once halfway through.
11. Serve warm.

Nutritional Information per Serving:
Calories 151; Total Fat 2.3 g; Saturated Fat 0.3 g; Cholesterol 0 mg; Sodium 234 mg

Cheddar Mustard Toasts

Preparation Time: 10 minutes; Cooking Time: 10 minutes; Servings: 2
Ingredients:
- 4 bread slices
- 2 tablespoons cheddar cheese, shredded
- 2 eggs, whites and yolks, separated
- 1 tablespoon mustard
- 1 tablespoon paprika

Method:
1. In a clean glass bowl, add the egg whites in and beat until they form soft peaks.
2. In another bowl, mix together the cheese, egg yolks, mustard, and paprika.
3. Gently, fold in the egg whites.

4. Spread the mustard mixture over the toasted bread slices.
5. Press "Power Button" of Air Fry Oven and turn the dial to select the "Air Fry" mode.
6. Press the Time button and again turn the dial to set the cooking time to 10 minutes.
7. Now push the Temp button and rotate the dial to set the temperature at 355 degrees F.
8. Press "Start/Pause" button to start.
9. When the unit beeps to show that it is preheated, open the lid and lightly, grease the sheet pan.
10. Arrange the bread slices into "Air Fry Basket" and insert in the oven.
11. Serve warm.

Nutritional Information per Serving:
Calories 175; Total Fat 9.4 g; Saturated Fat 3.1 g; Cholesterol 171 mg; Sodium 229 mg

Pickled Toasts

Preparation Time: 10 minutes; Cooking Time: 5 minutes; Servings: 2
Ingredients:
- 4 bread slices, toasted
- 2 tablespoons unsalted butter, softened
- 2 tablespoons Branston pickle
- ¼ cup Parmesan cheese, grated

Method:
1. Spread butter over bread slices evenly, followed by Branston pickle.
2. Top with cheese evenly.
3. Press "Power Button" of Air Fry Oven and turn the dial to select the "Air Fry" mode.
4. Press the Time button and again turn the dial to set the cooking time to 5 minutes.
5. Now push the Temp button and rotate the dial to set the temperature at 390 degrees F.
6. Press "Start/Pause" button to start.
7. When the unit beeps to show that it is preheated, open the lid and lightly, grease the sheet pan.
8. Arrange the bread slices into "Air Fry Basket" and insert in the oven.
9. Serve warm.

Nutritional Information per Serving:
Calories 211; Total Fat 14.5 g; Saturated Fat 8.6 g; Cholesterol 39 mg; Sodium 450 mg

Ricotta Toasts with Salmon

Preparation Time: 10 minutes; Cooking Time: 4 minutes; Servings: 2
Ingredients:
- 4 bread slices
- 1 garlic clove, minced
- 8 oz. ricotta cheese
- 1 teaspoon lemon zest
- Freshly ground black pepper, to taste
- 4 oz. smoked salmon

Method:
1. In a food processor, add the garlic, ricotta, lemon zest and black pepper and pulse until smooth.
2. Spread ricotta mixture over each bread slices evenly.
3. Press "Power Button" of Air Fry Oven and turn the dial to select the "Air Fry" mode.
4. Press the Time button and again turn the dial to set the cooking time to 4 minutes.
5. Now push the Temp button and rotate the dial to set the temperature at 355 degrees F.
6. Press "Start/Pause" button to start.
7. When the unit beeps to show that it is preheated, open the lid and lightly, grease the sheet pan.
8. Arrange the bread slices into "Air Fry Basket" and insert in the oven.
9. Top with salmon and serve.

Calories 274; Total Fat 12 g; Saturated Fat 6.3 g; Cholesterol 48 mg; Sodium 1300 mg

Pumpkin Pancakes

Preparation Time: 15 minutes; Cooking Time: 12 minutes; Servings: 4

Ingredients:

- 1 square puff pastry
- 3 tablespoons pumpkin filling
- 1 small egg, beaten

Method:

1. Roll out a square of puff pastry and layer it with pumpkin pie filling, leaving about ¼-inch space around the edges.
2. Cut it up into 8 equal sized square pieces and coat the edges with beaten egg.
3. Press "Power Button" of Air Fry Oven and turn the dial to select the "Air Fry" mode.
4. Press the Time button and again turn the dial to set the cooking time to 12 minutes.
5. Now push the Temp button and rotate the dial to set the temperature at 355 degrees F.
6. Press "Start/Pause" button to start.
7. When the unit beeps to show that it is preheated, open the lid.
8. Arrange the squares into a greased "Sheet Pan" and insert in the oven.
9. Serve warm.

Nutritional Information per Serving:

Calories 109; Total Fat 6.7 g; Saturated Fat 1.8 g; Cholesterol 34 mg; Sodium 87 mg

Zucchini Fritters

Preparation Time: 15 minutes; Cooking Time: 7 minutes; Servings: 4

Ingredients:

- 10½ oz. zucchini, grated and squeezed
- 7 oz. Halloumi cheese
- ¼ cup all-purpose flour
- 2 eggs
- 1 teaspoon fresh dill, minced
- Salt and ground black pepper, as required

Method:

1. In a large bowl and mix together all the ingredients.
2. Make a small-sized fritter from the mixture.
3. Press "Power Button" of Air Fry Oven and turn the dial to select the "Air Fry" mode.
4. Press the Time button and again turn the dial to set the cooking time to 7 minutes.
5. Now push the Temp button and rotate the dial to set the temperature at 355 degrees F.
6. Press "Start/Pause" button to start.
7. When the unit beeps to show that it is preheated, open the lid.
8. Arrange fritters into grease "Sheet Pan" and insert in the oven.
9. Serve warm.

Nutritional Information per Serving:

Calories 253; Total Fat 17.2 g; Saturated Fat 11 g; Cholesterol 121 mg; Sodium 333 mg

Sweet Potato Rosti

Preparation Time: 15 minutes; Cooking Time: 15 minutes; Servings: 2

Ingredients:

- ½ lb. sweet potatoes, peeled, grated and squeezed
- 1 tablespoon fresh parsley, chopped finely
- Salt and ground black pepper, as required
- 2 tablespoons sour cream

Method:

1. In a large bowl, mix together the grated sweet potato, parsley, salt, and black pepper.
2. Press "Power Button" of Air Fry Oven and turn the dial to select the "Air Fry" mode.
3. Press the Time button and again turn the dial to set the cooking time to 15 minutes.
4. Now push the Temp button and rotate the dial to set the temperature at 355 degrees F.
5. Press "Start/Pause" button to start.
6. When the unit beeps to show that it is preheated, open the lid and lightly, grease the sheet pan.
7. Arrange the sweet potato mixture into the "Sheet Pan" and shape it into an even circle.
8. Insert the "Sheet Pan" in the oven.
9. Cut the potato rosti into wedges.
10. Top with the sour cream and serve immediately.

Nutritional Information per Serving:
Calories 160; Total Fat 2.7 g; Saturated Fat 1.6 g; Cholesterol 5 mg; Sodium 95mg

Cheddar & Cream Omelet

Preparation Time: 10 minutes; Cooking Time: 8 minutes; Servings: 2
Ingredients:
- 4 eggs
- ¼ cup cream
- Salt and ground black pepper, as required
- ¼ cup Cheddar cheese, grated

Method:
1. In a bowl, add the eggs, cream, salt, and black pepper and beat well.
2. Place the egg mixture into a small baking pan.
3. Press "Power Button" of Air Fry Oven and turn the dial to select the "Air Fry" mode.
4. Press the Time button and again turn the dial to set the cooking time to 8 minutes.
5. Now push the Temp button and rotate the dial to set the temperature at 350 degrees F.
6. Press "Start/Pause" button to start.
7. When the unit beeps to show that it is preheated, open the lid.
8. Arrange pan over the "Wire Rack" and insert in the oven.
9. After 4 minutes, sprinkle the omelet with cheese evenly.
10. Cut the omelet into 2 portions and serve hot.
11. Cut into equal-sized wedges and serve hot.

Nutritional Information per Serving:
Calories 202; Total Fat 15.1 g; Saturated Fat 6.8 g; Cholesterol 348 mg; Sodium 298 mg

Onion Omelet

Preparation Time: 10 minutes; Cooking Time: 15 minutes; Servings: 2
Ingredients:
- 4 eggs
- ¼ teaspoon low-sodium soy sauce
- Ground black pepper, as required
- 1 teaspoon butter
- 1 medium yellow onion, sliced
- ¼ cup Cheddar cheese, grated

Method:
1. In a skillet, melt the butter over medium heat and cook the onion and cook for about 8-10 minutes.
2. Remove from the heat and set aside to cool slightly.
3. Meanwhile, in a bowl, add the eggs, soy sauce and black pepper and beat well.
4. Add the cooked onion and gently, stir to combine.
5. Place the zucchini mixture into a small baking pan.
6. Press "Power Button" of Air Fry Oven and turn the dial to select the "Air Fry" mode.
7. Press the Time button and again turn the dial to set the cooking time to 5 minutes.

8. Now push the Temp button and rotate the dial to set the temperature at 355 degrees F.
9. Press "Start/Pause" button to start.
10. When the unit beeps to show that it is preheated, open the lid.
11. Arrange pan over the "Wire Rack" and insert in the oven.
12. Cut the omelet into 2 portions and serve hot.

Nutritional Information per Serving:
Calories 222; Total Fat 15.4 g; Saturated Fat 6.9 g; Cholesterol 347 mg; Sodium 264 mg

Zucchini Omelet

Preparation Time: 15 minutes; Cooking Time: 14 minutes; Servings: 2
Ingredients:
- 1 teaspoon butter
- 1 zucchini, julienned
- 4 eggs
- ¼ teaspoon fresh basil, chopped
- ¼ teaspoon red pepper flakes, crushed
- Salt and ground black pepper, as required

Method:
1. In a skillet, melt the butter over medium heat and cook the zucchini for about 3-4 minutes.
2. Remove from the heat and set aside to cool slightly.
3. Meanwhile, in a bowl, mix together the eggs, basil, red pepper flakes, salt, and black pepper.
4. Add the cooked zucchini and gently, stir to combine.
5. Place the zucchini mixture into a small baking pan.
6. Press "Power Button" of Air Fry Oven and turn the dial to select the "Air Fry" mode.
7. Press the Time button and again turn the dial to set the cooking time to 10 minutes.
8. Now push the Temp button and rotate the dial to set the temperature at 355 degrees F.
9. Press "Start/Pause" button to start.
10. When the unit beeps to show that it is preheated, open the lid.
11. Arrange pan over the "Wire Rack" and insert in the oven.
12. Cut the omelet into 2 portions and serve hot.

Nutritional Information per Serving:
Calories 159; Total Fat 10.9 g; Saturated Fat 4 g; Cholesterol 332 mg; Sodium 224 mg

Mushroom & Pepperoncini Omelet

Preparation Time: 15 minutes; Cooking Time: 20 minutes; Servings: 2
Ingredients:
- 3 large eggs
- ¼ c milk
- Salt and ground black pepper, as required
- ½ cup cheddar cheese, shredded
- ¼ cup cooked mushrooms
- 3 pepperoncini peppers, sliced thinly
- ½ tablespoon scallion, sliced thinly

Method:
1. In a bowl, add the eggs, milk, salt and black pepper and beat well.
2. Place the mixture into a greased baking pan.
3. Press "Power Button" of Air Fry Oven and turn the dial to select the "Air Bake" mode.
4. Press the Time button and again turn the dial to set the cooking time to 20 minutes.
5. Now push the Temp button and rotate the dial to set the temperature at 350 degrees F.
6. Press "Start/Pause" button to start.
7. When the unit beeps to show that it is preheated, open the lid.
8. Arrange pan over the "Wire Rack" and insert in the oven.
9. Cut into equal-sized wedges and serve hot.

Nutritional Information per Serving:

Calories 254; Total Fat 17.5 g; Saturated Fat 8.7 g; Cholesterol 311 mg; Sodium 793 mg

Chicken Omelet

Preparation Time: 10 minutes; Cooking Time: 16 minutes; Servings: 2
Ingredients:

- 1 teaspoon butter
- 1 small yellow onion, chopped
- ½ jalapeño pepper, seeded and chopped
- 3 eggs
- Salt and ground black pepper, as required
- ¼ cup cooked chicken, shredded

Method:

1. In a frying pan, melt the butter over medium heat and cook the onion for about 4-5 minutes.
2. Add the jalapeño pepper and cook for about 1 minute.
3. Remove from the heat and set aside to cool slightly.
4. Meanwhile, in a bowl, add the eggs, salt, and black pepper and beat well.
5. Add the onion mixture and chicken and stir to combine.
6. Place the chicken mixture into a small baking pan.
7. Press "Power Button" of Air Fry Oven and turn the dial to select the "Air Fry" mode.
8. Press the Time button and again turn the dial to set the cooking time to 6 minutes.
9. Now push the Temp button and rotate the dial to set the temperature at 355 degrees F.
10. Press "Start/Pause" button to start.
11. When the unit beeps to show that it is preheated, open the lid.
12. Arrange pan over the "Wire Rack" and insert in the oven.
13. Cut the omelet into 2 portions and serve hot.

Nutritional Information per Serving:

Calories 153; Total Fat 9.1 g; Saturated Fat 3.4 g; Cholesterol 264 mg; Sodium 196 mg

Chicken & Zucchini Omelet

Preparation Time: 15 minutes; Cooking Time: 35 minutes; Servings: 6
Ingredients:

- 8 eggs
- ½ cup milk
- Salt and ground black pepper, as required
- 1 cup cooked chicken, chopped
- 1 cup Cheddar cheese, shredded
- ½ cup fresh chives, chopped
- ¾ cup zucchini, chopped

Method:

1. In a bowl, add the eggs, milk, salt and black pepper and beat well.
2. Add the remaining ingredients and stir to combine.
3. Place the mixture into a greased baking pan.
4. Press "Power Button" of Air Fry Oven and turn the dial to select the "Air Bake" mode.
5. Press the Time button and again turn the dial to set the cooking time to 35 minutes.
6. Now push the Temp button and rotate the dial to set the temperature at 315 degrees F.
7. Press "Start/Pause" button to start.
8. When the unit beeps to show that it is preheated, open the lid.
9. Arrange pan over the "Wire Rack" and insert in the oven.
10. Cut into equal-sized wedges and serve hot.

Nutritional Information per Serving:

Calories 209; Total Fat 13.3 g; Saturated Fat 6.3 g; Cholesterol 258 mg; Sodium 252 mg

Pepperoni Omelet

Preparation Time: 15 minutes; Cooking Time: 12 minutes; Servings: 2
Ingredients:

- 4 eggs
- 2 tablespoons milk
- Pinch of salt
- Ground black pepper, as required
- 8-10 turkey pepperoni slices

Method:

1. In a bowl, crack the eggs and beat well.
2. Add the remaining ingredients and gently, stir to combine.
3. Place the mixture into a baking pan.
4. Press "Power Button" of Air Fry Oven and turn the dial to select the "Air Fry" mode.
5. Press the Time button and again turn the dial to set the cooking time to 12 minutes.
6. Now push the Temp button and rotate the dial to set the temperature at 355 degrees F.
7. Press "Start/Pause" button to start.
8. When the unit beeps to show that it is preheated, open the lid.
9. Arrange pan over the "Wire Rack" and insert in the oven.
10. Cut into equal-sized wedges and serve hot.

Nutritional Information per Serving:
Calories 149; Total Fat 10 g; Saturated Fat 3.3 g; Cholesterol 337 mg; Sodium 350 mg

Sausage Omelet

Preparation Time: 10 minutes; Cooking Time: 13 minutes; Servings: 2
Ingredients:

- 4 eggs
- 1 bacon slice, chopped
- 2 sausages, chopped
- 1 yellow onion, chopped

Method:

1. In a bowl, crack the eggs and beat well.
2. Add the remaining ingredients and gently, stir to combine.
3. Place the mixture into a baking pan.
4. Press "Power Button" of Air Fry Oven and turn the dial to select the "Air Fry" mode.
5. Press the Time button and again turn the dial to set the cooking time to 13 minutes.
6. Now push the Temp button and rotate the dial to set the temperature at 320 degrees F.
7. Press "Start/Pause" button to start.
8. When the unit beeps to show that it is preheated, open the lid.
9. Arrange pan over the "Wire Rack" and insert in the oven.
10. Cut into equal-sized wedges and serve hot.

Nutritional Information per Serving:
Calories 325; Total Fat 23.1 g; Saturated Fat 7.4 g; Cholesterol 368 mg; Sodium 678 mg

Pancetta & Hot Dogs Omelet

Preparation Time: 10 minutes; Cooking Time: 10 minutes; Servings: 2
Ingredients:

- 4 eggs
- ¼ teaspoon dried parsley
- ¼ teaspoon dried rosemary
- 1 pancetta slice, chopped
- 2 hot dogs, chopped
- 2 small onions, chopped

Method:

1. In a bowl, crack the eggs and beat well.
2. Add the remaining ingredients and gently, stir to combine.
3. Place the mixture into a baking pan.

4. Press "Power Button" of Air Fry Oven and turn the dial to select the "Air Fry" mode.
5. Press the Time button and again turn the dial to set the cooking time to 10 minutes.
6. Now push the Temp button and rotate the dial to set the temperature at 320 degrees F.
7. Press "Start/Pause" button to start.
8. When the unit beeps to show that it is preheated, open the lid.
9. Arrange pan over the "Wire Rack" and insert in the oven.
10. Cut into equal-sized wedges and serve hot.

Nutritional Information per Serving:
Calories 282; Total Fat 19.3 g; Saturated Fat 6.5 g; Cholesterol 351mg; Sodium 632 mg

Egg & Tofu Omelet

Preparation Time: 15 minutes; Cooking Time: 10 minutes; Servings: 2
Ingredients:
- 1 teaspoon arrowroot starch
- 2 teaspoons water
- 3 eggs
- 2 teaspoons fish sauce
- 1 teaspoon olive oil
- Ground black pepper, as required
- 8 oz. silken tofu, pressed and sliced

Method:
1. In a large bowl, dissolve arrowroot starch in water.
2. Add the eggs, fish sauce, oil and black pepper and beat well.
3. Place tofu in the bottom of a greased baking pan and top with the egg mixture.
4. Press "Power Button" of Air Fry Oven and turn the dial to select the "Air Fry" mode.
5. Press the Time button and again turn the dial to set the cooking time to 10 minutes.
6. Now push the Temp button and rotate the dial to set the temperature at 390 degrees F.
7. Press "Start/Pause" button to start.
8. When the unit beeps to show that it is preheated, open the lid.
9. Arrange pan over the "Wire Rack" and insert in the oven.
10. Cut into equal-sized wedges and serve hot.

Nutritional Information per Serving:
Calories 192; Total Fat 12 g; Saturated Fat 2.8g; Cholesterol 246mg; Sodium 597 mg

Eggs, Tofu & Mushroom Omelet

Preparation Time: 15 minutes; Cooking Time: 35 minutes; Servings: 2
Ingredients:
- 2 teaspoons canola oil
- ¼ of onion, chopped
- 1 garlic clove, minced
- 8 oz. silken tofu, pressed and sliced
- 3½ oz. fresh mushrooms, sliced
- Salt and ground black pepper, as needed
- 3 eggs, beaten

Method:
1. In a skillet, heat the oil over medium heat and sauté the onion, and garlic for about 4-5 minutes.
2. Add the mushrooms and cook for about 4-5 minutes.
3. Remove from the heat and stir in the tofu, salt and black pepper.
4. Place the tofu mixture into a pan and top with the beaten eggs.
5. Press "Power Button" of Air Fry Oven and turn the dial to select the "Air Fry" mode.
6. Press the Time button and again turn the dial to set the cooking time to 25 minutes.
7. Now push the Temp button and rotate the dial to set the temperature at 355 degrees F.
8. Press "Start/Pause" button to start.
9. When the unit beeps to show that it is preheated, open the lid.
10. Arrange pan over the "Wire Rack" and insert in the oven.

11. Cut into equal-sized wedges and serve hot.
Nutritional Information per Serving:
Calories 224; Total Fat 14.5 g; Saturated Fat 2.9 g; Cholesterol 246 mg; Sodium 214 mg

Mini Mushroom Frittatas

Preparation Time: 15 minutes; Cooking Time: 17 minutes; Servings: 2
Ingredients:
- 1 tablespoon olive oil
- ½ of onion, sliced thinly
- 2 cups button mushrooms, sliced thinly
- 3 eggs
- Salt and ground black pepper, as required
- 3 tablespoons feta cheese, crumbled

Method:
1. In a frying pan, heat the oil over medium heat and cook the onion and mushroom for about 5 minutes.
2. Remove from the heat and set aside to cool slightly.
3. Meanwhile, in a small bowl, add the eggs, salt and black pepper and beat well.
4. Divide the beaten eggs in 2 greased ramekins evenly and top with the mushroom mixture.
5. Press "Power Button" of Air Fry Oven and turn the dial to select the "Air Fry" mode.
6. Press the Time button and again turn the dial to set the cooking time to 12 minutes.
7. Now push the Temp button and rotate the dial to set the temperature at 330 degrees F.
8. Press "Start/Pause" button to start.
9. When the unit beeps to show that it is preheated, open the lid.
10. Arrange the ramekins over the "Wire Rack" and insert in the oven.
11. Serve hot.

Nutritional Information per Serving:
Calories 218; Total Fat 16.8 g; Saturated Fat 5.2 g; Cholesterol 258 mg; Sodium 332 mg

Tomato Frittata

Preparation Time: 10 minutes; Cooking Time: 30 minutes; Servings: 2
Ingredients:
- 4 eggs
- ¼ cup onion, chopped
- ½ cup tomatoes, chopped
- ½ cup milk
- 1 cup Gouda cheese, shredded
- Salt, as required

Method:
1. In a small baking pan, add all the ingredients and mix well.
2. Press "Power Button" of Air Fry Oven and turn the dial to select the "Air Fry" mode.
3. Press the Time button and again turn the dial to set the cooking time to 30 minutes.
4. Now push the Temp button and rotate the dial to set the temperature at 340 degrees F.
5. Press "Start/Pause" button to start.
6. When the unit beeps to show that it is preheated, open the lid.
7. Arrange the baking pan over the "Wire Rack" and insert in the oven.
8. Cut into 2 wedges and serve.

Nutritional Information per Serving:
Calories 247; Total Fat 16.1 g; Saturated Fat 7.5 g; Cholesterol 332 mg; Sodium 417 mg

Mushroom Frittata

Preparation Time: 15 minutes; Cooking Time: 36 minutes; Servings: 4
Ingredients:
- 2 tablespoons olive oil
- 1 shallot, sliced thinly
- 2 garlic cloves, minced
- 4 cups white mushrooms, chopped

- 6 large eggs
- ¼ teaspoon red pepper flakes, crushed
- Salt and ground black pepper, as required
- ½ teaspoon fresh dill, minced
- ½ cup cream cheese, softened

Method:
1. In a skillet, heat the oil over medium heat and cook the shallot, mushrooms and garlic for about 5-6 minutes, stirring frequently.
2. Remove from the heat and transfer the mushroom mixture into a bowl.
3. In another bowl, add the eggs, red pepper flakes, salt and black peppers and beat well.
4. Add the mushroom mixture and stir to combine.
5. Place the egg mixture into a greased baking pan and sprinkle with the dill.
6. Spread cream cheese over egg mixture evenly.
7. Press "Power Button" of Air Fry Oven and turn the dial to select the "Air Fry" mode.
8. Press the Time button and again turn the dial to set the cooking time to 30 minutes.
9. Now push the Temp button and rotate the dial to set the temperature at 330 degrees F.
10. Press "Start/Pause" button to start.
11. When the unit beeps to show that it is preheated, open the lid.
12. Arrange pan over the "Wire Rack" and insert in the oven.
13. Cut into equal-sized wedges and serve

Nutritional Information per Serving:
Calories 290; Total Fat 24.8g; Saturated Fat 9.7 g; Cholesterol 311 mg; Sodium 236 mg

Mixed Veggies Frittata

Preparation Time: 15 minutes; Cooking Time: 21 minutes; Servings: 4
Ingredients:
- ½ teaspoon olive oil
- 4 fresh mushrooms, sliced
- 4 eggs
- 3 tablespoons heavy cream
- Salt, as required
- 4 tablespoons Cheddar cheese, grated
- 4 tablespoons fresh spinach, chopped
- 3 grape tomatoes, halved
- 2 tablespoons fresh mixed herbs, chopped
- 1 scallion, sliced

Method:
1. In a skillet, heat the oil over medium heat and cook the mushrooms for about 5-6 minutes, stirring frequently.
2. Remove from the heat and transfer the mushroom into a bowl.
3. In a bowl, add the eggs, cream and salt and beat well.
4. Add the mushroom and remaining ingredients and stir to combine.
5. Place the mixture into a greased baking pan evenly.
6. Press "Power Button" of Air Fry Oven and turn the dial to select the "Air Fry" mode.
7. Press the Time button and again turn the dial to set the cooking time to 15 minutes.
8. Now push the Temp button and rotate the dial to set the temperature at 350 degrees F.
9. Press "Start/Pause" button to start.
10. When the unit beeps to show that it is preheated, open the lid.
11. Arrange pan over the "Wire Rack" and insert in the oven.
12. Cut into equal-sized wedges and serve.

Nutritional Information per Serving:
Calories 159; Total Fat 11.7 g; Saturated Fat 5.6 g; Cholesterol 187 mg; Sodium 156 mg

Pancetta & Spinach Frittata

Preparation Time: 15 minutes; Cooking Time: 16 minutes; Servings: 2

Ingredients:
- ¼ cup pancetta
- ½ of tomato, cubed
- ¼ cup fresh baby spinach
- 3 eggs
- Salt and ground black pepper, as required
- ¼ cup Parmesan cheese, grated

Method:
1. Heat a nonstick skillet over medium heat and cook the pancetta for about 5 minutes.
2. Add the tomato and spinach cook for about 2-3 minutes.
3. Remove from the heat and drain the grease from skillet.
4. Set aside to cool slightly.
5. Meanwhile, in a small bowl, add the eggs, salt and black pepper and beat well.
6. In the bottom of a greased baking pan, place the pancetta mixture and top with the eggs, followed by the cheese.
7. Press "Power Button" of Air Fry Oven and turn the dial to select the "Air Fry" mode.
8. Press the Time button and again turn the dial to set the cooking time to 8 minutes.
9. Now push the Temp button and rotate the dial to set the temperature at 355 degrees F.
10. Press "Start/Pause" button to start.
11. When the unit beeps to show that it is preheated, open the lid.
12. Arrange pan over the "Wire Rack" and insert in the oven.
13. Cut into equal-sized wedges and serve.

Nutritional Information per Serving:
Calories 287; Total Fat 20.8g; Saturated Fat 7.2 g; Cholesterol 285 mg; Sodium 915 mg

Bacon, Mushroom & Tomato Frittata

Preparation Time: 15 minutes; Cooking Time: 16 minutes; Servings: 2
Ingredients:
- 1 cooked bacon slice, chopped
- 6 cherry tomatoes, halved
- 6 fresh mushrooms, sliced
- Salt and ground black pepper, as required
- 3 eggs
- 1 tablespoon fresh parsley, chopped
- ¼ cup Parmesan cheese, grated

Method:
1. In a baking pan, add the bacon, tomatoes, mushrooms, salt, and black pepper and mix well.
2. Press "Power Button" of Air Fry Oven and turn the dial to select the "Air Fry" mode.
3. Press the Time button and again turn the dial to set the cooking time to 16 minutes.
4. Now push the Temp button and rotate the dial to set the temperature at 320 degrees F.
5. Press "Start/Pause" button to start.
6. When the unit beeps to show that it is preheated, open the lid.
7. Arrange pan over the "Wire Rack" and insert in the oven.
8. Meanwhile, in a bowl, add the eggs and beat well.
9. Add the parsley and cheese and mix well.
10. After 6 minutes of cooking, top the bacon mixture with egg mixture evenly.
11. Cut into equal-sized wedges and serve.

Nutritional Information per Serving:
Calories 228; Total Fat 15.5 g; Saturated Fat 5.3 g; Cholesterol 270 mg; Sodium 608 mg

Sausage, Spinach & Broccoli Frittata

Preparation Time: 15 minutes; Cooking Time: 30 minutes; Servings: 4
Ingredients:

- 1 teaspoon butter
- 6 turkey sausage links, cut into small pieces
- 1 cup broccoli florets, cut into small pieces
- ½ cup fresh spinach, chopped up
- 6 eggs
- 1/8 teaspoon hot sauce
- 2 tablespoons half-and-half
- 1/8 teaspoon garlic salt
- Salt and ground black pepper, as required
- ¾ cup Cheddar cheese, shredded

Method:
1. In a skillet, melt the butter over medium heat and cook the sausage for about 7-8 minutes or until browned.
2. Add the broccoli and cook for about 3-4 minutes.
3. Add the spinach and cook for about 2-3 minutes.
4. Remove from the heat and set aside to cool slightly.
5. Meanwhile, in a bowl, add the eggs, half-and-half, hot sauce, garlic salt, salt and black pepper and beat until well combined.
6. Add the cheese and stir to combine.
7. In the bottom of a lightly greased pan, place the broccoli mixture and to with the egg mixture.
8. Press "Power Button" of Air Fry Oven and turn the dial to select the "Air Bake" mode.
9. Press the Time button and again turn the dial to set the cooking time to 15 minutes.
10. Now push the Temp button and rotate the dial to set the temperature at 400 degrees F.
11. Press "Start/Pause" button to start.
12. When the unit beeps to show that it is preheated, open the lid.
13. Arrange pan over the "Wire Rack" and insert in the oven.
14. Cut into equal-sized wedges and serve hot.

Nutritional Information per Serving:
Calories 339; Total Fat 27.4g; Saturated Fat 11.6 g; Cholesterol 229 mg; Sodium 596 mg

Sausage & Scallion Frittata

Preparation Time: 15 minutes; Cooking Time: 20 minutes; Servings: 2
Ingredients:
- ¼ lb. cooked breakfast sausage, crumbled
- ½ cup Cheddar cheese, shredded
- 4 eggs, beaten lightly
- 2 scallions, chopped
- Pinch of cayenne pepper

Method:
1. In a bowl, add the sausage, cheese, eggs, scallion and cayenne and mix until well combined.
2. Place the mixture into a greased baking pan.
3. Press "Power Button" of Air Fry Oven and turn the dial to select the "Air Fry" mode.
4. Press the Time button and again turn the dial to set the cooking time to 20 minutes.
5. Now push the Temp button and rotate the dial to set the temperature at 360 degrees F.
6. Press "Start/Pause" button to start.
7. When the unit beeps to show that it is preheated, open the lid.
8. Arrange pan over the "Wire Rack" and insert in the oven.
9. Cut into equal-sized wedges and serve hot.

Nutritional Information per Serving:
Calories 437; Total Fat 32.4 g; Saturated Fat 13.9 g; Cholesterol 405 mg; Sodium 726 mg

Trout Frittata

Preparation Time: 15 minutes; Cooking Time: 25 minutes; Servings: 4

Ingredients:

- 1 tablespoon olive oil
- 1 onion, sliced
- 6 eggs
- ½ tablespoon horseradish sauce
- 2 tablespoons crème fraiche
- 2 hot-smoked trout fillets, chopped
- ¼ cup fresh dill, chopped

Method:

1. In a skillet, heat the oil over medium heat and cook the onion for about 4-5 minutes.
2. Remove from the heat and set aside.
3. Meanwhile, in a bowl, add the eggs, horseradish sauce, and crème fraiche and mix well.
4. In the bottom of a baking pan, place the cooked onion and top with the egg mixture, followed by trout.
5. Press "Power Button" of Air Fry Oven and turn the dial to select the "Air Fry" mode.
6. Press the Time button and again turn the dial to set the cooking time to 20 minutes.
7. Now push the Temp button and rotate the dial to set the temperature at 320 degrees F.
8. Press "Start/Pause" button to start.
9. When the unit beeps to show that it is preheated, open the lid.
10. Arrange pan over the "Wire Rack" and insert in the oven.
11. Cut into equal-sized wedges and serve with the garnishing of dill.

Nutritional Information per Serving:
Calories 258; Total Fat 15.7 g; Saturated Fat 3.9g; Cholesterol 288 mg; Sodium 141 mg

Mini Macaroni Quiches

Preparation Time: 15 minutes; Cooking Time: 20 minutes; Servings: 4
Ingredients:

- 1 short crust pastry
- ½ cup leftover macaroni n' cheese
- 2 tablespoons plain Greek yogurt
- 1 teaspoon garlic puree
- 11 oz. milk
- 2 large eggs
- 2 tablespoons Parmesan cheese, grated

Method:

1. Dust 4 ramekins with a little flour.
2. Line the bottom of prepared ramekins with short crust pastry.
3. In a bowl, mix together macaroni, yogurt and garlic.
4. Transfer the macaroni mixture between ramekins about ¾ full.
5. In a small bowl, add the milk and eggs and beat well.
6. Place the egg mixture over the macaroni mixture and top with the cheese evenly.
7. Press "Power Button" of Air Fry Oven and turn the dial to select the "Air Fry" mode.
8. Press the Time button and again turn the dial to set the cooking time to 20 minutes.
9. Now push the Temp button and rotate the dial to set the temperature at 355 degrees F.
10. Press "Start/Pause" button to start.
11. When the unit beeps to show that it is preheated, open the lid.
12. Arrange the ramekins over the "Wire Rack" and insert in the oven.
13. Serve hot.

Nutritional Information per Serving:
Calories 209; Total Fat 10.4 g; Saturated Fat 2.9 g; Cholesterol 102 mg; Sodium 135 mg

Tomato Quiche

Preparation Time: 15 minutes; Cooking Time: 30 minutes; Servings: 2
Ingredients:

- 4 eggs
- ¼ cup onion, chopped
- ½ cup tomatoes, chopped
- ½ cup milk

- 1 cup Gouda cheese, shredded
- Salt, as required

Method:
1. In a small baking pan, add all the ingredients and mix well.
2. Press "Power Button" of Air Fry Oven and turn the dial to select the "Air Fry" mode.
3. Press the Time button and again turn the dial to set the cooking time to 30 minutes.
4. Now push the Temp button and rotate the dial to set the temperature at 340 degrees F.
5. Press "Start/Pause" button to start.
6. When the unit beeps to show that it is preheated, open the lid.
7. Arrange pan over the "Wire Rack" and insert in the oven.
8. Cut into equal-sized wedges and serve.

Nutritional Information per Serving:
Calories 247; Total Fat 16.1 g; Saturated Fat 7.5 g; Cholesterol 332 mg; Sodium 417 mg

Chicken & Broccoli Quiche

Preparation Time: 15 minutes; Cooking Time: 12 minutes; Servings: 2
Ingredients:
- ½ of frozen ready-made pie crust
- ¼ tablespoon olive oil
- 1 small egg
- 3 tablespoons cheddar cheese, grated
- 1½ tablespoons whipping cream
- Salt and freshly ground black pepper, as needed
- 3 tablespoons boiled broccoli, chopped
- 2 tablespoons cooked chicken, chopped

Method:
1. Cut 1 (5-inch) round from the pie crust.
2. Arrange the pie crust round in a small pie pan and gently, press in the bottom and sides.
3. In a bowl, mix together the egg, cheese, cream, salt, and black pepper.
4. Pour the egg mixture over dough base and top with the broccoli and chicken.
5. Press "Power Button" of Air Fry Oven and turn the dial to select the "Air Fry" mode.
6. Press the Time button and again turn the dial to set the cooking time to 12 minutes.
7. Now push the Temp button and rotate the dial to set the temperature at 390 degrees F.
8. Press "Start/Pause" button to start.
9. When the unit beeps to show that it is preheated, open the lid.
10. Arrange pan over the "Wire Rack" and insert in the oven.
11. Cut into equal-sized wedges and serve.

Nutritional Information per Serving:
Calories 197; Total Fat 15 g; Saturated Fat 5.9 g; Cholesterol 99 mg; Sodium 184 mg

Salmon Quiche

Preparation Time: 15 minutes; Cooking Time: 20 minutes; Servings: 2
Ingredients:
- 5½ oz. salmon fillet, chopped
- Salt and ground black pepper, as required
- ½ tablespoon fresh lemon juice
- 1 egg yolk
- 3½ tablespoons chilled butter
- 2/3 cup flour
- 1 tablespoon cold water
- 2 eggs
- 3 tablespoons whipping cream
- 1 scallion, chopped

Method:
1. In a bowl, mix together the salmon, salt, black pepper and lemon juice.
2. In another bowl, add the egg yolk, butter, flour and water and mix until a dough forms.
3. Place the dough onto a floured smooth surface and roll into about 7-inch round.

4. Place the dough in a quiche pan and press firmly in the bottom and along the edges.
5. Trim the excess edges.
6. In a small bowl, add the eggs, cream, salt and black pepper and beat until well combined.
7. Place the cream mixture over crust evenly and top with the salmon mixture, followed by the scallion.
8. Press "Power Button" of Air Fry Oven and turn the dial to select the "Air Fry" mode.
9. Press the Time button and again turn the dial to set the cooking time to 20 minutes.
10. Now push the Temp button and rotate the dial to set the temperature at 355 degrees F.
11. Press "Start/Pause" button to start.
12. When the unit beeps to show that it is preheated, open the lid.
13. Arrange pan over the "Wire Rack" and insert in the oven.
14. Cut into equal-sized wedges and serve.

Nutritional Information per Serving:
Calories 592; Total Fat 39 g; Saturated Fat 20.1 g; Cholesterol 381 mg; Sodium 331 mg

Bacon & Spinach Quiche

Preparation Time: 15 minutes; Cooking Time: 10 minutes; Servings: 4
Ingredients:
- 2 cooked bacon slices, chopped
- ½ cup fresh spinach, chopped
- ¼ cup mozzarella cheese, shredded
- ½ cup Parmesan cheese, shredded
- 2 tablespoons milk
- 2 dashes Tabasco sauce
- Salt and ground black pepper, as required

Method:
1. In a bowl, add all ingredients and mix well.
2. Transfer the mixture into a baking pan.
3. Press "Power Button" of Air Fry Oven and turn the dial to select the "Air Fry" mode.
4. Press the Time button and again turn the dial to set the cooking time to 10 minutes.
5. Now push the Temp button and rotate the dial to set the temperature at 320 degrees F.
6. Press "Start/Pause" button to start.
7. When the unit beeps to show that it is preheated, open the lid.
8. Arrange pan over the "Wire Rack" and insert in the oven.
9. Cut into equal-sized wedges and serve hot.

Nutritional Information per Serving:
Calories 130; Total Fat 9.3 g; Saturated Fat 4 g; Cholesterol 25 mg; Sodium 561 mg

Sausage & Mushroom Casserole

Preparation Time: 15 minutes; Cooking Time: 19 minutes; Servings: 6
Ingredients:
- 1 tablespoon olive oil
- ½ lb. spicy ground sausage
- ¾ cup yellow onion, chopped
- 5 fresh mushrooms, sliced
- 8 eggs, beaten
- ½ teaspoon garlic salt
- ¾ cup Cheddar cheese, shredded and divided
- ¼ cup Alfredo sauce

Method:
1. In a skillet, heat the oil over medium heat and cook the sausage and onions for about 4-5 minutes.
2. Add the mushrooms and cook for about 6-7 minutes.
3. Remove from the oven and drain the grease from skillet.
4. In a bowl, add the sausage mixture, beaten eggs, garlic salt, ½ cup of cheese and Alfredo sauce and stir to combine.

5. Place the sausage mixture into a baking pan.
6. Press "Power Button" of Air Fry Oven and turn the dial to select the "Air Fry" mode.
7. Press the Time button and again turn the dial to set the cooking time to 12 minutes.
8. Now push the Temp button and rotate the dial to set the temperature at 390 degrees F.
9. Press "Start/Pause" button to start.
10. When the unit beeps to show that it is preheated, open the lid.
11. Arrange pan over the "Wire Rack" and insert in the oven.
12. After 6 minutes of cooking, stir the sausage mixture well.
13. Cut into equal-sized wedges and serve with the topping of remaining cheese.

Nutritional Information per Serving:
Calories 319; Total Fat 24.5 g; Saturated Fat 9.1 g; Cholesterol 267 mg; Sodium 698 mg

Sausage & Bell Pepper Casserole

Preparation Time: 15 minutes; Cooking Time: 25 minutes; Servings: 6
Ingredients:

- 1 teaspoon olive oil
- 1 lb. ground sausage
- 1 green bell pepper, seeded and chopped
- ¼ cup onion, chopped
- 8 eggs, beaten
- ½ cup Colby Jack cheese, shredded
- 1 teaspoon fennel seed
- ½ teaspoon garlic salt

Method:
1. In a skillet, heat the oil over medium heat and cook the sausage for about 4-5 minutes.
2. Add the bell pepper and onion and cook for about 4-5 minutes.
3. Remove from the heat and transfer the sausage mixture into a bowl to cool slightly.
4. In a baking pan, place the sausage mixture and top with the cheese, followed by the beaten eggs, fennel seed and garlic salt.
5. Press "Power Button" of Air Fry Oven and turn the dial to select the "Air Fry" mode.
6. Press the Time button and again turn the dial to set the cooking time to 15 minutes.
7. Now push the Temp button and rotate the dial to set the temperature at 390 degrees F.
8. Press "Start/Pause" button to start.
9. When the unit beeps to show that it is preheated, open the lid.
10. Arrange pan over the "Wire Rack" and insert in the oven.
11. Cut into equal-sized wedges and serve hot.

Nutritional Information per Serving:
Calories 394; Total Fat 1.1 g; Saturated Fat 10.8 g; Cholesterol 290 mg; Sodium 709 mg

Turkey & Yogurt Casserole

Preparation Time: 10 minutes; Cooking Time: 25 minutes; Servings: 4
Ingredients:

- 6 eggs
- ½ cup plain Greek yogurt
- ½ cup cooked turkey meat, chopped
- Salt and ground black pepper, as required
- ½ cup sharp Cheddar cheese, shredded

Method:
1. In a bowl, add the egg and yogurt and beat well.
2. Add the remaining ingredients and stir to combine.
3. In a greased baking pan, place the egg mixture.
4. Press "Power Button" of Air Fry Oven and turn the dial to select the "Air Bake" mode.
5. Press the Time button and again turn the dial to set the cooking time to 25 minutes.
6. Now push the Temp button and rotate the dial to set the temperature at 375 degrees F.

7. Press "Start/Pause" button to start.
8. When the unit beeps to show that it is preheated, open the lid.
9. Arrange pan over the "Wire Rack" and insert in the oven.
10. Cut into equal-sized wedges and serve.

Nutritional Information per Serving:

Calories 203; Total Fat 12.5 g; Saturated Fat 5.6 g; Cholesterol 275 mg; Sodium 253 mg

Ham & Hashbrown Casserole

Preparation Time: 15 minutes; Cooking Time: 35 minutes; Servings: 5

Ingredients:

- 1½ tablespoons olive oil
- ½ of large onion, chopped
- 24 oz. frozen hashbrowns
- 3 eggs
- 2 tablespoons milk
- Salt and ground black pepper, as required
- ½ lb. ham, chopped
- ¼ cup Cheddar cheese, shredded

Method:

1. In a skillet, heat the oil over medium heat and sauté the onion for about 4-5 minutes.
2. Remove from the heat and transfer the onion into a bowl.
3. Add the hashbrowns and mix well.
4. Place the mixture into a baking pan.
5. Press "Power Button" of Air Fry Oven and turn the dial to select the "Air Bake" mode.
6. Press the Time button and again turn the dial to set the cooking time to 32 minutes.
7. Now push the Temp button and rotate the dial to set the temperature at 350 degrees F.
8. Press "Start/Pause" button to start.
9. When the unit beeps to show that it is preheated, open the lid.
10. Arrange pan over the "Wire Rack" and insert in the oven.
11. Stir the mixture once after 8 minutes.
12. Meanwhile, in a bowl, add the eggs, milk, salt and black pepper and beat well.
13. After 15 minutes of cooking, place the egg mixture over hashbrown mixture evenly and top with the ham.
14. After 30 minutes of cooking, sprinkle the casserole with the cheese.
15. Cut into equal-sized wedges and serve.

Nutritional Information per Serving:

Calories 540; Total Fat 29.8 g; Saturated Fat 6.5 g; Cholesterol 131 mg; Sodium 1110 mg

Eggs with Ham

Preparation Time: 15 minutes; Cooking Time: 13 minutes; Servings: 2

Ingredients:

- 2 teaspoons unsalted butter, softened
- 2 oz. ham, sliced thinly
- 4 large eggs, divided
- Salt and ground black pepper, as required
- 2 tablespoons heavy cream
- 1/8 teaspoon smoked paprika
- 3 tablespoons Parmesan cheese, grated finely
- 2 teaspoons fresh chives, minced

Method:

1. In the bottom of a baking pan, spread butter.
2. Arrange the ham slices over the butter.
3. In a bowl, add 1egg, salt, black pepper and cream and beat until smooth.
4. Place the egg mixture over the ham slices evenly.
5. Carefully, crack the remaining eggs on top and sprinkle with paprika, salt, black pepper, cheese and chives evenly.

6. Press "Power Button" of Air Fry Oven and turn the dial to select the "Air Fry" mode.
7. Press the Time button and again turn the dial to set the cooking time to 13 minutes.
8. Now push the Temp button and rotate the dial to set the temperature at 320 degrees F.
9. Press "Start/Pause" button to start.
10. When the unit beeps to show that it is preheated, open the lid.
11. Arrange pan over the "Wire Rack" and insert in the oven.
12. Cut into equal-sized wedges and serve.

Nutritional Information per Serving:
Calories 302; Total Fat 23.62 g; Saturated Fat 10.7 g; Cholesterol 425 mg; Sodium 685 mg

Eggs with Turkey & Spinach

Preparation Time: 15 minutes; Cooking Time: 23 minutes; Servings: 4
Ingredients:

- 1 tablespoon unsalted butter
- 1 lb. fresh baby spinach
- 4 eggs
- 7 oz. cooked turkey, chopped
- 4 teaspoons milk
- Salt and ground black pepper, as required

Method:
1. In a skillet, melt the butter over medium heat and cook the spinach for about 2-3 minutes or until just wilted.
2. Remove from the heat and transfer the spinach into a bowl.
3. Set aside to cool slightly.
4. Divide the spinach into 4 greased ramekins, followed by the turkey.
5. Crack 1 egg into each ramekin and drizzle with milk.
6. Sprinkle with salt and black pepper.
7. Press "Power Button" of Air Fry Oven and turn the dial to select the "Air Fry" mode.
8. Press the Time button and again turn the dial to set the cooking time to 20 minutes.
9. Now push the Temp button and rotate the dial to set the temperature at 355 degrees F.
10. Press "Start/Pause" button to start.
11. When the unit beeps to show that it is preheated, open the lid.
12. Arrange ramekins over the "Wire Rack" and insert in the oven.
13. Serve hot.

Nutritional Information per Serving:
Calories 201; Total Fat 10.3 g; Saturated Fat 4.1 g; Cholesterol 209 mg; Sodium 248 mg

Eggs with Ham & Veggies

Preparation Time: 15 minutes; Cooking Time: 15 minutes; Servings: 2
Ingredients:

- 1 teaspoon olive oil
- 6 small button mushroom, quartered
- 6 cherry tomatoes, halved
- 4 slices shaved ham
- 2 tablespoons spinach, chopped
- 1 cup cheddar cheese, shredded
- 2 eggs
- 1 tablespoon fresh rosemary, chopped
- Salt and ground black pepper, as required

Method:
1. In a skillet, heat the oil over medium heat and cook the mushrooms for about 6-7 minutes.
2. Remove from the heat and set aside to cool slightly.
3. In a bowl, mix together the mushrooms, tomatoes, ham and greens.
4. Place half of the vegetable mixture in a greased baking pan and top with half of the cheese.

5. Repeat the layers once.
6. Make 2 wells in the mixture.
7. Carefully, crack 1 eggs in each well and sprinkle with rosemary, salt and black pepper.
8. Press "Power Button" of Air Fry Oven and turn the dial to select the "Air Fry" mode.
9. Press the Time button and again turn the dial to set the cooking time to 8 minutes.
10. Now push the Temp button and rotate the dial to set the temperature at 390 degrees F.
11. Press "Start/Pause" button to start.
12. When the unit beeps to show that it is preheated, open the lid.
13. Arrange ramekins over the "Wire Rack" and insert in the oven.
14. Serve hot.

Nutritional Information per Serving:
Calories 424; Total Fat 30.7 g; Saturated Fat 15.4 g; Cholesterol 255 mg; Sodium 1140 mg

Eggs in Bread & Tomato Cups

Preparation Time: 15 minutes; Cooking Time: 12 minutes; Servings: 2
Ingredients:
- ½ teaspoon butter
- 2 bread slices
- 1 pancetta slice, chopped
- 4 tomato slices
- 1 tablespoon Mozzarella cheese, shredded
- 2 eggs
- 1/8 teaspoon maple syrup
- 1/8 teaspoon balsamic vinegar
- ¼ teaspoon fresh parsley, chopped
- Salt and freshly ground pepper, to taste

Method:
1. Line each prepared ramekin with 1 bread slice.
2. Divide bacon and tomato slices over bread slice evenly in each ramekin.
3. Top with the cheese evenly.
4. Crack 1 egg in each ramekin over cheese.
5. Drizzle with maple syrup and balsamic vinegar and then sprinkle with parsley, salt and black pepper.
6. Press "Power Button" of Air Fry Oven and turn the dial to select the "Air Fry" mode.
7. Press the Time button and again turn the dial to set the cooking time to 12 minutes.
8. Now push the Temp button and rotate the dial to set the temperature at 320 degrees F.
9. Press "Start/Pause" button to start.
10. When the unit beeps to show that it is preheated, open the lid.
11. Arrange the ramekins over the "Wire Rack" and insert in the oven.
12. Serve warm.

Nutritional Information per Serving:
Calories 219; Total Fat 14.2 g; Saturated Fat 5.5 g; Cholesterol 190 mg; Sodium 628 mg

Eggs in Bread & Sausage Cups

Preparation Time: 10 minutes; Cooking Time: 22 minutes; Servings: 2
Ingredients:
- ¼ cup cream
- 3 eggs
- 2 cooked sausages, sliced
- 1 bread slice, cut into sticks
- ¼ cup mozzarella cheese, grated

Method:
1. In a bowl, add the cream and eggs and beat well.
2. Transfer the egg mixture into ramekins.
3. Place the sausage slices and bread sticks around the edges and gently push them in the egg mixture.

4. Sprinkle with the cheese evenly.
5. Press "Power Button" of Air Fry Oven and turn the dial to select the "Air Fry" mode.
6. Press the Time button and again turn the dial to set the cooking time to 22 minutes.
7. Now push the Temp button and rotate the dial to set the temperature at 355 degrees F.
8. Press "Start/Pause" button to start.
9. When the unit beeps to show that it is preheated, open the lid.
10. Arrange the ramekins over the "Wire Rack" and insert in the oven.
11. Serve warm.

Nutritional Information per Serving:
Calories 229; Total Fat 18.6 g; Saturated Fat 6 g; Cholesterol 278 mg; Sodium 360 mg

Eggs in Bread & Bacon Cups

Preparation Time: 10 minutes; Cooking Time: 15 minutes; Servings: 4
Ingredients:

- 4 bacon slices
- 4 bread slices
- 1 scallion, chopped
- 2 tablespoons bell pepper, seeded and chopped
- 1½ tablespoons mayonnaise
- 4 eggs

Method:
1. Grease 6 cups muffin tin with cooking spray.
2. Line the sides of each prepared muffin cup with 1 bacon slice.
3. Cut bread slices with round cookie cutter.
4. Arrange the bread slice in the bottom of each muffin cup.
5. Top with, scallion, bell pepper and mayonnaise evenly.
6. Carefully, crack one egg in each muffin cup.
7. Press "Power Button" of Air Fry Oven and turn the dial to select the "Air Fry" mode.
8. Press the Time button and again turn the dial to set the cooking time to 15 minutes.
9. Now push the Temp button and rotate the dial to set the temperature at 375 degrees F.
10. Press "Start/Pause" button to start.
11. When the unit beeps to show that it is preheated, open the lid.
12. Arrange the ramekins over the "Wire Rack" and insert in the oven.
13. Serve warm.

Nutritional Information per Serving:
Calories 298; Total Fat 20.7 g; Saturated Fat 6 g; Cholesterol 197 mg; Sodium 829 mg

Spinach & Mozzarella Muffins

Preparation Time: 10 minutes; Cooking Time: 10 minutes; Servings: 2
Ingredients:

- 2 large eggs
- 2 tablespoons half-and-half
- 2 tablespoons frozen spinach, thawed
- 4 teaspoons mozzarella cheese, grated
- Salt and ground black pepper, as required

Method:
1. Grease 2 ramekins.
2. In each prepared ramekin, crack 1 egg.
3. Divide the half-and-half, spinach, cheese, salt and black pepper and each ramekin and gently stir to combine, without breaking the yolks.
4. Press "Power Button" of Air Fry Oven and turn the dial to select the "Air Fry" mode.
5. Press the Time button and again turn the dial to set the cooking time to 10 minutes.
6. Now push the Temp button and rotate the dial to set the temperature at 330 degrees F.
7. Press "Start/Pause" button to start.

8. When the unit beeps to show that it is preheated, open the lid.
9. Arrange the ramekins over the "Wire Rack" and insert in the oven.
10. Serve warm.

Nutritional Information per Serving:

Calories 251; Total Fat 16.7 g; Saturated Fat 8.6 g; Cholesterol 222 mg; Sodium 495 mg

Bacon & Spinach Muffins

Preparation Time: 10 minutes; Cooking Time: 17 minutes; Servings: 6

Ingredients:

- 6 eggs
- ½ cup milk
- Salt and ground black pepper, as required
- 1 cup fresh spinach, chopped
- 4 cooked bacon slices, crumbled

Method:

1. In a bowl, add the eggs, milk, salt and black pepper and beat until well combined.
2. Add the spinach and stir to combine.
3. Divide the spinach mixture into 6 greased cups of an egg bite mold evenly.
4. Press "Power Button" of Air Fry Oven and turn the dial to select the "Air Fry" mode.
5. Press the Time button and again turn the dial to set the cooking time to 17 minutes.
6. Now push the Temp button and rotate the dial to set the temperature at 325 degrees F.
7. Press "Start/Pause" button to start.
8. When the unit beeps to show that it is preheated, open the lid.
9. Arrange the mold over the "Wire Rack" and insert in the oven.
10. Place the mold onto a wire rack to cool for about 5 minutes.
11. Top with bacon pieces and serve warm.

Nutritional Information per Serving:

Calories 179; Total Fat 12.9 g; Saturated Fat 4.3g; Cholesterol 187 mg; Sodium 549 mg

Ham Muffins

Preparation Time: 10 minutes; Cooking Time: 18 minutes; Servings: 6

Ingredients:

- 6 ham slices
- 6 eggs
- 6 tablespoons cream
- 3 tablespoon mozzarella cheese, shredded
- ¼ teaspoon dried basil, crushed

Method:

1. Lightly, grease 6 cups of a silicone muffin tin.
2. Line each prepared muffin cup with 1 ham slice.
3. Crack 1 egg into each muffin cup and top with cream.
4. Sprinkle with cheese and basil.
5. Press "Power Button" of Air Fry Oven and turn the dial to select the "Air Fry" mode.
6. Press the Time button and again turn the dial to set the cooking time to 18 minutes.
7. Now push the Temp button and rotate the dial to set the temperature at 350 degrees F.
8. Press "Start/Pause" button to start.
9. When the unit beeps to show that it is preheated, open the lid.
10. Arrange the muffin tin over the "Wire Rack" and insert in the oven.
11. Place the muffin tin onto a wire rack to cool for about 5 minutes.
12. Carefully, invert the muffins onto the platter and serve warm.

Nutritional Information per Serving:

Calories 156; Total Fat 10 g; Saturated Fat 4.1 g; Cholesterol 189 mg; Sodium 516 mg

Savory Carrot Muffins

Preparation Time: 15 minutes; Cooking Time: 7 minutes; Servings: 6
Ingredients:
For Muffins:
- ¼ cup whole-wheat flour
- ¼ cup all-purpose flour
- ½ teaspoon baking powder
- 1/8 teaspoon baking soda
- ½ teaspoon dried parsley, crushed
- ½ teaspoon salt
- ½ cup plain yogurt
- 1 teaspoon vinegar
- 1 tablespoon vegetable oil
- 3 tablespoons cottage cheese, grated
- 1 carrot, peeled and grated
- 2-4 tablespoons water (if needed)

For Topping:
- 7 oz. Parmesan cheese, grated
- ¼ cup walnuts, chopped

Method:
1. For muffin: in a large bowl, mix together the flours, baking powder, baking soda, parsley, and salt.
2. In another large bowl, mix well the yogurt, and vinegar.
3. Add the remaining ingredients except water and beat them well. (add some water if needed)
4. Make a well in the center of the yogurt mixture.
5. Slowly, add the flour mixture in the well and mix until well combined.
6. Place the mixture into lightly greased muffin molds evenly and top with the Parmesan cheese and walnuts.
7. Press "Power Button" of Air Fry Oven and turn the dial to select the "Air Fry" mode.
8. Press the Time button and again turn the dial to set the cooking time to 7 minutes.
9. Now push the Temp button and rotate the dial to set the temperature at 355 degrees F.
10. Press "Start/Pause" button to start.
11. When the unit beeps to show that it is preheated, open the lid.
12. Arrange the ramekins over "Wire Rack" and insert in the oven.
13. Place the muffin molds onto a wire rack to cool for about 5 minutes.
14. Carefully, invert the muffins onto the platter and serve warm.

Nutritional Information per Serving:
Calories 292; Total Fat 13.1 g; Saturated Fat 5.7 g; Cholesterol 25 mg; Sodium 579 mg

Potato & Bell Pepper Hash

Preparation Time: 15 minutes; Cooking Time: 25 minutes; Servings: 4
Ingredients:
- 2 cups water
- 5 russet potatoes, peeled and cubed
- ½ tablespoon extra-virgin olive oil
- ½ of onion, chopped
- ½ of jalapeño, chopped
- 1 green bell pepper, seeded and chopped
- ¼ teaspoon dried oregano, crushed
- ¼ teaspoon garlic powder
- ¼ teaspoon ground cumin
- ¼ teaspoon red chili powder
- Salt and freshly ground black pepper, as needed

Method:
1. In a large bowl, add the water and potatoes and set aside for about 30 minutes.
2. Drain well and pat dry with the paper towels.
3. In a bowl, add the potatoes and oil and toss to coat well.
4. Press "Power Button" of Air Fry Oven and turn the dial to select the "Air Fry" mode.
5. Press the Time button and again turn the dial to set the cooking time to 5 minutes.

6. Now push the Temp button and rotate the dial to set the temperature at 330 degrees F.
7. Press "Start/Pause" button to start.
8. When the unit beeps to show that it is preheated, open the lid.
9. Arrange the potato cubes in "Air Fry Basket" and insert in the oven.
10. Transfer the potatoes onto a plate.
11. In a bowl, add the potatoes and remaining ingredients and toss to coat well.
12. Press "Power Button" of Air Fry Oven and turn the dial to select the "Air Fry" mode.
13. Press the Time button and again turn the dial to set the cooking time to 20 minutes.
14. Now push the Temp button and rotate the dial to set the temperature at 390 degrees F.
15. Press "Start/Pause" button to start.
16. When the unit beeps to show that it is preheated, open the lid.
17. Arrange the veggie mixture in "Air Fry Basket" and insert in the oven.
18. Serve hot.

Nutritional Information per Serving:
Calories 216; Total Fat 2.2 g; Saturated Fat 0.3 g; Cholesterol 0 mg; Sodium 58 mg

Chapter 2: Snacks & Appetizer Recipes

Spicy Chickpeas

Preparation Time: 5 minutes; Cooking Time: 10 minutes; Servings: 4

Ingredients:

- 1 (15-oz.) can chickpeas, rinsed and drained
- 1 tablespoon olive oil
- ½ teaspoon ground cumin
- ½ teaspoon cayenne pepper
- ½ teaspoon smoked paprika
- Salt, as required

Method:

1. In a bowl, add all the ingredients and toss to coat well.
2. Press "Power Button" of Air Fry Oven and turn the dial to select the "Air Fry" mode.
3. Press the Time button and again turn the dial to set the cooking time to 10 minutes.
4. Now push the Temp button and rotate the dial to set the temperature at 390 degrees F.
5. Press "Start/Pause" button to start.
6. When the unit beeps to show that it is preheated, open the lid.
7. Arrange the chickpeas in "Air Fry Basket" and insert in the oven.
8. Serve warm.

Nutritional Information per Serving:

Calories 146; Total Fat 4.5 g; Saturated Fat 0.5 g; Cholesterol 0 mg; Sodium 66 mg

Roasted Peanuts

Preparation Time: 5 minutes; Cooking Time: 14 minutes; Servings: 6

Ingredients:

- 1½ cups raw peanuts
- Nonstick cooking spray

Method:

1. Press "Power Button" of Air Fry Oven and turn the dial to select the "Air Fry" mode.
2. Press the Time button and again turn the dial to set the cooking time to 14 minutes.
3. Now push the Temp button and rotate the dial to set the temperature at 320 degrees F.
4. Press "Start/Pause" button to start.
5. When the unit beeps to show that it is preheated, open the lid.
6. Arrange the peanuts in "Air Fry Basket" and insert in the oven.
7. Toss the peanuts twice.
8. After 9 minutes of cooking, spray the peanuts with cooking spray.
9. Serve warm.

Nutritional Information per Serving:

Calories 207; Total Fat 18 g; Saturated Fat 2.5 g; Cholesterol 0 mg; Sodium 7 mg

Roasted Cashews

Preparation Time: 5 minutes; Cooking Time: 5 minutes; Servings: 6

Ingredients:

- 1½ cups raw cashew nuts
- 1 teaspoon butter, melted
- Salt and freshly ground black pepper, as needed

Method:

1. In a bowl, mix together all the ingredients.
2. Press "Power Button" of Air Fry Oven and turn the dial to select the "Air Fry" mode.
3. Press the Time button and again turn the dial to set the cooking time to 5 minutes.
4. Now push the Temp button and rotate the dial to set the temperature at 355 degrees F.
5. Press "Start/Pause" button to start.
6. When the unit beeps to show that it is preheated, open the lid.

7. Arrange the cashews in "Air Fry Basket" and insert in the oven.
8. Shake the cashews once halfway through.

Nutritional Information per Serving:
Calories 202; Total Fat 16.5 g; Saturated Fat 3.5 g; Cholesterol 2 mg; Sodium 37 mg

French Fries

Preparation Time: 15 minutes; Cooking Time: 30 minutes; Servings: 4

Ingredients:
- 1 lb. potatoes, peeled and cut into strips
- 3 tablespoons olive oil
- ½ teaspoon onion powder
- ½ teaspoon garlic powder
- 1 teaspoon paprika

Method:
1. In a large bowl of water, soak the potato strips for about 1 hour.
2. Drain the potato strips well and pat them dry with the paper towels.
3. In a large bowl, add the potato strips and the remaining ingredients and toss to coat well.
4. Press "Power Button" of Air Fry Oven and turn the dial to select the "Air Fry" mode.
5. Press the Time button and again turn the dial to set the cooking time to 30 minutes.
6. Now push the Temp button and rotate the dial to set the temperature at 375 degrees F.
7. Press "Start/Pause" button to start.
8. When the unit beeps to show that it is preheated, open the lid.
9. Arrange the potato fries in "Air Fry Basket" and insert in the oven.
10. Serve warm.

Nutritional Information per Serving:
Calories 172; Total Fat 10.7 g; Saturated Fat 1.5 g; Cholesterol 0 mg; Sodium 7 mg

Zucchini Fries

Preparation Time: 10 minutes; Cooking Time: 20 minutes; Servings: 4

Ingredients:
- 1 lb. zucchini, sliced into 2½-inch sticks
- Salt, as required
- 2 tablespoons olive oil
- ¾ cup panko breadcrumbs

Method:
1. In a colander, add the zucchini and sprinkle with salt. Set aside for about 10 minutes.
2. Gently pat dry the zucchini sticks with the paper towels and coat with oil.
3. In a shallow dish, add the breadcrumbs.
4. Coat the zucchini sticks with breadcrumbs evenly.
5. Press "Power Button" of Air Fry Oven and turn the dial to select the "Air Fry" mode.
6. Press the Time button and again turn the dial to set the cooking time to 12 minutes.
7. Now push the Temp button and rotate the dial to set the temperature at 400 degrees F.
8. Press "Start/Pause" button to start.
9. When the unit beeps to show that it is preheated, open the lid.
10. Arrange the zucchini fries in "Air Fry Basket" and insert in the oven.
11. Serve warm.

Nutritional Information per Serving:
Calories 151; Total Fat 8.6 g; Saturated Fat 1.6 g; Cholesterol 0 mg; Sodium 50 mg

Spicy Carrot Fries

Preparation Time: 10 minutes; Cooking Time: 12 minutes; Servings: 2
Ingredients:

- 1 large carrot, peeled and cut into sticks
- 1 tablespoon fresh rosemary, chopped finely
- 1 tablespoon olive oil
- ¼ teaspoon cayenne pepper
- Salt and ground black pepper, as required

Method:
1. In a bowl, add all the ingredients and mix well.
2. Press "Power Button" of Air Fry Oven and turn the dial to select the "Air Fry" mode.
3. Press the Time button and again turn the dial to set the cooking time to 12 minutes.
4. Now push the Temp button and rotate the dial to set the temperature at 390 degrees F.
5. Press "Start/Pause" button to start.
6. When the unit beeps to show that it is preheated, open the lid.
7. Arrange the carrot fries in "Air Fry Basket" and insert in the oven.
8. Serve warm.

Nutritional Information per Serving:
Calories 81; Total Fat 8.3 g; Saturated Fat 1.1 g; Cholesterol 0 mg; Sodium 36 mg

Maple Carrot Fries

Preparation Time: 10 minutes; Cooking Time: 12 minutes; Servings: 6
Ingredients:
- 1 lb. carrots, peeled and cut into sticks
- 1 teaspoon maple syrup
- 1 teaspoon olive oil
- ½ teaspoon ground cinnamon
- Salt, to taste

Method:
1. In a bowl, add all the ingredients and mix well.
2. Press "Power Button" of Air Fry Oven and turn the dial to select the "Air Fry" mode.
3. Press the Time button and again turn the dial to set the cooking time to 12 minutes.
4. Now push the Temp button and rotate the dial to set the temperature at 400 degrees F.
5. Press "Start/Pause" button to start.
6. When the unit beeps to show that it is preheated, open the lid.
7. Arrange the carrot fries in "Air Fry Basket" and insert in the oven.
8. Serve warm.

Nutritional Information per Serving:
Calories 41; Total Fat 0.8 g; Saturated Fat 0.1 g; Cholesterol 0 mg; Sodium 79 mg

Squash Fries

Preparation Time: 10 minutes; Cooking Time: 35 minutes; Servings: 2
Ingredients:
- 14 oz. butternut squash, peeled, seeded and cut into strips
- 2 teaspoons olive oil
- ½ teaspoon ground cinnamon
- ½ teaspoon red chili powder
- ¼ teaspoon garlic salt
- Salt and freshly ground black pepper, as needed

Method:
1. In a bowl, add all the ingredients and toss to coat well.
2. Press "Power Button" of Air Fry Oven and turn the dial to select the "Air Fry" mode.
3. Press the Time button and again turn the dial to set the cooking time to 30 minutes.
4. Now push the Temp button and rotate the dial to set the temperature at 400 degrees F.
5. Press "Start/Pause" button to start.
6. When the unit beeps to show that it is preheated, open the lid.
7. Arrange the squash fries in "Air Fry Basket" and insert in the oven.
8. Serve warm.

Nutritional Information per Serving:
   Calories 134; Total Fat 5 g; Saturated Fat 0.7 g; Cholesterol 0 mg; Sodium 92 mg

Avocado Fries

Preparation Time: 15 minutes; Cooking Time: 7 minutes; Servings: 2
Ingredients:
- ¼ cup all-purpose flour
- Salt and freshly ground black pepper, as needed
- 1 egg
- 1 teaspoon water
- ½ cup panko breadcrumbs
- 1 avocado, peeled, pitted and sliced into 8 pieces
- Non-stick cooking spray

Method:
1. In a shallow bowl, mix together the flour, salt, and black pepper.
2. In a second bowl, mix well egg and water.
3. In a third bowl, put the breadcrumbs.
4. Coat the avocado slices with flour mixture, then dip into egg mixture and finally, coat evenly with the breadcrumbs.
5. Now, spray the avocado slices evenly with cooking spray.
6. Press "Power Button" of Air Fry Oven and turn the dial to select the "Air Fry" mode.
7. Press the Time button and again turn the dial to set the cooking time to 7 minutes.
8. Now push the Temp button and rotate the dial to set the temperature at 400 degrees F.
9. Press "Start/Pause" button to start.
10. When the unit beeps to show that it is preheated, open the lid.
11. Arrange the avocado fries in "Air Fry Basket" and insert in the oven.
12. Serve warm.

Nutritional Information per Serving:
   Calories 391; Total Fat 23.8g; Saturated Fat 5.6 g; Cholesterol 82 mg; Sodium 115 mg

Dill Pickle Fries

Preparation Time: 15 minutes; Cooking Time: 15 minutes; Servings: 8
Ingredients:
- 1 (16-oz.) jar spicy dill pickle spears, drained and pat dried
- ¾ cup all-purpose flour
- ½ teaspoon paprika
- 1 egg, beaten
- ¼ cup milk
- 1 cup panko breadcrumbs
- Nonstick cooking spray

Method:
1. In a shallow dish, mix together the flour, and paprika.
2. In a second dish, place the milk and egg and mix well.
3. In a third dish, put the breadcrumbs.
4. Coat the pickle spears with flour mixture, then dip into egg mixture and finally, coat evenly with the breadcrumbs.
5. Now, spray the pickle spears evenly with cooking spray.
6. Press "Power Button" of Air Fry Oven and turn the dial to select the "Air Fry" mode.
7. Press the Time button and again turn the dial to set the cooking time to 15 minutes.
8. Now push the Temp button and rotate the dial to set the temperature at 400 degrees F.
9. Press "Start/Pause" button to start.
10. When the unit beeps to show that it is preheated, open the lid.
11. Arrange the squash fries in "Air Fry Basket" and insert in the oven.
12. Serve warm.
13. Flip the fries once halfway through.

14. Serve warm.

Nutritional Information per Serving:
Calories 110; Total Fat 1.9 g; Saturated Fat 0.7 g; Cholesterol 21 mg; Sodium 697 mg

Mozzarella Sticks

Preparation Time: 15 minutes; Cooking Time: 12 minutes; Servings: 3

Ingredients:

- ¼ cup white flour
- 2 eggs
- 3 tablespoons nonfat milk
- 1 cup plain breadcrumbs
- 1 lb. Mozzarella cheese block cut into 3x½-inch sticks

Method:

1. In a shallow dish, add the flour.
2. In a second shallow dish, mix together the eggs, and milk.
3. In a third shallow dish, place the breadcrumbs.
4. Coat the Mozzarella sticks with flour, then dip into egg mixture and finally, coat evenly with the breadcrumbs.
5. Press "Power Button" of Air Fry Oven and turn the dial to select the "Air Fry" mode.
6. Press the Time button and again turn the dial to set the cooking time to 12 minutes.
7. Now push the Temp button and rotate the dial to set the temperature at 400 degrees F.
8. Press "Start/Pause" button to start.
9. When the unit beeps to show that it is preheated, open the lid.
10. Arrange the mozzarella sticks in "Air Fry Basket" and insert in the oven.
11. Serve warm

Nutritional Information per Serving:
Calories 254; Total Fat 6.6 g; Saturated Fat 2.4 g; Cholesterol 114 mg; Sodium 370 mg

Tortilla Chips

Preparation Time: 10 minutes; Cooking Time: 3 minutes; Servings: 3

Ingredients:

- 4 corn tortillas, cut into triangles
- 1 tablespoon olive oil
- Salt, to taste

Method:

1. Coat the tortilla chips with oi and then, sprinkle each side of the tortillas with salt.
2. Press "Power Button" of Air Fry Oven and turn the dial to select the "Air Fry" mode.
3. Press the Time button and again turn the dial to set the cooking time to 3 minutes.
4. Now push the Temp button and rotate the dial to set the temperature at 390 degrees F.
5. Press "Start/Pause" button to start.
6. When the unit beeps to show that it is preheated, open the lid.
7. Arrange the tortilla chips in "Air Fry Basket" and insert in the oven.
8. Serve warm.

Nutritional Information per Serving:
Calories 110; Total Fat 5.6 g; Saturated Fat 0.8 g; Cholesterol 0 mg; Sodium 65 mg

Apple Chips

Preparation Time: 10 minutes; Cooking Time: 8 minutes; Servings: 2

Ingredients:

- 1 apple, peeled, cored and thinly sliced
- 1 tablespoon sugar
- ½ teaspoon ground cinnamon
- Pinch of ground cardamom
- Pinch of ground ginger
- Pinch of salt

Method:

1. In a bowl, add all the ingredients and toss to coat well.
2. Press "Power Button" of Air Fry Oven and turn the dial to select the "Air Fry" mode.
3. Press the Time button and again turn the dial to set the cooking time to 8 minutes.
4. Now push the Temp button and rotate the dial to set the temperature at 390 degrees F.
5. Press "Start/Pause" button to start.
6. When the unit beeps to show that it is preheated, open the lid.
7. Arrange the apple chips in "Air Fry Basket" and insert in the oven.

Nutritional Information per Serving:
Calories 83; Total Fat 0.2 g; Saturated Fat 0 g; Cholesterol 0 mg; Sodium 79 mg

Kale Chips

Preparation Time: 10 minutes; Cooking Time: 3 minutes; Servings: 4
Ingredients:

- 1 head fresh kale, stems and ribs removed and cut into 1½ inch pieces
- 1 tablespoon olive oil
- 1 teaspoon soy sauce
- 1/8 teaspoon cayenne pepper
- Pinch of freshly ground black pepper

Method:
1. In a large bowl and mix together all the ingredients.
2. Press "Power Button" of Air Fry Oven and turn the dial to select the "Air Fry" mode.
3. Press the Time button and again turn the dial to set the cooking time to 3 minutes.
4. Now push the Temp button and rotate the dial to set the temperature at 390 degrees F.
5. Press "Start/Pause" button to start.
6. When the unit beeps to show that it is preheated, open the lid.
7. Arrange the apple chips in "Air Fry Basket" and insert in the oven.
8. Toss the kale chips once halfway through.

Nutritional Information per Serving:
Calories 115; Total Fat 3.5 g; Saturated Fat 0.5 g; Cholesterol 0 mg; Sodium 149 mg

Beet Chips

Preparation Time: 10 minutes; Cooking Time: 15 minutes; Servings: 6
Ingredients:

- 4 medium beetroots, peeled and thinly sliced
- 2 tablespoons olive oil
- ¼ teaspoon smoked paprika
- Salt, to taste

Method:
1. In a large bowl and mix together all the ingredients.
2. Press "Power Button" of Air Fry Oven and turn the dial to select the "Air Fry" mode.
3. Press the Time button and again turn the dial to set the cooking time to 15 minutes.
4. Now push the Temp button and rotate the dial to set the temperature at 325 degrees F.
5. Press "Start/Pause" button to start.
6. When the unit beeps to show that it is preheated, open the lid.
7. Arrange the apple chips in "Air Fry Basket" and insert in the oven.
8. Toss the beet chips once halfway through.
9. Serve at room temperature.

Nutritional Information per Serving:
Calories 70; Total Fat 4.8 g; Saturated Fat 0.7 g; Cholesterol 0mg; Sodium 79 mg

Potato Chips

Preparation Time: 15 minutes; Cooking Time: 30 minutes; Servings: 6
Ingredients:

- 4 small russet potatoes, thinly sliced
- 1 tablespoon olive oil
- 2 tablespoons fresh rosemary, finely chopped
- ¼ teaspoon salt

Method:
1. In a large bowl of water, soak the potato slices for about 30 minutes, changing the water once halfway through.
2. Drain the potato slices well and pat them dry with the paper towels.
3. Press "Power Button" of Air Fry Oven and turn the dial to select the "Air Fry" mode.
4. Press the Time button and again turn the dial to set the cooking time to 25 minutes.
5. Now push the Temp button and rotate the dial to set the temperature at 350 degrees F.
6. Press "Start/Pause" button to start.
7. When the unit beeps to show that it is preheated, open the lid.
8. Arrange the potato chips in "Air Fry Basket" and insert in the oven.
9. Toss the potato chips once halfway through.

Nutritional Information per Serving:
Calories 102; Total Fat 2.6 g; Saturated Fat 0.4 g; Cholesterol 0 mg; Sodium 104 mg

Buttered Corn

Preparation Time: 5 minutes; Cooking Time: 20 minutes; Servings: 2
Ingredients:
- 2 corn on the cob
- Salt and freshly ground black pepper, as needed
- 2 tablespoons butter, softened and divided

Method:
1. Sprinkle the cobs evenly with salt and black pepper.
2. Then, rub with 1 tablespoon of butter.
3. With 1 piece of foil, wrap each cob.
4. Press "Power Button" of Air Fry Oven and turn the dial to select the "Air Fry" mode.
5. Press the Time button and again turn the dial to set the cooking time to 20 minutes.
6. Now push the Temp button and rotate the dial to set the temperature at 320 degrees F.
7. Press "Start/Pause" button to start.
8. When the unit beeps to show that it is preheated, open the lid.
9. Arrange the cobs in "Air Fry Basket" and insert in the oven.
10. Serve warm.

Nutritional Information per Serving:
Calories 186; Total Fat 12.2 g; Saturated Fat 7.4 g; Cholesterol 31 mg; Sodium 163 mg

Bread Sticks

Preparation Time: 15 minutes; Cooking Time: 6 minutes; Servings: 6
Ingredients:
- 1 egg
- 1/8 teaspoon ground cinnamon
- Pinch of ground nutmeg
- Pinch of ground cloves
- Salt, to taste
- 2 bread slices
- 1 tablespoon butter, softened
- Nonstick cooking spray
- 1 tablespoon icing sugar

Method:
1. In a bowl, add the eggs, cinnamon, nutmeg, cloves and salt and beat until well combined.
2. Spread the butter over both sides of the slices evenly.
3. Cut each bread slice into strips.
4. Dip bread strips into egg mixture evenly.

5. Press "Power Button" of Air Fry Oven and turn the dial to select the "Air Fry" mode.
6. Press the Time button and again turn the dial to set the cooking time to 6 minutes.
7. Now push the Temp button and rotate the dial to set the temperature at 355 degrees F.
8. Press "Start/Pause" button to start.
9. When the unit beeps to show that it is preheated, open the lid.
10. Arrange the breadsticks in "Air Fry Basket" and insert in the oven.
11. After 2 minutes of cooking, spray the both sides of the bread strips with cooking spray.
12. Serve immediately with the topping of icing sugar.

Nutritional Information per Serving:
Calories 41; Total Fat 2.8 g; Saturated Fat 1.5 g; Cholesterol 32 mg; Sodium 72 mg

Polenta Sticks

Preparation Time: 15 minutes; Cooking Time: 6 minutes; Servings: 4
Ingredients:
- 1 tablespoon oil
- 2½ cups cooked polenta
- Salt, to taste
- ¼ cup Parmesan cheese

Method:
1. Place the polenta in a lightly greased baking pan.
2. With a plastic wrap, cover and refrigerate for about 1 hour or until set.
3. Remove from the refrigerator and cut into desired sized slices.
4. Sprinkle with salt.
5. Press "Power Button" of Air Fry Oven and turn the dial to select the "Air Fry" mode.
6. Press the Time button and again turn the dial to set the cooking time to 6 minutes.
7. Now push the Temp button and rotate the dial to set the temperature at 350 degrees F.
8. Press "Start/Pause" button to start.
9. When the unit beeps to show that it is preheated, open the lid.
10. Arrange the pan over the "Wire Rack" and insert in the oven.
11. Top with cheese and serve.

Nutritional Information per Serving:
Calories 397; Total Fat 5.6g; Saturated Fat 1.3 g; Cholesterol 4mg; Sodium 127 mg

Crispy Eggplant Slices

Preparation Time: 15 minutes; Cooking Time: 8 minutes; Servings: 4
Ingredients:
- 1 medium eggplant, peeled and cut into ½-inch round slices
- Salt, as required
- ½ cup all-purpose flour
- 2 eggs, beaten
- 1 cup Italian-style breadcrumbs
- ¼ cup olive oil

Method:
1. In a colander, add the eggplant slices and sprinkle with salt. Set aside for about 45 minutes.
2. With paper towels, pat dry the eggplant slices.
3. In a shallow dish, place the flour.
4. Crack the eggs in a second dish and beat well.
5. In a third dish, mix together the oil, and breadcrumbs.
6. Coat each eggplant slice with flour, then dip into beaten eggs and finally, coat with the breadcrumbs mixture.
7. Press "Power Button" of Air Fry Oven and turn the dial to select the "Air Fry" mode.
8. Press the Time button and again turn the dial to set the cooking time to 8 minutes.
9. Now push the Temp button and rotate the dial to set the temperature at 390 degrees F.

10. Press "Start/Pause" button to start.
11. When the unit beeps to show that it is preheated, open the lid.
12. Arrange the eggplant slices in "Air Fry Basket" and insert in the oven.
13. Serve warm.

Nutritional Information per Serving:
Calories 332; Total Fat 16.6 g; Saturated Fat 2.8 g; Cholesterol 82 mg; Sodium 270 mg

Simple Cauliflower Poppers

Preparation Time: 10 minutes; Cooking Time: 8 minutes; Servings: 4

Ingredients:

- ½ large head cauliflower, cut into bite-sized florets
- 1 tablespoon olive oil
- Salt and ground black pepper, as required

Method:

1. In a bowl, add all the ingredients and toss to coat well.
2. Press "Power Button" of Air Fry Oven and turn the dial to select the "Air Fry" mode.
3. Press the Time button and again turn the dial to set the cooking time to 8 minutes.
4. Now push the Temp button and rotate the dial to set the temperature at 390 degrees F.
5. Press "Start/Pause" button to start.
6. When the unit beeps to show that it is preheated, open the lid.
7. Arrange the cauliflower florets in "Air Fry Basket" and insert in the oven.
8. Toss the cauliflower florets once halfway through.
9. Serve warm.

Nutritional Information per Serving:
Calories 38; Total Fat 23.5 g; Saturated Fat 0.5 g; Cholesterol 0 mg; Sodium 49 mg

Crispy Cauliflower Poppers

Preparation Time: 10 minutes; Cooking Time: 20 minutes; Servings: 4

Ingredients:

- 1 egg white
- 1½ tablespoons ketchup
- 1 tablespoon hot sauce
- 1/3 cup panko breadcrumbs
- 2 cups cauliflower florets

Method:

1. In a shallow bowl, mix together the egg white, ketchup and hot sauce.
2. In another bowl, place the breadcrumbs.
3. Dip the cauliflower florets in ketchup mixture and then coat with the breadcrumbs.
4. Press "Power Button" of Air Fry Oven and turn the dial to select the "Air Fry" mode.
5. Press the Time button and again turn the dial to set the cooking time to 20 minutes.
6. Now push the Temp button and rotate the dial to set the temperature at 320 degrees F.
7. Press "Start/Pause" button to start.
8. When the unit beeps to show that it is preheated, open the lid.
9. Arrange the cauliflower florets in "Air Fry Basket" and insert in the oven.
10. Toss the cauliflower florets once halfway through.
11. Serve warm.

Nutritional Information per Serving:
Calories 55; Total Fat 0.7 g; Saturated Fat 0.3g; Cholesterol 0 mg; Sodium 181 mg

Broccoli Poppers

Preparation Time: 15 minutes; Cooking Time: 10 minutes; Servings: 4

Ingredients:

- 2 tablespoons plain yogurt
- ½ teaspoon red chili powder
- ¼ teaspoon ground cumin
- ¼ teaspoon ground turmeric
- Salt, to taste
- 1 lb. broccoli, cut into small florets
- 2 tablespoons chickpea flour

Method:
1. In a bowl, mix together the yogurt, and spices.
2. Add the broccoli and coat with marinade generously.
3. Refrigerate for about 20 minutes.
4. Press "Power Button" of Air Fry Oven and turn the dial to select the "Air Fry" mode.
5. Press the Time button and again turn the dial to set the cooking time to 10 minutes.
6. Now push the Temp button and rotate the dial to set the temperature at 400 degrees F.
7. Press "Start/Pause" button to start.
8. When the unit beeps to show that it is preheated, open the lid.
9. Arrange the broccoli florets in "Air Fry Basket" and insert in the oven.
10. Toss the broccoli florets once halfway through.
11. Serve warm.

Nutritional Information per Serving:
    Calories 69; Total Fat 0.9 g; Saturated Fat 0.1 g; Cholesterol 0 mg; Sodium 87 mg

Cheesy Broccoli Bites

Preparation Time: 15 minutes; Cooking Time: 12 minutes; Servings: 5
Ingredients:
- 1 cup broccoli florets
- 1 egg, beaten
- ¾ cup cheddar cheese, grated
- 2 tablespoons Parmesan cheese, grated
- ¾ cup panko breadcrumbs
- Salt and freshly ground black pepper, as needed

Method:
1. In a food processor, add the broccoli and pulse until finely crumbled.
2. In a large bowl, mix together the broccoli, and remaining ingredients.
3. Make small equal-sized balls from the mixture.
4. Press "Power Button" of Air Fry Oven and turn the dial to select the "Air Fry" mode.
5. Press the Time button and again turn the dial to set the cooking time to 12 minutes.
6. Now push the Temp button and rotate the dial to set the temperature at 350 degrees F.
7. Press "Start/Pause" button to start.
8. When the unit beeps to show that it is preheated, open the lid.
9. Arrange the broccoli balls in "Air Fry Basket" and insert in the oven.
10. Serve warm.

Nutritional Information per Serving:
    Calories 153; Total Fat 8.2 g; Saturated Fat 4.5g; Cholesterol 52 mg; Sodium 172 mg

Mixed Veggie Bites

Preparation Time: 15 minutes; Cooking Time: 10 minutes; Servings: 5
Ingredients:
- ¾ lb. fresh spinach, blanched, drained and chopped
- ¼ of onion, chopped
- ½ of carrot, peeled and chopped
- 1 garlic clove, minced
- 1 American cheese slice, cut into tiny pieces
- 1 bread slice, toasted and processed into breadcrumbs
- ½ tablespoon corn flour
- ½ teaspoon red chili flakes
- Salt, as required

Method:

1. In a bowl, add all the ingredients except breadcrumbs and mix until well combined.
2. Add the breadcrumbs and gently stir to combine.
3. Make 10 equal-sized balls from the mixture.
4. Press "Power Button" of Air Fry Oven and turn the dial to select the "Air Fry" mode.
5. Press the Time button and again turn the dial to set the cooking time to 10 minutes.
6. Now push the Temp button and rotate the dial to set the temperature at 355 degrees F.
7. Press "Start/Pause" button to start.
8. When the unit beeps to show that it is preheated, open the lid.
9. Arrange the veggie balls in "Air Fry Basket" and insert in the oven.
10. Serve warm.

Nutritional Information per Serving:

Calories 43; Total Fat 1.4 g; Saturated Fat 0.7 g; Cholesterol 3 mg; Sodium 155 mg

Risotto Bites

Preparation Time: 15 minutes; Cooking Time: 10 minutes; Servings: 4

Ingredients:

- 1½ cups cooked risotto
- 3 tablespoons Parmesan cheese, grated
- ½ egg, beaten
- 1½ oz. mozzarella cheese, cubed
- 1/3 cup breadcrumbs

Method:

1. In a bowl, add the risotto, Parmesan and egg and mix until well combined.
2. Make 20 equal-sized balls from the mixture.
3. Insert a mozzarella cube in the center of each ball.
4. With your fingers smooth the risotto mixture to cover the ball.
5. In a shallow dish, place the breadcrumbs.
6. Coat the balls with the breadcrumbs evenly.
7. Press "Power Button" of Air Fry Oven and turn the dial to select the "Air Fry" mode.
8. Press the Time button and again turn the dial to set the cooking time to 10 minutes.
9. Now push the Temp button and rotate the dial to set the temperature at 390 degrees F.
10. Press "Start/Pause" button to start.
11. When the unit beeps to show that it is preheated, open the lid.
12. Arrange the balls in "Air Fry Basket" and insert in the oven.
13. Serve warm.

Nutritional Information per Serving:

Calories 340; Total Fat 4.3 g; Saturated Fat 2 g; Cholesterol 29 mg; Sodium 173 mg

Rice Flour Bites

Preparation Time: 15 minutes; Cooking Time: 12 minutes; Servings: 4

Ingredients:

- 6 tablespoons milk
- ½ teaspoon vegetable oil
- ¾ cup rice flour
- 1 oz. Parmesan cheese, shredded

Method:

1. In a bowl, add milk, flour, oil and cheese and mix until a smooth dough forms.
2. Make small equal-sized balls from the dough.
3. Press "Power Button" of Air Fry Oven and turn the dial to select the "Air Fry" mode.
4. Press the Time button and again turn the dial to set the cooking time to 12 minutes.
5. Now push the Temp button and rotate the dial to set the temperature at 300 degrees F.
6. Press "Start/Pause" button to start.
7. When the unit beeps to show that it is preheated, open the lid.

8. Arrange the balls in "Air Fry Basket" and insert in the oven.
9. Serve warm.

Nutritional Information per Serving:
Calories 148; Total Fat 3 g; Saturated Fat 1.5 g; Cholesterol 7 mg; Sodium 77 mg

Potato Croquettes

Preparation Time: 15 minutes; Cooking Time: 8 minutes; Servings: 4

Ingredients:
- 2 medium Russet potatoes, peeled and cubed
- 2 tablespoons all-purpose flour
- ½ cup Parmesan cheese, grated
- 1 egg yolk
- 2 tablespoons chives, minced
- Pinch of ground nutmeg
- Salt and freshly ground black pepper, as needed
- 2 eggs
- ½ cup breadcrumbs
- 2 tablespoons vegetable oil

Method:
1. In a pan of a boiling water, add the potatoes and cook for about 15 minutes.
2. Drain the potatoes well and transfer into a large bowl.
3. With a potato masher, mash the potatoes and set aside to cool completely.
4. In the bowl of mashed potatoes, add the flour, Parmesan cheese, egg yolk, chives, nutmeg, salt, and black pepper and mix until well combined.
5. Make small equal-sized balls from the mixture.
6. Now, roll each ball into a cylinder shape.
7. In a shallow dish, crack the eggs and beat well.
8. In another dish, mix together the breadcrumbs, and oil.
9. Dip the croquettes in egg mixture and then coat with the breadcrumbs mixture.
10. Press "Power Button" of Air Fry Oven and turn the dial to select the "Air Fry" mode.
11. Press the Time button and again turn the dial to set the cooking time to 8 minutes.
12. Now push the Temp button and rotate the dial to set the temperature at 390 degrees F.
13. Press "Start/Pause" button to start.
14. When the unit beeps to show that it is preheated, open the lid.
15. Arrange the croquettes in "Air Fry Basket" and insert in the oven.
16. Serve warm.

Nutritional Information per Serving:
Calories 283; Total Fat 13.4 g; Saturated Fat 3.8 g; Cholesterol 142 mg; Sodium 263mg

Salmon Croquettes

Preparation Time: 15 minutes; Cooking Time: 7 minutes; Servings: 8

Ingredients:
- ½ of large can red salmon, drained
- 1 egg, lightly beaten
- 1 tablespoon fresh parsley, chopped
- Salt and freshly ground black pepper, as needed
- 3 tablespoons vegetable oil
- ½ cup breadcrumbs

Method:
1. In a bowl, add the salmon and with a fork, mash it completely.
2. Add the eggs, parsley, salt, and black pepper and mix until well combined.
3. Make 8 equal-sized croquettes from the mixture.
4. In a shallow dish, mix together the oil, and breadcrumbs.
5. Coat the croquettes with the breadcrumb mixture.
6. Press "Power Button" of Air Fry Oven and turn the dial to select the "Air Fry" mode.
7. Press the Time button and again turn the dial to set the cooking time to 7 minutes.

8. Now push the Temp button and rotate the dial to set the temperature at 390 degrees F.
9. Press "Start/Pause" button to start.
10. When the unit beeps to show that it is preheated, open the lid.
11. Arrange the croquettes in "Air Fry Basket" and insert in the oven.
12. Serve warm.

Nutritional Information per Serving:
Calories 117; Total Fat 7.8 g; Saturated Fat 1.5 g; Cholesterol 33 mg; Sodium 89 mg

Bacon Croquettes

Preparation Time: 15 minutes; Cooking Time: 8 minutes; Servings: 8

Ingredients:
- 1 pound sharp cheddar cheese block
- 1 pound thin bacon slices
- 1 cup all-purpose flour
- 3 eggs
- 1 cup breadcrumbs
- Salt, as required
- ¼ cup olive oil

Method:
1. Cut the cheese block into 1-inch rectangular pieces.
2. Wrap 2 bacon slices around 1 piece of cheddar cheese, covering completely.
3. Repeat with the remaining bacon and cheese pieces.
4. Arrange the croquettes in a baking dish and freeze for about 5 minutes.
5. In a shallow dish, place the flour.
6. In a second dish, crack the eggs and beat well.
7. In a third dish, mix together the breadcrumbs, salt, and oil.
8. Coat the croquettes with flour, then dip into beaten eggs and finally, coat with the breadcrumbs mixture.
9. Press "Power Button" of Air Fry Oven and turn the dial to select the "Air Fry" mode.
10. Press the Time button and again turn the dial to set the cooking time to 8 minutes.
11. Now push the Temp button and rotate the dial to set the temperature at 390 degrees F.
12. Press "Start/Pause" button to start.
13. When the unit beeps to show that it is preheated, open the lid.
14. Arrange the croquettes in "Air Fry Basket" and insert in the oven.
15. Serve warm.

Nutritional Information per Serving:
Calories 723; Total Fat 51.3 g; Saturated Fat 21.3 g; Cholesterol 183 mg; Sodium 1880 mg

Chicken Nuggets

Preparation Time: 15 minutes; Cooking Time: 10 minutes; Servings: 6

Ingredients:
- 2 large chicken breasts, cut into 1-inch cubes
- 1 cup breadcrumbs
- 1/3 tablespoon Parmesan cheese, shredded
- 1 teaspoon onion powder
- ¼ teaspoon smoked paprika
- Salt and ground black pepper, as required

Method:
1. In a large resealable bag, add all the ingredients.
2. Seal the bag and shake well to coat completely.
3. Press "Power Button" of Air Fry Oven and turn the dial to select the "Air Fry" mode.
4. Press the Time button and again turn the dial to set the cooking time to 10 minutes.
5. Now push the Temp button and rotate the dial to set the temperature at 400 degrees F.
6. Press "Start/Pause" button to start.

7. When the unit beeps to show that it is preheated, open the lid.
8. Arrange the nuggets in "Air Fry Basket" and insert in the oven.
9. Serve warm.

Nutritional Information per Serving:
Calories 218; Total Fat 6.6 g; Saturated Fat 1.8 g; Cholesterol 67 mg; Sodium 229 mg

Chicken & Veggie Nuggets

Preparation Time: 20 minutes; Cooking Time: 10 minutes; Servings: 4
Ingredients:
- ½ of zucchini, roughly chopped
- ½ of carrot, roughly chopped
- 14 oz. chicken breast, cut into chunks
- ½ tablespoon mustard powder
- 1 tablespoon garlic powder
- 1 tablespoon onion powder
- Salt and freshly ground black pepper, as needed
- 1 cup all-purpose flour
- 2 tablespoons milk
- 1 egg
- 1 cup panko breadcrumbs

Method:
1. In a food processor, add the zucchini, and carrot and pulse until finely chopped.
2. Add the chicken, mustard powder, garlic powder, onion powder, salt, and black pepper and pulse until well combined.
3. In a shallow dish, place the flour.
4. In a second dish, mix together the milk, and egg.
5. In a third dish, put the breadcrumbs.
6. Coat the nuggets with flour, then dip into egg mixture and finally, coat with the breadcrumbs.
7. Press "Power Button" of Air Fry Oven and turn the dial to select the "Air Fry" mode.
8. Press the Time button and again turn the dial to set the cooking time to 10 minutes.
9. Now push the Temp button and rotate the dial to set the temperature at 390 degrees F.
10. Press "Start/Pause" button to start.
11. When the unit beeps to show that it is preheated, open the lid.
12. Arrange the nuggets in "Air Fry Basket" and insert in the oven.
13. Serve warm.

Nutritional Information per Serving:
Calories 371; Total Fat 6.4 g; Saturated Fat 1.3 g; Cholesterol 105 mg; Sodium 118 mg

Cod Nuggets

Preparation Time: 15 minutes; Cooking Time: 8 minutes; Servings: 5
Ingredients:
- 1 cup all-purpose flour
- 2 eggs
- ¾ cup breadcrumbs
- Pinch of salt
- 2 tablespoons olive oil
- 1 lb. cod, cut into 1x2½-inch strips

Method:
1. In a shallow dish, place the flour.
2. Crack the eggs in a second dish and beat well.
3. In a third dish, mix together the breadcrumbs, salt, and oil.
4. Coat the nuggets with flour, then dip into beaten eggs and finally, coat with the breadcrumbs.
5. Press "Power Button" of Air Fry Oven and turn the dial to select the "Air Fry" mode.
6. Press the Time button and again turn the dial to set the cooking time to 8 minutes.
7. Now push the Temp button and rotate the dial to set the temperature at 390 degrees F.
8. Press "Start/Pause" button to start.

9. When the unit beeps to show that it is preheated, open the lid.
10. Arrange the nuggets in "Air Fry Basket" and insert in the oven.
11. Serve warm.

Nutritional Information per Serving:
Calories 323; Total Fat 9.2 g; Saturated Fat 1.7 g; Cholesterol 115 mg; Sodium 245 mg

BBQ Chicken Wings

Preparation Time: 15 minutes; Cooking Time: 19 minutes; Servings: 4
Ingredients:
- 2 lbs. chicken wings
- 1 teaspoon olive oil
- 1 teaspoon smoked paprika
- 1 teaspoon garlic powder
- Salt and ground black pepper, as required
- ¼ cup BBQ sauce

Method:
1. In a large bowl combine chicken wings, smoked paprika, garlic powder, oil, salt, and pepper and mix well.
2. Press "Power Button" of Air Fry Oven and turn the dial to select the "Air Fry" mode.
3. Press the Time button and again turn the dial to set the cooking time to 19 minutes.
4. Now push the Temp button and rotate the dial to set the temperature at 360 degrees F.
5. Press "Start/Pause" button to start.
6. When the unit beeps to show that it is preheated, open the lid.
7. Arrange the chicken wings in "Air Fry Basket" and insert in the oven.
8. After 12 minutes of cooking, flip the wings and coat with barbecue sauce evenly.
9. Serve immediately.

Nutritional Information per Serving:
Calories 468; Total Fat 18.1 g; Saturated Fat 4.8 g; Cholesterol 202mg; Sodium 409 mg

Buffalo Chicken Wings

Preparation Time: 15 minutes; Cooking Time: 16 minutes; Servings: 5
Ingredients:
- 2 lbs. frozen chicken wings, drums and flats separated
- 2 tablespoons olive oil
- 2 tablespoons Buffalo sauce
- ½ teaspoon red pepper flakes, crushed
- Salt, as required

Method:
1. Coat the chicken wings with oi evenly.
2. Press "Power Button" of Air Fry Oven and turn the dial to select the "Air Fry" mode.
3. Press the Time button and again turn the dial to set the cooking time to 16 minutes.
4. Now push the Temp button and rotate the dial to set the temperature at 390 degrees F.
5. Press "Start/Pause" button to start.
6. When the unit beeps to show that it is preheated, open the lid.
7. Arrange the chicken wings in "Air Fry Basket" and insert in the oven.
8. After 12 minutes of cooking, flip the wings and coat with barbecue sauce evenly.
9. After 7 minutes, flip the wings.
10. Meanwhile, in a large bowl, add Buffalo sauce, red pepper flakes and salt and mix well.
11. Transfer the wings into the bowl of Buffalo sauce and toss to coat well.
12. Serve immediately.

Nutritional Information per Serving:
Calories 394; Total Fat 19.1 g; Saturated Fat 4.5 g; Cholesterol 161 mg; Sodium 339mg

Crispy Prawns

Preparation Time: 15 minutes; Cooking Time: 8 minutes; Servings: 4
Ingredients:
- 1 egg
- ½ pound nacho chips, crushed
- 12 prawns, peeled and deveined

Method:
1. In a shallow dish, beat the egg.
2. In another shallow dish, place the crushed nacho chips.
3. Coat the prawn into egg and then roll into nacho chips.
4. Press "Power Button" of Air Fry Oven and turn the dial to select the "Air Fry" mode.
5. Press the Time button and again turn the dial to set the cooking time to 8 minutes.
6. Now push the Temp button and rotate the dial to set the temperature at 355 degrees F.
7. Press "Start/Pause" button to start.
8. When the unit beeps to show that it is preheated, open the lid.
9. Arrange the prawns in "Air Fry Basket" and insert in the oven.
10. Serve immediately.

Nutritional Information per Serving:
Calories 386; Total Fat 17 g; Saturated Fat 2.9 g; Cholesterol 182 mg; Sodium 525 mg

Breaded Shrimp

Preparation Time: 20 minutes; Cooking Time: 12 minutes; Servings: 4
Ingredients:
- 8 large shrimp, peeled and deveined
- Salt and ground black pepper, as required
- 8 ounces coconut milk
- ½ cup panko breadcrumbs
- ½ teaspoon cayenne pepper

Method:
1. In a shallow dish, mix together salt, black pepper and coconut milk.
2. In another shallow dish, mix together breadcrumbs, cayenne pepper, salt and black pepper.
3. Dip the shrimp in coconut milk mixture and then roll into breadcrumbs mixture.
4. Press "Power Button" of Air Fry Oven and turn the dial to select the "Air Fry" mode.
5. Press the Time button and again turn the dial to set the cooking time to 12 minutes.
6. Now push the Temp button and rotate the dial to set the temperature at 350 degrees F.
7. Press "Start/Pause" button to start.
8. When the unit beeps to show that it is preheated, open the lid.
9. Arrange the shrimp in "Air Fry Basket" and insert in the oven.
10. Serve immediately.

Nutritional Information per Serving:
Calories 193; Total Fat 14.7 g; Saturated Fat 2.4 g; Cholesterol 23 mg; Sodium 74 mg

Bacon Wrapped Shrimp

Preparation Time: 15 minutes; Cooking Time: 7 minutes; Servings: 6
Ingredients:
- 1 lb. bacon, sliced thinly
- 1 lb. shrimp, peeled and deveined

Method:
1. Wrap one slice of bacon around each shrimp completely.
2. Arrange the shrimp in a baking dish and refrigerate for about 20 minutes.
3. Press "Power Button" of Air Fry Oven and turn the dial to select the "Air Fry" mode.
4. Press the Time button and again turn the dial to set the cooking time to 6 minutes.

5. Now push the Temp button and rotate the dial to set the temperature at 390 degrees F.
6. Press "Start/Pause" button to start.
7. When the unit beeps to show that it is preheated, open the lid.
8. Arrange the shrimp in "Air Fry Basket" and insert in the oven.
9. Serve immediately.

Nutritional Information per Serving:
Calories 499; Total Fat 32.9 g; Saturated Fat 10.8 g; Cholesterol 242 mg; Sodium 1931 mg

Feta Tater Tots

Preparation Time: 15 minutes; Cooking Time: 25 minutes; Servings: 6
Ingredients:
- 2 lbs. frozen tater tots
- ½ cup feta cheese, crumbled
- ½ cup tomato, chopped
- ¼ cup black olives, pitted and sliced
- ¼ cup red onion, chopped

Method:
1. Press "Power Button" of Air Fry Oven and turn the dial to select the "Air Fry" mode.
2. Press the Time button and again turn the dial to set the cooking time to 25 minutes.
3. Now push the Temp button and rotate the dial to set the temperature at 450 degrees F.
4. Press "Start/Pause" button to start.
5. When the unit beeps to show that it is preheated, open the lid.
6. Arrange the tater tots in "Air Fry Basket" and insert in the oven.
7. After 15 minutes of cooking, press "Start/Pause" button to pause the unit
8. Remove basket from oven and transfer tots into a large bowl.
9. Add the feta cheese, tomatoes, olives and onion and toss to coat well.
10. Now, place the mixture into "Sheet Pan" and insert in the oven.
11. Press "Start/Pause" button to resume cooking.
12. Serve warm.

Nutritional Information per Serving:
Calories 332; Total Fat 17.7 g; Saturated Fat 5.6 g; Cholesterol 11 mg; Sodium 784 mg

Buttermilk Biscuits

Preparation Time: 15 minutes; Cooking Time: 8 minutes; Servings: 8
Ingredients:
- ½ cup cake flour
- 1¼ cups all-purpose flour
- ¼ teaspoon baking soda
- ½ teaspoon baking powder
- 1 teaspoon granulated sugar
- Salt, to taste
- ¼ cup cold unsalted butter, cut into cubes
- ¾ cup buttermilk
- 2 tablespoons butter, melted

Method:
1. In a large bowl, sift together flours, baking soda, baking powder, sugar and salt.
2. With a pastry cutter, cut cold butter and mix until a coarse crumb forms.
3. Slowly, add buttermilk and mix until a smooth dough forms.
4. Place the dough onto a floured surface and with your hands, press it into ½ inch thickness.
5. With a 1¾-inch round cookie cutter, cut the biscuits.
6. Arrange the biscuits into a baking pan in a single layer and coat with the butter.
7. Press "Power Button" of Air Fry Oven and turn the dial to select the "Air Fry" mode.
8. Press the Time button and again turn the dial to set the cooking time to 8 minutes.
9. Now push the Temp button and rotate the dial to set the temperature at 400 degrees F.
10. Press "Start/Pause" button to start.

11. When the unit beeps to show that it is preheated, open the lid.
12. Arrange pan over the "Wire Rack" and insert in the oven.
13. Place the baking pan onto a wire rack for about 5 minutes.
14. Carefully, invert the biscuits onto the wire rack to cool completely before serving.

Nutritional Information per Serving:
Calories 187; Total Fat 9.1 g; Saturated Fat 5.6 g; Cholesterol 24 mg; Sodium 144 mg

Cheddar Biscuits

Preparation Time: 15 minutes; Cooking Time: 10 minutes; Servings: 8

Ingredients:
- 1/3 cup unbleached all-purpose flour
- 1/8 teaspoon cayenne pepper
- 1/8 teaspoon smoked paprika
- Pinch of garlic powder
- Salt and ground black pepper, as required
- ½ cup sharp cheddar cheese, shredded
- 2 tablespoons butter, softened
- Nonstick cooking spray

Method:
1. In a food processor, add the flour, spices, salt and black pepper and pulse until well combined.
2. Add the cheese and butter and pulse until a smooth dough forms.
3. Place the dough onto a lightly floured surface.
4. Make 16 small equal-sized balls from the dough and press each slightly.
5. Press "Power Button" of Air Fry Oven and turn the dial to select the "Air Bake" mode.
6. Press the Time button and again turn the dial to set the cooking time to 10 minutes.
7. Now push the Temp button and rotate the dial to set the temperature at 330 degrees F.
8. Press "Start/Pause" button to start.
9. When the unit beeps to show that it is preheated, open the lid.
10. Arrange the biscuits in greased "Air Fry Basket" and insert in the oven.
11. Place the basket onto a wire rack for about 10 minutes.
12. Carefully, invert the biscuits onto the wire rack to cool completely before serving.

Nutritional Information per Serving:
Calories 73; Total Fat 5.3 g; Saturated Fat 3.3 g; Cholesterol 15 mg; Sodium 84 mg

Lemon Biscuits

Preparation Time: 15 minutes; Cooking Time: 5 minutes; Servings: 10

Ingredients:
- 8½ oz. self-rising flour
- 3½ oz. caster sugar
- 3½ oz. cold butter
- 1 small egg
- 1 teaspoon fresh lemon zest, grated finely
- 2 tablespoons fresh lemon juice
- 1 teaspoon vanilla extract

Method:
1. In a large bowl, mix together flour and sugar.
2. With a pastry cutter, cut cold butter and mix until a coarse crumb forms.
3. Add the egg, lemon zest and lemon juice and mix until a soft dough forms.
4. Place the dough onto a floured surface and roll the dough.
5. Cut the dough into medium-sized biscuits.
6. Arrange the biscuits into a baking pan in a single layer and coat with the butter.
7. Press "Power Button" of Air Fry Oven and turn the dial to select the "Air Fry" mode.
8. Press the Time button and again turn the dial to set the cooking time to 5 minutes.
9. Now push the Temp button and rotate the dial to set the temperature at 355 degrees F.
10. Press "Start/Pause" button to start.

11. When the unit beeps to show that it is preheated, open the lid.
12. Arrange pan over the "Wire Rack" and insert in the oven.
13. Place the baking pan onto a wire rack for about 10 minutes.
14. Carefully, invert the biscuits onto the wire rack to cool completely before serving.

Nutritional Information per Serving:

Calories 203; Total Fat 8.7 g; Saturated Fat 5.3 g; Cholesterol 35 mg; Sodium 63 mg

Potato Bread Rolls

Preparation Time: 20 minutes; Cooking Time: 33 minutes; Servings: 8

Ingredients:

- 5 large potatoes, peeled
- 2 tablespoons vegetable oil, divided
- 2 small onions, finely chopped
- 2 green chilies, seeded and chopped
- 2 curry leaves
- ½ teaspoon ground turmeric
- Salt, as required
- 8 bread slices, trimmed

Method:

1. In a pan of a boiling water, add the potatoes and cook for about 15-20 minutes.
2. Drain the potatoes well and with a potato masher, mash the potatoes.
3. In a skillet, heat 1 teaspoon of oil over a medium heat and sauté the onion for about 4-5 minutes.
4. Add the green chilies, curry leaves, and turmeric and sauté for about 1 minute.
5. Add the mashed potatoes, and salt and mix well.
6. Remove from the heat and set aside to cool completely.
7. Make 8 equal-sized oval-shaped patties from the mixture.
8. Wet the bread slices completely with water.
9. Press each bread slice between your hands to remove the excess water.
10. Place 1 bread slice in your palm and place 1 patty in the center.
11. Roll the bread slice in a spindle shape and seal the edges to secure the filling.
12. Coat the roll with some oil.
13. Repeat with the remaining slices, filling and oil.
14. Press "Power Button" of Air Fry Oven and turn the dial to select the "Air Fry" mode.
15. Press the Time button and again turn the dial to set the cooking time to 13 minutes.
16. Now push the Temp button and rotate the dial to set the temperature at 390 degrees F.
17. Press "Start/Pause" button to start.
18. When the unit beeps to show that it is preheated, open the lid.
19. Arrange the bread rolls in "Air Fry Basket" and insert in the oven.
20. Serve warm.

Nutritional Information per Serving:

Calories 222; Total Fat 4 g; Saturated Fat 0.8 g; Cholesterol 0 mg; Sodium 95 mg

Veggie Spring Rolls

Preparation Time: 20 minutes; Cooking Time: 5 minutes; Servings: 6

Ingredients:

- 1 tablespoon vegetable oil, divided
- 14 oz. fresh mushrooms, sliced
- ½ oz. canned water chestnuts, sliced
- ½ teaspoon fresh ginger, finely grated
- ½ oz. bean sprouts
- ½ of small carrot, peeled and cut into matchsticks
- 1 scallion (green part), chopped
- ½ tablespoon soy sauce
- ½ teaspoon Chinese five-spice powder
- 1½ oz. cooked shrimps
- 6 spring roll wrappers
- 1 small egg, beaten

Method:

1. In a skillet, heat 1 tablespoon of oil over medium heat and sauté the mushrooms, water chestnuts, and ginger for about 2-3 minutes.
2. Add the beans sprouts, carrot, scallion, soy sauce, and five-spice powder and sauté for about 1 minute.
3. Stir in the shrimps and remove from heat. Set aside to cool.
4. Arrange the spring rolls onto a smooth surface.
5. Divide the veggie mixture evenly between spring rolls.
6. Roll the wrappers around the filling and seal with beaten egg.
7. Coat each roll with the remaining oil.
8. Repeat with the remaining slices, filling and oil.
9. Press "Power Button" of Air Fry Oven and turn the dial to select the "Air Fry" mode.
10. Press the Time button and again turn the dial to set the cooking time to 5 minutes.
11. Now push the Temp button and rotate the dial to set the temperature at 390 degrees F.
12. Press "Start/Pause" button to start.
13. When the unit beeps to show that it is preheated, open the lid.
14. Arrange the rolls in "Air Fry Basket" and insert in the oven.
15. Serve warm.

Nutritional Information per Serving:
Calories 153; Total Fat 3.7 g; Saturated Fat 0.8 g; Cholesterol 41 mg; Sodium 292 mg

Spinach Rolls

Preparation Time: 20 minutes; Cooking Time: 4 minutes; Servings: 6

Ingredients:
- 1 red onion, chopped
- 1 cup fresh parsley, chopped
- 1 cup fresh mint leaves, chopped
- 1 egg
- 1 cup feta cheese, crumbled
- ½ cup Romano cheese, grated
- ¼ teaspoon ground cardamom
- Salt and freshly ground black pepper, as needed
- 1 package frozen phyllo dough, thawed
- 1 (16-oz.) package frozen spinach, thawed
- 2 tablespoons olive oil

Method:
1. In a food processor, add all the ingredients except phyllo dough and oil and pulse until smooth.
2. Place one phyllo sheet on the cutting board and cut into three rectangular strips.
3. Brush each strip with the oil.
4. Place about 1 teaspoon of spinach mixture along with the short side of a strip.
5. Roll the dough to secure the filling.
6. Repeat with the remaining phyllo sheets and spinach mixture.
7. Press "Power Button" of Air Fry Oven and turn the dial to select the "Air Fry" mode.
8. Press the Time button and again turn the dial to set the cooking time to 4 minutes.
9. Now push the Temp button and rotate the dial to set the temperature at 355 degrees F.
10. Press "Start/Pause" button to start.
11. When the unit beeps to show that it is preheated, open the lid.
12. Arrange the rolls in "Air Fry Basket" and insert in the oven.
13. Serve warm.

Nutritional Information per Serving:
Calories 206; Total Fat 13.8 g; Saturated Fat 6.2 g; Cholesterol 56 mg; Sodium 512 mg

Cheese Pastries

Preparation Time: 15 minutes; Cooking Time: 10 minutes; Servings: 6

Ingredients:
- 1 egg yolk
- 4 oz. feta cheese, crumbled
- 1 scallion, finely chopped
- 2 tablespoons fresh parsley, finely chopped
- Salt and ground black pepper, as needed
- 2 frozen phyllo pastry sheets, thawed
- 2 tablespoons olive oil

Method:
1. In a large bowl, add the egg yolk, and beat well.
2. Add the feta cheese, scallion, parsley, salt, and black pepper and mix well.
3. Cut each pastry sheet in three strips.
4. Add about 1 teaspoon of feta mixture on the underside of a strip.
5. Fold the tip of sheet over the filling in a zigzag manner to form a triangle.
6. Repeat with the remaining strips and fillings.
7. Coat each pastry with oil evenly.
8. Press "Power Button" of Air Fry Oven and turn the dial to select the "Air Fry" mode.
9. Press the Time button and again turn the dial to set the cooking time to 3 minutes.
10. Now push the Temp button and rotate the dial to set the temperature at 390 degrees F.
11. Press "Start/Pause" button to start.
12. When the unit beeps to show that it is preheated, open the lid.
13. Arrange the pastries in "Air Fry Basket" and insert in the oven.
14. After 3 minutes, set the temperature at 390 degrees F for 2 minutes.
15. Repeat with remaining pastries.
16. Serve warm.

Nutritional Information per Serving:
Calories 128; Total Fat 10 g; Saturated Fat 3.9 g; Cholesterol 52 mg; Sodium 286 mg

Veggie Pastries

Preparation Time: 20 minutes; Cooking Time: 10 minutes; Servings: 8
Ingredients:
- 2 large potatoes, peeled
- 1 tablespoon olive oil
- ½ cup carrot, peeled and chopped
- ½ cup onion, chopped
- 2 garlic cloves, minced
- 2 tablespoons fresh ginger, minced
- ½ cup green peas, shelled
- Salt and ground black pepper, as needed
- 3 puff pastry sheets

Method:
1. In a pan of a boiling water, cOok the potatoes for about 15-20 minutes.
2. Drain the potatoes well and with a potato masher, mash the potatoes.
3. In a skillet, heat the oil over medium heat and sauté the carrot, onion, ginger, and garlic for about 4-5 minutes.
4. Drain all the fat from the skillet.
5. Stir in the mashed potatoes, peas, salt, and black pepper and cook for about 1-2 minutes.
6. Remove the potato mixture from heat and set aside to cool completely.
7. Arrange the puff pastry onto a smooth surface.
8. Cut each puff pastry sheet into four pieces and then cut each piece in a round shape.
9. Place about 2 tablespoons of veggie filling over each pastry round.
10. With your wet fingers, moisten the edges.
11. Fold each pastry round in half to seal the filling.
12. With a fork, firmly press the edges.
13. Press "Power Button" of Air Fry Oven and turn the dial to select the "Air Fry" mode.
14. Press the Time button and again turn the dial to set the cooking time to 5 minutes.

15. Now push the Temp button and rotate the dial to set the temperature at 390 degrees F.
16. Press "Start/Pause" button to start.
17. When the unit beeps to show that it is preheated, open the lid.
18. Arrange half of the pastries in "Air Fry Basket" and insert in the oven.
19. Repeat with remaining pastries.
20. Serve warm.

Nutritional Information per Serving:
Calories 146; Total Fat 5.3 g; Saturated Fat 1.2 g; Cholesterol 0 mg; Sodium 53 mg

Spinach Dip

Preparation Time: 15 minutes; Cooking Time: 35 minutes; Servings: 8

Ingredients:
- 1 (8-oz.) package cream cheese, softened
- 1 cup mayonnaise
- 1 cup Parmesan cheese, grated
- 1 cup frozen spinach, thawed and squeezed
- 1/3 cup water chestnuts, drained and chopped
- ½ cup onion, minced
- ¼ teaspoon garlic powder
- Ground black pepper, as required

Method:
1. In a bowl, add all the ingredients and mix until well combined.
2. Transfer the mixture into a baking pan and spread in an even layer.
3. Press "Power Button" of Air Fry Oven and turn the dial to select the "Air Fry" mode.
4. Press the Time button and again turn the dial to set the cooking time to 35 minutes.
5. Now push the Temp button and rotate the dial to set the temperature at 300 degrees F.
6. Press "Start/Pause" button to start.
7. When the unit beeps to show that it is preheated, open the lid.
8. Arrange pan over the "Wire Rack" and insert in the oven.
9. Stir the dip once halfway through.
10. Serve hot.

Nutritional Information per Serving:
Calories 258; Total Fat 22.1 g; Saturated Fat 8.9 g; Cholesterol 47 mg; Sodium 384 mg

Chili Dip

Preparation Time: 10 minutes; Cooking Time: 15 minutes; Servings: 8

Ingredients:
- 1 (8-oz.) package cream cheese, softened
- 1 (16-oz.) can Hormel chili without beans
- 1 (16-oz.) package mild cheddar cheese, shredded

Method:
1. In a baking pan, place the cream cheese and spread in an even layer.
2. Top with chili evenly, followed by the cheese.
3. Press "Power Button" of Air Fry Oven and turn the dial to select the "Air Bake" mode.
4. Press the Time button and again turn the dial to set the cooking time to 15 minutes.
5. Now push the Temp button and rotate the dial to set the temperature at 375 degrees F.
6. Press "Start/Pause" button to start.
7. When the unit beeps to show that it is preheated, open the lid.
8. Arrange pan over the "Wire Rack" and insert in the oven.
9. Serve hot.

Nutritional Information per Serving:

Calories 388; Total Fat 31.3 g; Saturated Fat 19.2 g; Cholesterol 103 mg; Sodium 674 mg

Onion Dip

Preparation Time: 10 minutes; Cooking Time: 45 minutes; Servings: 10

Ingredients:

- 2/3 cup onion, chopped
- 1 cup cheddar jack cheese, shredded
- ½ cup Swiss cheese, shredded
- ¼ cup Parmesan cheese, shredded
- 2/3 cup whipped salad dressing
- ½ cup milk
- Salt, as required

Method:

1. In a large bowl, add all the ingredients and mix well.
2. Transfer the mixture into a baking pan and spread in an even layer.
3. Press "Power Button" of Air Fry Oven and turn the dial to select the "Air Bake" mode.
4. Press the Time button and again turn the dial to set the cooking time to 45 minutes.
5. Now push the Temp button and rotate the dial to set the temperature at 375 degrees F.
6. Press "Start/Pause" button to start.
7. When the unit beeps to show that it is preheated, open the lid.
8. Arrange pan over the "Wire Rack" and insert in the oven.
9. Serve hot.

Nutritional Information per Serving:

Calories 87; Total Fat 6 g; Saturated Fat 3.5 g; Cholesterol 18 mg; Sodium 140 mg

Chapter 3: Poultry Recipes

Buttermilk Marinated Chicken

Prep Time: 10 minutes; Cooking Time: 25 minutes; Serving: 6

Ingredients

- 3-lb. whole chicken
- 1 tablespoon salt
- 1-pint buttermilk

Method:

1. Place the whole chicken in a large bowl and drizzle salt on top.
2. Pour the buttermilk over it and leave the chicken soaked overnight.
3. Cover the chicken bowl and refrigerate overnight.
4. Remove the chicken from the marinade and fix it on the rotisserie rod in the Air fryer oven.
5. Turn the dial to select the "Air Roast" mode.
6. Hit the Time button and again use the dial to set the cooking time to 25 minutes.
7. Now push the Temp button and rotate the dial to set the temperature at 370 degrees F.
8. Close its lid and allow the chicken to roast.
9. Serve warm.

Nutritional Information per Serving:

Calories 284; Total Fat 7.9 g; Saturated Fat 1.4 g; Cholesterol 36 mg; Sodium 704 mg

Thyme Turkey Breast

Prep Time: 10 minutes; Cooking Time: 40 minutes; Serving: 4

Ingredients

- 2 lb. turkey breast
- Salt, to taste
- Black pepper, to taste
- 4 tablespoon butter, melted
- 3 cloves garlic, minced
- 1 teaspoon thyme, chopped
- 1 teaspoon rosemary, chopped

Method:

1. Mix butter with salt, black pepper, garlic, thyme, and rosemary in a bowl.
2. Rub this seasoning over the turkey breast liberally and place in the Air Fryer basket.
3. Turn the dial to select the "Air Fry" mode.
4. Hit the Time button and again use the dial to set the cooking time to 40 minutes.
5. Now push the Temp button and rotate the dial to set the temperature at 375 degrees F.
6. Once preheated, place the Air fryer basket inside the oven.
7. Slice and serve fresh.

Nutritional Information per Serving:

Calories 334; Total Fat 4.7 g; Saturated Fat 0.6 g; Cholesterol 124mg; Sodium 1 mg

Roasted Duck

Prep Time: 10 minutes; Cooking Time: 3 hours; Serving: 12

Ingredients

- 6 lb. whole Pekin duck
- salt
- 5 garlic cloves chopped
- 1 lemon, chopped

Glaze

- 1/2 cup balsamic vinegar
- 1 lemon, juiced
- 1/4 cup honey

Method:

1. Place the Pekin duck in a baking tray and add garlic, lemon, and salt on top.
2. Whisk honey, vinegar, and honey in a bowl.

3. Brush this glaze over the duck liberally. Marinate overnight in the refrigerator.
4. Remove the duck from the marinade and fix it on the rotisserie rod in the Air fryer oven.
5. Turn the dial to select the "Air Roast" mode.
6. Hit the Time button and again use the dial to set the cooking time to 3 hours.
7. Now push the Temp button and rotate the dial to set the temperature at 350 degrees F.
8. Close its lid and allow the duck to roast.
9. Serve warm.

Nutritional Information per Serving:
Calories 387; Total Fat 6 g; Saturated Fat 9.9 g; Cholesterol 41 mg; Sodium 154 mg

Chicken Drumsticks

Prep Time: 10 minutes; Cooking Time: 20 minutes; Serving: 8

Ingredients
- 8 chicken drumsticks
- 2 tablespoon olive oil
- 1 teaspoon salt
- 1 teaspoon pepper
- 1 teaspoon garlic powder
- 1 teaspoon paprika
- 1/2 teaspoon cumin

Method:
1. Mix olive oil with salt, black pepper, garlic powder, paprika, and cumin in a bowl.
2. Rub this mixture liberally over all the drumsticks.
3. Place these drumsticks in the Air fryer basket.
4. Turn the dial to select the "Air Fry" mode.
5. Hit the Time button and again use the dial to set the cooking time to 20 minutes.
6. Now push the Temp button and rotate the dial to set the temperature at 375 degrees F.
7. Once preheated, place the Air fryer basket inside the oven.
8. Flip the drumsticks when cooked halfway through.
9. Resume air frying for another rest of the 10 minutes.
10. Serve warm.

Nutritional Information per Serving:
Calories 212; Total Fat 11.8 g; Saturated Fat 2.2 g; Cholesterol 23mg; Sodium 321 mg

Blackened Chicken Bake

Prep Time: 10 minutes; Cooking Time: 18 minutes; Serving: 4

Ingredients
- 4 chicken breasts
- 2 teaspoon olive oil

Seasoning:
- 1 1/2 tablespoon brown sugar
- 1 teaspoon paprika
- 1 teaspoon dried oregano
- 1/4 teaspoon garlic powder
- 1/2 teaspoon salt and pepper

Garnish:
- Chopped parsley

Method:
1. Mix olive oil with brown sugar, paprika, oregano, garlic powder, salt, and black pepper in a bowl.
2. Place the chicken breasts in the baking tray of the Ninja Oven.
3. Pour and rub this mixture liberally over all the chicken breasts.
4. Turn the dial to select the "Bake" mode.
5. Hit the Time button and again use the dial to set the cooking time to 18 minutes.
6. Now push the Temp button and rotate the dial to set the temperature at 425 degrees F.
7. Once preheated, place the baking tray inside the oven.

8. Serve warm.
Nutritional Information per Serving:
Calories 412; Total Fat 24.8 g; Saturated Fat 12.4 g; Cholesterol 3 mg; Sodium 132 mg

Crusted Chicken Drumsticks

Prep Time: 10 minutes; Cooking Time: 10 minutes; Serving: 4
Ingredients
- 1 lb. chicken drumsticks
- 1/2 cup buttermilk
- 1/2 cup panko breadcrumbs
- 1/2 cup flour
- 1/4 teaspoon baking powder

Spice Mixture
- 1/2 teaspoon salt
- 1/2 teaspoon celery salt
- 1/4 teaspoon oregano
- 1/4 teaspoon cayenne
- 1 teaspoon paprika
- 1/4 teaspoon garlic powder
- 1/4 teaspoon dried thyme
- 1/2 teaspoon ground ginger
- 1/2 teaspoon white pepper
- 1/2 teaspoon black pepper
- 3 tablespoon butter melted

Method:
1. Soak chicken in the buttermilk and cover to marinate overnight in the refrigerator.
2. Mix spices with flour, breadcrumbs, and baking powder in a shallow tray.
3. Remove the chicken from the milk and coat them well with the flour spice mixture
4. Place the chicken drumsticks in the Air fryer basket of the Ninja Oven.
5. Pour the melted butter over the drumsticks
6. Turn the dial to select the "Air fry" mode.
7. Hit the Time button and again use the dial to set the cooking time to 10 minutes.
8. Now push the Temp button and rotate the dial to set the temperature at 425 degrees F.
9. Once preheated, place the baking tray inside the oven.
10. Flip the drumsticks and resume cooking for another 10 minutes.
11. Serve warm.
Nutritional Information per Serving:
Calories 331; Total Fat 2.5 g; Saturated Fat 0.5 g; Cholesterol 35 mg; Sodium 595 mg

Roasted Turkey Breast

Prep Time: 10 minutes; Cooking Time: 50 minutes; Serving: 6
Ingredients
- 3 lb. boneless turkey breast
- ¼ cup mayonnaise
- 2 teaspoon poultry seasoning
- 1 teaspoon salt
- ½ teaspoon garlic powder
- ¼ teaspoon black pepper

Method:
1. Whisk all the ingredients, including turkey in a bowl, and coat it well.
2. Place the boneless turkey breast in the Air fryer basket.
3. Rotate the dial to select the "Air fry" mode.
4. Press the Time button and again use the dial to set the cooking time to 50 minutes.
5. Now press the Temp button and rotate the dial to set the temperature at 350 degrees F.
6. Once preheated, place the air fryer basket in the Ninja oven and Close its lid to bake.
7. Slice and serve.
Nutritional Information per Serving:
Calories 322; Total Fat 11.8 g; Saturated Fat 2.2 g; Cholesterol 56 mg; Sodium 321 mg

Brine Soaked Turkey

Prep Time: 10 minutes; Cooking Time: 45 minutes; Serving: 8

Ingredients
- 7 lb. bone-in, skin-on turkey breast

Brine:
- 1/2 cup salt
- 1 lemon
- 1/2 onion
- 3 cloves garlic, smashed
- 5 sprigs fresh thyme
- 3 bay leaves
- black pepper

Turkey Breast:
- 4 tablespoon butter, softened
- 1/2 teaspoon black pepper
- 1/2 teaspoon garlic powder
- 1/4 teaspoon dried thyme
- 1/4 teaspoon dried oregano

Method:
1. Mix the turkey brine ingredients in a pot and soak the turkey in the brine overnight.
2. Next day, remove the soaked turkey from the brine.
3. Whisk the butter, black pepper, garlic powder, oregano, and thyme.
4. Brush the butter mixture over the turkey then place it in a baking tray.
5. Press "Power Button" of Air Fry Oven and turn the dial to select the "Air Roast" mode.
6. Press the Time button and again turn the dial to set the cooking time to 45 minutes.
7. Now push the Temp button and rotate the dial to set the temperature at 370 degrees F.
8. Once preheated, place the turkey baking tray in the oven and close its lid.
9. Slice and serve warm.

Nutritional Information per Serving:
Calories 397; Total Fat 15.4 g; Saturated Fat 4.2 g; Cholesterol 168 mg; Sodium 203 mg

Turkey Meatballs

Prep Time: 10 minutes; Cooking Time: 20 minutes; Serving: 6

Ingredients
- 1.5 lb. turkey mince
- 1 red bell pepper, deseeded and chopped
- 1 large egg, beaten
- 4 tablespoons parsley, minced
- 1 tablespoon cilantro, minced
- Salt, to taste
- Black pepper, to taste

Method:
1. Toss all the meatball ingredients in a bowl and mix well.
2. Make small meatballs out this mixture and place them in the air fryer basket.
3. Press "Power Button" of Air Fry Oven and turn the dial to select the "Air Fry" mode.
4. Press the Time button and again turn the dial to set the cooking time to 20 minutes.
5. Now push the Temp button and rotate the dial to set the temperature at 375 degrees F.
6. Once preheated, place the air fryer basket inside and close its lid.
7. Serve warm.

Nutritional Information per Serving:
Calories 338; Total Fat 9.7 g; Saturated Fat 4.7 g; Cholesterol 181 mg; Sodium 245 mg

Lemon Pepper Turkey

Prep Time: 10 minutes; Cooking Time: 45 minutes; Serving: 6

Ingredients
- 3 lbs. turkey breast
- 2 tablespoons oil
- 1 tablespoon Worcestershire sauce
- 1 teaspoon lemon pepper

- 1/2 teaspoon salt

Method:
1. Whisk everything in a bowl and coat the turkey liberally.
2. Place the turkey in the Air fryer basket.
3. Press "Power Button" of Air Fry Oven and turn the dial to select the "Air Fry" mode.
4. Press the Time button and again turn the dial to set the cooking time to 45 minutes.
5. Now push the Temp button and rotate the dial to set the temperature at 375 degrees F.
6. Once preheated, place the air fryer basket inside and close its lid.
7. Serve warm.

Nutritional Information per Serving:
Calories 391; Total Fat 2.8 g; Saturated Fat 0.6 g; Cholesterol 330 mg; Sodium 62 mg

Ground Chicken Meatballs

Prep Time: 10 minutes; Cooking Time: 10 minutes; Serving: 4

Ingredients
- 1-lb. ground chicken
- 1/3 cup panko
- 1 teaspoon salt
- 2 teaspoons chives
- 1/2 teaspoon garlic powder
- 1 teaspoon thyme
- 1 egg

Method:
1. Toss all the meatball ingredients in a bowl and mix well.
2. Make small meatballs out this mixture and place them in the air fryer basket.
3. Press "Power Button" of Air Fry Oven and turn the dial to select the "Air Fry" mode.
4. Press the Time button and again turn the dial to set the cooking time to 10 minutes.
5. Now push the Temp button and rotate the dial to set the temperature at 350 degrees F.
6. Once preheated, place the air fryer basket inside and close its lid.
7. Serve warm.

Nutritional Information per Serving:
Calories 453; Total Fat 2.4 g; Saturated Fat 3 g; Cholesterol 21 mg; Sodium 216 mg

Parmesan Chicken Meatballs

Prep Time: 10 minutes; Cooking Time: 12 minutes; Serving: 4

Ingredients
- 1-lb. ground chicken
- 1 large egg, beaten
- ½ cup Parmesan cheese, grated
- ½ cup pork rinds, ground
- 1 teaspoon garlic powder
- 1 teaspoon paprika
- 1 teaspoon kosher salt
- ½ teaspoon pepper

Crust:
- ½ cup pork rinds, ground

Method:
1. Toss all the meatball ingredients in a bowl and mix well.
2. Make small meatballs out this mixture and roll them in the pork rinds.
3. Place the coated meatballs in the air fryer basket.
4. Press "Power Button" of Air Fry Oven and turn the dial to select the "Bake" mode.
5. Press the Time button and again turn the dial to set the cooking time to 12 minutes.
6. Now push the Temp button and rotate the dial to set the temperature at 400 degrees F.
7. Once preheated, place the air fryer basket inside and close its lid.
8. Serve warm.

Nutritional Information per Serving:
Calories 529; Total Fat 17 g; Saturated Fat 3 g; Cholesterol 65 mg; Sodium 391 mg

Easy Italian Meatballs

Prep Time: 10 minutes; Cooking Time: 13 minutes; Serving: 4

Ingredients

- 2-lb. lean ground turkey
- ¼ cup onion, minced
- 2 cloves garlic, minced
- 2 tablespoons parsley, chopped
- 2 eggs
- 1½ cup parmesan cheese, grated
- ½ teaspoon red pepper flakes
- ½ teaspoon Italian seasoning
- Salt and black pepper to taste

Method:

1. Toss all the meatball ingredients in a bowl and mix well.
2. Make small meatballs out this mixture and place them in the air fryer basket.
3. Press "Power Button" of Air Fry Oven and turn the dial to select the "Air Fry" mode.
4. Press the Time button and again turn the dial to set the cooking time to 13 minutes.
5. Now push the Temp button and rotate the dial to set the temperature at 350 degrees F.
6. Once preheated, place the air fryer basket inside and close its lid.
7. Flip the meatballs when cooked halfway through.
8. Serve warm.

Nutritional Information per Serving:

Calories 472; Total Fat 25.8 g; Saturated Fat .4 g; Cholesterol 268 mg; Sodium 503 mg

Oregano Chicken Breast

Prep Time: 10 minutes; Cooking Time: 25 minutes; Serving: 6

Ingredients

- 2 lbs. chicken breasts, minced
- 1 tablespoon avocado oil
- 1 teaspoon smoked paprika
- 1 teaspoon garlic powder
- 1 teaspoon oregano
- 1/2 teaspoon salt
- Black pepper, to taste

Method:

1. Toss all the meatball ingredients in a bowl and mix well.
2. Make small meatballs out this mixture and place them in the air fryer basket.
3. Press "Power Button" of Air Fry Oven and turn the dial to select the "Air Fry" mode.
4. Press the Time button and again turn the dial to set the cooking time to 25 minutes.
5. Now push the Temp button and rotate the dial to set the temperature at 375 degrees F.
6. Once preheated, place the air fryer basket inside and close its lid.
7. Serve warm.

Nutritional Information per Serving:

Calories 352; Total Fat 14 g; Saturated Fat 2 g; Cholesterol 65 mg; Sodium 220 mg

Lemon Chicken Breasts

Prep Time: 10 minutes; Cooking Time: 30 minutes; Serving: 4

Ingredients

- 1/4 cup olive oil
- 3 tablespoons garlic, minced
- 1/3 cup dry white wine
- 1 tablespoon lemon zest, grated
- 2 tablespoons lemon juice
- 1 1/2 teaspoons dried oregano, crushed
- 1 teaspoon thyme leaves, minced
- Salt and black pepper
- 4 skin-on boneless chicken breasts
- 1 lemon, sliced

Method:

1. Whisk everything in a baking pan to coat the chicken breasts well.

2. Place the lemon slices on top of the chicken breasts.
3. Spread the mustard mixture over the toasted bread slices.
4. Press "Power Button" of Air Fry Oven and turn the dial to select the "Bake" mode.
5. Press the Time button and again turn the dial to set the cooking time to 30 minutes.
6. Now push the Temp button and rotate the dial to set the temperature at 370 degrees F.
7. Once preheated, place the baking pan inside and close its lid.
8. Serve warm.

Nutritional Information per Serving:
Calories 388; Total Fat 8 g; Saturated Fat 1 g; Cholesterol 153mg; sodium 339 mg

Maple Chicken Thighs

Prep Time: 10 minutes; Cooking Time: 30 minutes; Serving: 4
Ingredients

- 4 large chicken thighs, bone-in
- 2 tablespoons French mustard
- 2 tablespoons Dijon mustard
- 1 clove minced garlic
- 1/2 teaspoon dried marjoram
- 2 tablespoons maple syrup

Method:
1. Mix chicken with everything in a bowl and coat it well.
2. Place the chicken along with its marinade in the baking pan.
3. Press "Power Button" of Air Fry Oven and turn the dial to select the "Bake" mode.
4. Press the Time button and again turn the dial to set the cooking time to 30 minutes.
5. Now push the Temp button and rotate the dial to set the temperature at 370 degrees F.
6. Once preheated, place the baking pan inside and close its lid.
7. Serve warm.

Nutritional Information per Serving:
Calories 301; Total Fat 15.8 g; Saturated Fat 2.7 g; Cholesterol 75 mg; Sodium 189 mg

Orange Chicken Rice

Prep Time: 10 minutes; Cooking Time: 55 minutes; Serving: 4
Ingredients

- 3 tablespoons olive oil
- 1 medium onion, chopped
- 1 3/4 cups chicken broth
- 1 cup brown basmati rice
- Zest and juice of 2 oranges
- Salt to taste
- 4 (6-oz.) boneless, skinless chicken thighs
- Black pepper, to taste
- 2 tablespoons fresh mint, chopped
- 2 tablespoons pine nuts, toasted

Method:
1. Spread the rice in a casserole dish and place the chicken on top.
2. Toss the rest of the ingredients in a bowl and liberally pour over the chicken.
3. Press "Power Button" of Air Fry Oven and turn the dial to select the "Bake" mode.
4. Press the Time button and again turn the dial to set the cooking time to 55 minutes.
5. Now push the Temp button and rotate the dial to set the temperature at 350 degrees F.
6. Once preheated, place the casserole dish inside and close its lid.
7. Serve warm.

Nutritional Information per Serving:
Calories 231; Total Fat 20.1 g; Saturated Fat 2.4 g; Cholesterol 110 mg; Sodium 941 mg

Chicken & Rice Casserole

Prep Time: 10 minutes; Cooking Time: 40 minutes; Serving: 6
Ingredients

- 2 lbs. bone-in chicken thighs
- Salt and black pepper
- 1 teaspoon olive oil
- 5 cloves garlic, chopped
- 2 large onions, chopped
- 2 large red bell peppers, chopped
- 1 tablespoon sweet Hungarian paprika
- 1 teaspoon hot Hungarian paprika
- 2 tablespoons tomato paste
- 2 cups chicken broth
- 3 cups brown rice, thawed
- 2 tablespoons parsley, chopped
- 6 tablespoons sour cream

Method:
1. Mix broth, tomato paste, and all the spices in a bowl.
2. Add chicken and mix well to coat.
3. Spread the rice in a casserole dish and add chicken along with its marinade.
4. Top the casserole with the rest of the ingredients.
5. Press "Power Button" of Air Fry Oven and turn the dial to select the "Bake" mode.
6. Press the Time button and again turn the dial to set the cooking time to 40 minutes.
7. Now push the Temp button and rotate the dial to set the temperature at 350 degrees F.
8. Once preheated, place the baking pan inside and close its lid.
9. Serve warm.

Nutritional Information per Serving:
Calories 440; Total Fat 7.9 g; Saturated Fat 1.8 g; Cholesterol 5 mg; Sodium 581 mg

Deviled Chicken

Prep Time: 10 minutes; Cooking Time: 40 minutes; Serving: 8
Ingredients
- 2 tablespoons butter
- 2 cloves garlic, chopped
- 1 cup Dijon mustard
- 1/2 teaspoon cayenne pepper
- 1 1/2 cups panko breadcrumbs
- 3/4 cup Parmesan, freshly grated
- 1/4 cup chives, chopped
- 2 teaspoons paprika
- 8 small bone-in chicken thighs, skin removed

Method:
1. Toss the chicken thighs with crumbs, cheese, chives, butter, and spices in a bowl and mix well to coat.
2. Transfer the chicken along with its spice mix to a baking pan.
3. Press "Power Button" of Air Fry Oven and turn the dial to select the "Air Fry" mode.
4. Press the Time button and again turn the dial to set the cooking time to 40 minutes.
5. Now push the Temp button and rotate the dial to set the temperature at 350 degrees F.
6. Once preheated, place the baking pan inside and close its lid.
7. Serve warm.

Nutritional Information per Serving:
Calories 380; Total Fat 20 g; Saturated Fat 5 g; Cholesterol 151 mg; Sodium 686 mg

Marinated Chicken Parmesan

Prep Time: 10 minutes; Cooking Time: 20 minutes; Serving: 4
Ingredients
- 2 cups breadcrumbs
- 1 teaspoon dried oregano
- 1/2 teaspoon garlic powder
- 4 teaspoons paprika
- 1/2 teaspoon salt
- 1/2 teaspoon black pepper
- 2 egg whites
- 1/2 cup skim milk
- 1/2 cup flour
- 4 (6 oz.) chicken breast halves, lb.ed
- Cooking spray
- 1 jar marinara sauce
- 3/4 cup mozzarella cheese, shredded
- 2 tablespoons Parmesan, shredded

Method:
1. Whisk the flour with all the spices in a bowl and beat the eggs in another.
2. Coat the pounded chicken with flour then dip in the egg whites.
3. Dredge the chicken breast through the crumbs well.
4. Spread marinara sauce in a baking dish and place the crusted chicken on it.
5. Drizzle cheese on top of the chicken.
6. Press "Power Button" of Air Fry Oven and turn the dial to select the "Bake" mode.
7. Press the Time button and again turn the dial to set the cooking time to 20 minutes.
8. Now push the Temp button and rotate the dial to set the temperature at 400 degrees F.
9. Once preheated, place the baking pan inside and close its lid.
10. Serve warm.

Nutritional Information per Serving:
Calories 361; Total Fat 16.3 g; Saturated Fat 4.9 g; Cholesterol 114 mg; Sodium 515 mg

Rosemary Lemon Chicken

Prep Time: 10 minutes; Cooking Time: 45 minutes; Serving: 8
Ingredients
- 4-lb. chicken, cut into pieces
- Salt and black pepper, to taste
- Flour for dredging
- 3 tablespoons olive oil
- 1 large onion, sliced
- Peel of ½ lemon
- 2 large garlic cloves, minced
- 1 1/2 teaspoons rosemary leaves
- 1 tablespoon honey
- 1/4 cup lemon juice
- 1 cup chicken broth

Method:
1. Dredges the chicken through the flour then place in the baking pan.
2. Whisk broth with the rest of the ingredients in a bowl.
3. Pour this mixture over the dredged chicken in the pan.
4. Press "Power Button" of Air Fry Oven and turn the dial to select the "Bake" mode.
5. Press the Time button and again turn the dial to set the cooking time to 45 minutes.
6. Now push the Temp button and rotate the dial to set the temperature at 400 degrees F.
7. Once preheated, place the baking pan inside and close its lid.
8. Baste the chicken with its sauce every 15 minutes.
9. Serve warm.

Nutritional Information per Serving:
Calories 405; Total Fat 22.7 g; Saturated Fat 6.1 g; Cholesterol 4 mg; Sodium 227 mg

Garlic Chicken Potatoes

Prep Time: 10 minutes; Cooking Time: 30 minutes; Serving: 4
Ingredients
- 2 lbs. red potatoes, quartered
- 3 tablespoons olive oil
- 1/2 teaspoon cumin seeds
- Salt and black pepper, to taste
- 4 garlic cloves, chopped
- 2 tablespoons brown sugar
- 1 lemon (1/2 juiced and 1/2 cut into wedges)
- Pinch of red pepper flakes
- 4 skinless, boneless chicken breasts
- 2 tablespoons cilantro, chopped

Method:
1. Place the chicken, lemon, garlic, and potatoes in a baking pan.
2. Toss the spices, herbs, oil, and sugar in a bowl.
3. Add this mixture to the chicken and veggies then toss well to coat.
4. Press "Power Button" of Air Fry Oven and turn the dial to select the "Bake" mode.

5. Press the Time button and again turn the dial to set the cooking time to 30 minutes.
6. Now push the Temp button and rotate the dial to set the temperature at 400 degrees F.
7. Once preheated, place the baking pan inside and close its lid.
8. Serve warm.

Nutritional Information per Serving:

Calories 545; Total Fat 36.4 g; Saturated Fat 10.1 g; Cholesterol 200 mg; Sodium 272 mg

Chicken Potato Bake

Prep Time: 10 minutes; Cooking Time: 25 minutes; Serving: 4

Ingredients

- 4 potatoes, diced
- 1 tablespoon garlic, minced
- 1.5 tablespoons olive oil
- 1/8 teaspoon salt
- 1/8 teaspoon pepper
- 1.5 lbs. boneless skinless chicken
- 3/4 cup mozzarella cheese, shredded
- parsley chopped

Method:

1. Toss chicken and potatoes with all the spices and oil in a baking pan.
2. Drizzle the cheese on top of the chicken and potato.
3. Press "Power Button" of Air Fry Oven and turn the dial to select the "Bake" mode.
4. Press the Time button and again turn the dial to set the cooking time to 25 minutes.
5. Now push the Temp button and rotate the dial to set the temperature at 375 degrees F.
6. Once preheated, place the baking pan inside and close its lid.
7. Serve warm.

Nutritional Information per Serving:

Calories 695; Total Fat 17.5 g; Saturated Fat 4.8 g; Cholesterol 283 mg; Sodium 355 mg

Spanish Chicken Bake

Prep Time: 10 minutes; Cooking Time: 25 minutes; Serving: 4

Ingredients

- ½ onion, quartered
- ½ red onion, quartered
- ½ lb. potatoes, quartered
- 4 garlic cloves
- 4 tomatoes, quartered
- 1/8 cup chorizo
- ¼ teaspoon paprika powder
- 4 chicken thighs, boneless
- ¼ teaspoon dried oregano
- ½ green bell pepper, julienned
- Salt
- Black pepper

Method:

1. Toss chicken, veggies, and all the ingredients in a baking tray.
2. Press "Power Button" of Air Fry Oven and turn the dial to select the "Bake" mode.
3. Press the Time button and again turn the dial to set the cooking time to 25 minutes.
4. Now push the Temp button and rotate the dial to set the temperature at 425 degrees F.
5. Once preheated, place the baking pan inside and close its lid.
6. Serve warm.

Nutritional Information per Serving:

Calories 301; Total Fat 8.9 g; Saturated Fat 4.5 g; Cholesterol 57 mg; Sodium 340 mg

Chicken pasta Bake

Prep Time: 10 minutes; Cooking Time: 22 minutes; Serving: 4

Ingredients

- 9oz penne, boiled
- 1 onion, roughly chopped
- 3 chicken breasts, cut into strips
- 2 tablespoon olive oil
- 1 tablespoon paprika
- Salt and black pepper

Sauce
- 1¾oz butter
- 1¾oz plain flour
- 1 pint 6 fl oz hot milk
- 1 teaspoon Dijon mustard
- 3½oz Parmesan cheese, grated
- 2 large tomatoes, deseeded and cubed

Method:
1. Butter a casserole dish and toss chicken with pasta, onion, oil, paprika, salt, and black pepper in it.
2. Prepare the sauce in a suitable pan. Add butter and melt over moderate heat.
3. Stir in flour and whisk well for 2 minutes, then pour in hot milk.
4. Mix until smooth, then add tomatoes, mustard, and cheese.
5. Toss well and pour this sauce over the chicken mix in the casserole dish.
6. Press "Power Button" of Air Fry Oven and turn the dial to select the "Bake" mode.
7. Press the Time button and again turn the dial to set the cooking time to 20 minutes.
8. Now push the Temp button and rotate the dial to set the temperature at 375 degrees F.
9. Once preheated, place the casserole dish inside and close its lid.
10. Serve warm.

Nutritional Information per Serving:
Calories 548; Total Fat 22.9 g; Saturated Fat 9 g; Cholesterol 105 mg; Sodium 350 mg

Creamy Chicken Casserole

Prep Time: 10 minutes; Cooking Time: 45 minutes; Serving: 6
Ingredients
Chicken and Mushroom Casserole:
- 2 1/2 lbs. chicken breasts, cut into strips
- 1 1/2 teaspoon salt
- 1/4 teaspoon black pepper
- 1 cup all-purpose flour
- 6 tablespoon olive oil
- 1-lb. white mushrooms, sliced
- 1 medium onion, diced
- 3 garlic cloves, minced

Sauce:
- 3 tablespoon unsalted butter
- 3 tablespoon all-purpose flour
- 1 1/2 cups chicken broth
- 1 tablespoon lemon juice
- 1 cup half and half cream

Method:
1. Butter a casserole dish and toss in chicken with mushrooms and all the casserole ingredients.
2. Prepare the sauce in a suitable pan. Add butter and melt over moderate heat.
3. Stir in flour and whisk well for 2 minutes, then pour in milk, lemon juice, and cream.
4. Mix well and pour milk this sauce over the chicken mix in the casserole dish.
5. Press "Power Button" of Air Fry Oven and turn the dial to select the "Bake" mode.
6. Press the Time button and again turn the dial to set the cooking time to 45 minutes.
7. Now push the Temp button and rotate the dial to set the temperature at 350 degrees F.
8. Once preheated, place the casserole dish inside and close its lid.
9. Serve warm.

Nutritional Information per Serving:
Calories 409; Total Fat 50.5 g; Saturated Fat 11.7 g; Cholesterol 58 mg; Sodium 463 mg

Italian Chicken Bake

Prep Time: 10 minutes; Cooking Time: 25 minutes; Serving: 6
Ingredients:
- ¾ lbs. chicken breasts
- 2 tablespoons pesto sauce

- ½ (14 oz) can tomatoes, diced
- 1 cup Mozzarella cheese, shredded
- 2 tablespoon fresh basil, chopped

Method:

1. Place the flattened chicken breasts in a baking pan and top them with pesto.
2. Add tomatoes, cheese, and basil on top of each chicken piece.
3. Press "Power Button" of Air Fry Oven and turn the dial to select the "Bake" mode.
4. Press the Time button and again turn the dial to set the cooking time to 25 minutes.
5. Now push the Temp button and rotate the dial to set the temperature at 355 degrees F.
6. Once preheated, place the baking dish inside and close its lid.
7. Serve warm.

Nutritional Information per Serving:

Calories 537; Total Fat 19.8 g; Saturated Fat 1.4 g; Cholesterol 10 mg; Sodium 719 mg

Pesto Chicken Bake

Prep Time: 10 minutes; Cooking Time: 35 minutes; Serving: 3

Ingredients

- 3 chicken breasts
- 1 (6 oz.) jar basil pesto
- 2 medium fresh tomatoes, sliced
- 6 mozzarella cheese slices

Method:

1. Spread the tomato slices in a casserole dish and top them with chicken.
2. Add pesto and cheese on top of the chicken and spread evenly.
3. Press "Power Button" of Air Fry Oven and turn the dial to select the "Air Fry" mode.
4. Press the Time button and again turn the dial to set the cooking time to 30 minutes.
5. Now push the Temp button and rotate the dial to set the temperature at 350 degrees F.
6. Once preheated, place the casserole dish inside and close its lid.
7. After it is baked, switch the oven to broil mode and broil for 5 minutes.
8. Serve warm.

Nutritional Information per Serving:

Calories 452; Total Fat 4 g; Saturated Fat 2 g; Cholesterol 65 mg; Sodium 220 mg

Duck a la Orange

Prep Time: 10 minutes; Cooking Time: 60 minutes; Serving: 6

Ingredients

- 1 tablespoon salt
- 1 teaspoon ground coriander
- 1/2 teaspoon ground cumin
- 1 teaspoon black pepper
- 1 (5- to 6-lb) duck, skinned
- 1 juice orange, halved
- 4 fresh thyme sprigs
- 4 fresh marjoram sprigs
- 2 parsley sprigs
- 1 small onion, cut into wedges
- 1/2 cup dry white wine
- 1/2 cup chicken broth
- 1/2 carrot
- 1/2 celery rib

Method:

1. Place the Pekin duck in a roasting pan and whisk orange juice and rest of ingredients in a bowl.
2. Pour the herb sauce over the duck and brush it liberally
3. Press "Power Button" of Air Fry Oven and turn the dial to select the "Air Roast" mode.
4. Press the Time button and again turn the dial to set the cooking time to 1 hour.
5. Now push the Temp button and rotate the dial to set the temperature at 350 degrees F.
6. Once preheated, place the casserole dish inside and close its lid.
7. Continue basting the duck during baking.
8. Serve warm.

Nutritional Information per Serving:

Calories 301; Total Fat 15.8 g; Saturated Fat 2.7 g; Cholesterol 75 mg; Sodium 389 mg

Baked Duck

Prep Time: 10 minutes; Cooking Time: 20 minutes; Serving: 6

Ingredients

- 1 ½ sprig of fresh rosemary
- ½ nutmeg
- Black pepper
- Juice from 1 orange
- 1 whole duck
- 4 cloves garlic, chopped
- 1 ½ red onions, chopped
- a few stalks celery
- 1 ½ carrot
- 2 cm piece fresh ginger
- 1 ½ bay leaves
- 2 lbs. Piper potatoes
- 4 cups chicken stock

Method:

1. Place duck in a large cooking pot and add broth along with all the ingredients.
2. Cook this duck for 2 hours on a simmer then transfer to the baking tray.
3. Press "Power Button" of Air Fry Oven and turn the dial to select the "Air Fry" mode.
4. Press the Time button and again turn the dial to set the cooking time to 20 minutes.
5. Now push the Temp button and rotate the dial to set the temperature at 350 degrees F.
6. Once preheated, place the baking tray inside and close its lid.
7. Serve warm.

Nutritional Information per Serving:

Calories 308; Total Fat 20.5 g; Saturated Fat 3 g; Cholesterol 42 mg; Sodium 688 mg

Roasted Goose

Prep Time: 10 minutes; Cooking Time: 40 minutes; Serving: 12

Ingredients

- 8 lbs. goose
- Juice of a lemon
- Salt and pepper
- 1/2 yellow onion, peeled and chopped
- 1 head garlic, peeled and chopped
- 1/2 cup wine
- 1 teaspoon dried thyme

Method:

1. Place the goose in a baking tray and whisk the rest of the ingredients in a bowl.
2. Pour this thick sauce over the goose and brush it liberally.
3. Press "Power Button" of Air Fry Oven and turn the dial to select the "Air Roast" mode.
4. Press the Time button and again turn the dial to set the cooking time to 40 minutes.
5. Now push the Temp button and rotate the dial to set the temperature at 355 degrees F.
6. Once preheated, place the casserole dish inside and close its lid.
7. Serve warm.

Nutritional Information per Serving:

Calories 231; Total Fat 20.1 g; Saturated Fat 2.4 g; Cholesterol 110 mg; Sodium 941 mg

Christmas Roast Goose

Prep Time: 10 minutes; Cooking Time: 60 minutes; Serving: 12

Ingredients

- 2 goose
- 2 lemons, sliced
- 1 ½ lime, sliced
- ½ teaspoon Chinese five-spice powder
- ½ handful parsley, chopped
- ½ handful sprigs, chopped
- ½ handful thyme, chopped
- ½ handful sage, chopped
- 1 ½ tablespoon clear honey
- ½ tablespoon thyme leaves

Method:

1. Place the goose in a baking dish and brush it with honey.
2. Set the lemon and lime slices on top of the goose.
3. Add all the herbs and spice powder over the lemon slices.
4. Press "Power Button" of Air Fry Oven and turn the dial to select the "Air Roast" mode.
5. Press the Time button and again turn the dial to set the cooking time to 60 minutes.
6. Now push the Temp button and rotate the dial to set the temperature at 375 degrees F.
7. Once preheated, place the baking dish inside and close its lid.
8. Serve warm.

Nutritional Information per Serving:

Calories 472; Total Fat 11.1 g; Saturated Fat 5.8 g; Cholesterol 610 mg; Sodium 749 mg

Chicken Kebabs

Prep Time: 10 minutes; Cooking Time: 20 minutes; Serving: 2

Ingredients

- 16 oz skinless chicken breasts, cubed
- 2 tablespoons soy sauce
- ½ zucchini sliced
- 1 tablespoon chicken seasoning
- 1 teaspoon bbq seasoning
- salt and pepper to taste
- ½ green pepper sliced
- ½ red pepper sliced
- ½ yellow pepper sliced
- ¼ red onion sliced
- 4 cherry tomatoes
- cooking spray

Method:

1. Toss chicken and veggies with all the spices and seasoning in a bowl.
2. Alternatively, thread them on skewers and place these skewers in the Air fryer basket.
3. Press "Power Button" of Air Fry Oven and turn the dial to select the "Air Fry" mode.
4. Press the Time button and again turn the dial to set the cooking time to 20 minutes.
5. Now push the Temp button and rotate the dial to set the temperature at 350 degrees F.
6. Once preheated, place the baking dish inside and close its lid.
7. Flip the skewers when cooked halfway through then resume cooking.
8. Serve warm.

Nutritional Information per Serving:

Calories 327; Total Fat 3.5 g; Saturated Fat 0.5 g; Cholesterol 162 mg; Sodium 142 mg

Asian Chicken Kebabs

Prep Time: 10 minutes; Cooking Time: 12 minutes; Serving: 6

Ingredients

- 2 lbs. chicken breasts, cubed
- 1/2 cup soy sauce
- 6 cloves garlic, crushed
- 1 teaspoon fresh ginger, grated
- 1/2 cup golden sweetener
- 1 red pepper, chopped
- 1/2 red onion, chopped
- 8 mushrooms, halved
- 2 cups zucchini, chopped

Method:

1. Toss chicken and veggies with all the spices and seasoning in a bowl.
2. Alternatively, thread them on skewers and place these skewers in the Air fryer basket.
3. Press "Power Button" of Air Fry Oven and turn the dial to select the "Air Fry" mode.
4. Press the Time button and again turn the dial to set the cooking time to 12 minutes.
5. Now push the Temp button and rotate the dial to set the temperature at 380 degrees F.
6. Once preheated, place the baking dish inside and close its lid.
7. Flip the skewers when cooked halfway through then resume cooking.
8. Serve warm.

Nutritional Information per Serving:
   Calories 353; Total Fat 7.5 g; Saturated Fat 1.1 g; Cholesterol 20 mg; Sodium 297 mg

Kebab Tavuk Sheesh

Prep Time: 10 minutes; Cooking Time: 10 minutes; Serving: 2

Ingredients

- 1/4 cup plain yogurt
- 1 tablespoon garlic, minced
- 1 tablespoon tomato paste
- 1 tablespoon olive oil
- 1 tablespoon lemon juice
- 1 teaspoon salt
- 1 teaspoon ground cumin
- 1 teaspoon smoked paprika
- 1/2 teaspoon ground cinnamon
- 1/2 teaspoon ground black pepper
- 1/2 teaspoon cayenne
- 1 lb. boneless skinless chicken thighs, quartered

Method:

1. Mix chicken with yogurt and all the seasonings in a bowl.
2. Marinate the yogurt chicken for 30 minutes in the refrigerator.
3. Thread chicken pieces on the skewers and place these skewers in the Air fryer basket.
4. Press "Power Button" of Air Fry Oven and turn the dial to select the "Air Fry" mode.
5. Press the Time button and again turn the dial to set the cooking time to 10 minutes.
6. Now push the Temp button and rotate the dial to set the temperature at 370 degrees F.
7. Once preheated, place the baking dish inside and close its lid.
8. Flip the skewers when cooked halfway through then resume cooking.
9. Serve warm.

Nutritional Information per Serving:
   Calories 248; Total Fat 13 g; Saturated Fat 7 g; Cholesterol 387 mg; Sodium 353 mg

Chicken Mushroom Kebab

Prep Time: 10 minutes; Cooking Time: 15 minutes; Serving: 4

Ingredients

- 1/3 cup honey
- 1/3 cup soy sauce
- Salt, to taste
- 6 mushrooms chop in half
- 3 bell peppers, cubed
- 2 chicken breasts diced

Method:

1. Toss chicken, mushrooms and veggies with all the honey, and seasoning in a bowl.
2. Alternatively, thread them on skewers and place these skewers in the Air fryer basket.
3. Press "Power Button" of Air Fry Oven and turn the dial to select the "Air Fry" mode.
4. Press the Time button and again turn the dial to set the cooking time to 15 minutes.
5. Now push the Temp button and rotate the dial to set the temperature at 350 degrees F.
6. Once preheated, place the baking dish inside and close its lid.
7. Flip the skewers when cooked halfway through then resume cooking.
8. Serve warm.

Nutritional Information per Serving:
   Calories 457; Total Fat 19.1 g; Saturated Fat 11 g; Cholesterol 262 mg; Sodium 557 mg

Chicken Fajita Skewers

Prep Time: 10 minutes; Cooking Time: 8 minutes; Serving: 2

Ingredients

- 1 lb. chicken breasts, diced
- 1 tablespoon lemon juice
- 1 teaspoon chili powder
- 1 teaspoon cumin
- 1 orange bell pepper, cut into squares
- 1 red bell pepper, cut into squares

- 2 tablespoon olive oil
- 1 teaspoon garlic powder
- 1 large red onion, cut into squares
- 1 teaspoon salt
- 1 teaspoon ground black pepper
- 1 teaspoon oregano
- 1 teaspoon parsley flakes
- 1 teaspoon paprika

Method:
1. Toss chicken and veggies with all the spices and seasoning in a bowl.
2. Alternatively, thread them on skewers and place these skewers in the Air fryer basket.
3. Press "Power Button" of Air Fry Oven and turn the dial to select the "Air Fry" mode.
4. Press the Time button and again turn the dial to set the cooking time to 8 minutes.
5. Now push the Temp button and rotate the dial to set the temperature at 360 degrees F.
6. Once preheated, place the baking dish inside and close its lid.
7. Flip the skewers when cooked halfway through then resume cooking.
8. Serve warm.

Nutritional Information per Serving:
Calories 392; Total Fat 16.1 g; Saturated Fat 2.3 g; Cholesterol 231 mg; Sodium 466 mg

Zucchini Chicken Kebabs

Prep Time: 10 minutes; Cooking Time: 16 minutes; Serving: 4
Ingredients
- 1 large zucchini, cut into squares
- 2 chicken breasts boneless, skinless, cubed
- 1 onion yellow, cut into squares
- 1.5 cup grape tomatoes
- 1 clove garlic minced
- 1 lemon juiced
- 1/4 c olive oil
- 1 tablespoon olive oil
- 2 tablespoon red wine vinegar
- 1 teaspoon oregano

Method:
1. Toss chicken and veggies with all the spices and seasoning in a bowl.
2. Alternatively, thread them on skewers and place these skewers in the Air fryer basket.
3. Press "Power Button" of Air Fry Oven and turn the dial to select the "Air Fry" mode.
4. Press the Time button and again turn the dial to set the cooking time to 16 minutes.
5. Now push the Temp button and rotate the dial to set the temperature at 380 degrees F.
6. Once preheated, place the baking dish inside and close its lid.
7. Flip the skewers when cooked halfway through then resume cooking.
8. Serve warm.

Nutritional Information per Serving:
Calories 321; Total Fat 7.4 g; Saturated Fat 4.6 g; Cholesterol 105 mg; Sodium 353 mg

Chicken Soy Skewers

Prep Time: 10 minutes; Cooking Time: 7 minutes; Serving: 4
Ingredients
- 1-lb. boneless chicken tenders, diced
- 1/2 cup soy sauce
- 1/2 cup pineapple juice
- 1/4 cup sesame seed oil
- 4 garlic cloves, chopped
- 4 scallions, chopped
- 1 tablespoon grated ginger
- 2 teaspoons toasted sesame seeds
- black pepper

Method:
1. Toss chicken with all the sauces and seasonings in a baking pan.
2. Press "Power Button" of Air Fry Oven and turn the dial to select the "Air Fry" mode.
3. Press the Time button and again turn the dial to set the cooking time to 7 minutes.
4. Now push the Temp button and rotate the dial to set the temperature at 390 degrees F.

5. Once preheated, place the baking dish inside and close its lid.
6. Serve warm.

Nutritional Information per Serving:
Calories 248; Total Fat 15.7 g; Saturated Fat 2.7 g; Cholesterol 75 mg; Sodium 94 mg

Chicken Alfredo Bake

Prep Time: 10 minutes; Cooking Time: 25 minutes; Serving: 6
Ingredients

- 1 tablespoon olive oil
- 3 chicken breasts, cubed
- salt, to taste
- Black pepper, to taste
- 4 cloves garlic, minced
- 2 ½ cups chicken broth
- 2 ½ cups heavy cream
- 1 cup penne pasta, uncooked
- 2 cups parmesan cheese
- 2 cups mozzarella cheese
- 1 handful fresh parsley, chopped

Method:
1. Whisk cream, broth, chicken, pasta, and all the ingredients in a casserole dish.
2. Press "Power Button" of Air Fry Oven and turn the dial to select the "Bake" mode.
3. Press the Time button and again turn the dial to set the cooking time to 25 minutes.
4. Now push the Temp button and rotate the dial to set the temperature at 380 degrees F.
5. Once preheated, place the baking dish inside and close its lid.
6. Serve warm.

Nutritional Information per Serving:
Calories 378; Total Fat 21 g; Saturated Fat 4.3 g; Cholesterol 150 mg; Sodium 146 mg

Chapter 4: Beef Recipes

Basic Meatloaf

Prep Time: 10 minutes; Cooking Time: 40 minutes; Serving: 8

Ingredients

- 2 lbs. ground beef
- 1 shallot, chopped
- 2 eggs
- 3 garlic cloves minced
- 3 tablespoon tomato sauce
- 3 tablespoon parsley, chopped
- 3/4 cup Panko breadcrumbs
- 1/3 cup milk
- 1 ½ teaspoon salt or to taste
- 1 ½ teaspoon Italian seasoning
- ¼ teaspoon ground black pepper
- ½ teaspoon ground paprika

Method:

1. Thoroughly mix ground beef with egg, onion, garlic, crumbs, and all the ingredients in a bowl.
2. Grease a meatloaf pan with oil or butter and spread the minced beef in the pan.
3. Press "Power Button" of Air Fry Oven and turn the dial to select the "Bake" mode.
4. Press the Time button and again turn the dial to set the cooking time to 40 minutes.
5. Now push the Temp button and rotate the dial to set the temperature at 375 degrees F.
6. Once preheated, place the beef baking pan in the oven and close its lid.
7. Slice and serve.

Nutritional Information per Serving:

Calories 284; Total Fat 7.9 g; Saturated Fat 1.4 g; Cholesterol 36 mg; Sodium 704 mg

Sauce Glazed Meatloaf

Prep Time: 10 minutes; Cooking Time: 55 minutes; Serving: 4

Ingredients

- 1 lb. ground beef
- ½ onion chopped
- 1 egg
- 1 ½ garlic clove, minced
- 1 ½ tablespoon ketchup
- 1 ½ tablespoon fresh parsley, chopped
- 1/4 cup breadcrumbs
- 2 tablespoons milk
- Salt to taste
- 1 ½ teaspoon herb seasoning
- ¼ teaspoon black pepper
- ½ teaspoon ground paprika

Glaze:

- 3/4 cup ketchup
- 1 ½ teaspoon white vinegar
- 2 ½ tablespoon brown sugar
- 1 teaspoon garlic powder
- ½ teaspoon onion powder
- ¼ teaspoon ground black pepper
- ¼ teaspoon salt

Method:

1. Thoroughly mix ground beef with egg, onion, garlic, crumbs, and all the ingredients in a bowl.
2. Grease a meatloaf pan with oil or butter and spread the minced beef in the pan.
3. Press "Power Button" of Air Fry Oven and turn the dial to select the "Bake" mode.
4. Press the Time button and again turn the dial to set the cooking time to 40 minutes.
5. Now push the Temp button and rotate the dial to set the temperature at 375 degrees F.
6. Once preheated, place the beef baking pan in the oven and close its lid.
7. Meanwhile, prepare the glaze by whisking its ingredients in a saucepan.
8. Stir cook for 5 minutes until it thickens.
9. Brush this glaze over the meatloaf and bake it again for 15 minutes.
10. Slice and serve.

Nutritional Information per Serving:

Calories 134; Total Fat 4.7 g; Saturated Fat 0.6 g; Cholesterol 124mg; Sodium 1 mg

Zucchini Beef Meatloaf

Prep Time: 10 minutes; Cooking Time: 40 minutes; Serving: 8

Ingredients

- 2 lbs. ground beef
- 1 cup zucchini, shredded
- 2 eggs
- 3 garlic cloves minced
- 3 tablespoon Worcestershire sauce
- 3 tablespoon fresh parsley, chopped
- 3/4 cup Panko breadcrumbs
- 1/3 cup beef broth
- Salt to taste
- ¼ teaspoon ground black pepper
- ½ teaspoon ground paprika

Method:

1. Thoroughly mix ground beef with egg, zucchini, onion, garlic, crumbs, and all the ingredients in a bowl.
2. Grease a meatloaf pan with oil or butter and spread the minced beef in the pan.
3. Press "Power Button" of Air Fry Oven and turn the dial to select the "Bake" mode.
4. Press the Time button and again turn the dial to set the cooking time to 40 minutes.
5. Now push the Temp button and rotate the dial to set the temperature at 375 degrees F.
6. Once preheated, place the beef baking pan in the oven and close its lid.
7. Slice and serve.

Nutritional Information per Serving:

Calories 387; Total Fat 6 g; Saturated Fat 9.9 g; Cholesterol 41 mg; Sodium 154 mg

Carrot Beef Cake

Prep Time: 10 minutes; Cooking Time: 60 minutes; Serving: 10

Ingredients

- 3 eggs, beaten
- 1/2 cup almond milk
- 1-oz. onion soup mix
- 1 cup dry bread crumbs
- 2 cups shredded carrots
- 2 lbs. lean ground beef
- 1/2-lb. ground pork

Method:

1. Thoroughly mix ground beef with carrots and all other ingredients in a bowl.
2. Grease a meatloaf pan with oil or butter and spread the minced beef in the pan.
3. Press "Power Button" of Air Fry Oven and turn the dial to select the "Bake" mode.
4. Press the Time button and again turn the dial to set the cooking time to 60 minutes.
5. Now push the Temp button and rotate the dial to set the temperature at 350 degrees F.
6. Once preheated, place the beef baking pan in the oven and close its lid.
7. Slice and serve.

Nutritional Information per Serving:

Calories 212; Total Fat 11.8 g; Saturated Fat 2.2 g; Cholesterol 23mg; Sodium 321 mg

Crumbly Oat Meatloaf

Prep Time: 10 minutes; Cooking Time: 60 minutes; Serving: 8

Ingredients

- 2 lbs. ground beef
- 1 cup of salsa
- ¾ cup Quaker Oats
- ½ cup chopped onion
- 1 large egg, beaten
- 1 tablespoon Worcestershire sauce
- Salt and black pepper to taste

Method:

1. Thoroughly mix ground beef with salsa, oats, onion, egg, and all the ingredients in a bowl.

2. Grease a meatloaf pan with oil or butter and spread the minced beef in the pan.
3. Press "Power Button" of Air Fry Oven and turn the dial to select the "Bake" mode.
4. Press the Time button and again turn the dial to set the cooking time to 60 minutes.
5. Now push the Temp button and rotate the dial to set the temperature at 350 degrees F.
6. Once preheated, place the beef baking pan in the oven and close its lid.
7. Slice and serve.

Nutritional Information per Serving:
Calories 412; Total Fat 24.8 g; Saturated Fat 12.4 g; Cholesterol 3 mg; Sodium 132 mg

Creole Beef Meatloaf

Prep Time: 10 minutes; Cooking Time: 15 minutes; Serving: 6
Ingredients
- 1 lb. ground beef
- 1/2 tablespoon butter
- 1 red bell pepper diced
- 1/3 cup red onion diced
- 1/3 cup cilantro diced
- 1/3 cup zucchini diced
- 1 tablespoon creole seasoning
- 1/2 teaspoon turmeric
- 1/2 teaspoon cumin
- 1/2 teaspoon coriander
- 2 garlic cloves minced
- Salt and black pepper to taste

Method:
1. Mix the beef minced with all the meatball ingredients in a bowl.
2. Make small meatballs out of this mixture and place them in the Air fryer basket.
3. Press "Power Button" of Air Fry Oven and turn the dial to select the "Air Fry" mode.
4. Press the Time button and again turn the dial to set the cooking time to 15 minutes.
5. Now push the Temp button and rotate the dial to set the temperature at 370 degrees F.
6. Once preheated, place the Air fryer basket in the oven and close its lid.
7. Slice and serve warm.

Nutritional Information per Serving:
Calories 331; Total Fat 2.5 g; Saturated Fat 0.5 g; Cholesterol 35 mg; Sodium 595 mg

Healthy Mama Meatloaf

Prep Time: 10 minutes; Cooking Time: 40 minutes; Serving: 8
Ingredients
- 1 tablespoon olive oil
- 1 green bell pepper, diced
- 1/2 cup diced sweet onion
- 1/2 teaspoon minced garlic
- 1-lb. ground beef
- 1 cup whole wheat bread crumbs
- 2 large eggs
- 3/4 cup shredded carrot
- 3/4 cup shredded zucchini
- salt and ground black pepper to taste
- 1/4 cup ketchup, or to taste

Method:
1. Thoroughly mix ground beef with egg, onion, garlic, crumbs, and all the ingredients in a bowl.
2. Grease a meatloaf pan with oil or butter and spread the minced beef in the pan.
3. Press "Power Button" of Air Fry Oven and turn the dial to select the "Bake" mode.
4. Press the Time button and again turn the dial to set the cooking time to 40 minutes.
5. Now push the Temp button and rotate the dial to set the temperature at 375 degrees F.
6. Once preheated, place the beef baking pan in the oven and close its lid.
7. Slice and serve.

Nutritional Information per Serving:
Calories 322; Total Fat 11.8 g; Saturated Fat 2.2 g; Cholesterol 56 mg; Sodium 321 mg

Beef Short Ribs

Prep Time: 10 minutes; Cooking Time: 35 minutes; Serving: 4
Ingredients
- 1 2/3 lbs. short ribs
- Salt and black pepper, to taste
- 1 teaspoon grated garlic
- 1/2 teaspoon salt
- 1 teaspoon cumin seeds
- ¼ cup panko crumbs
- 1 teaspoon ground cumin
- 1 teaspoon avocado oil
- ½ teaspoon orange zest
- 1 egg, beaten

Method:
1. Place the beef ribs in a baking tray and pour the whisked egg on top.
2. Whisk rest of the crusting ingredients in a bowl and spread over the beef.
3. Press "Power Button" of Air Fry Oven and turn the dial to select the "Air Fry" mode.
4. Press the Time button and again turn the dial to set the cooking time to 35 minutes.
5. Now push the Temp button and rotate the dial to set the temperature at 350 degrees F.
6. Once preheated, place the beef baking tray in the oven and close its lid.
7. Serve warm.

Nutritional Information per Serving:
Calories 267; Total Fat 15.4 g; Saturated Fat 4.2 g; Cholesterol 168 mg; Sodium 203 mg

Tarragon Beef Shanks

Prep Time: 10 minutes; Cooking Time: 1hr 30 minutes; Serving: 6
Ingredients
- 2 tablespoons olive oil
- 2 lbs. beef shank
- Salt and black pepper to taste
- 1 onion, diced
- 2 stalks celery, diced
- 1 cup Marsala wine
- 2 tablespoons dried tarragon

Method:
1. Place the beef shanks in a baking pan.
2. Whisk rest of the ingredients in a bowl and pour over the shanks.
3. Place these shanks in the Air fryer basket.
4. Press "Power Button" of Air Fry Oven and turn the dial to select the "Air Fry" mode.
5. Press the Time button and again turn the dial to set the cooking time to 1 hr. 30 minutes.
6. Now push the Temp button and rotate the dial to set the temperature at 400 degrees F.
7. Once preheated, place the Air fryer basket in the oven and close its lid.
8. Serve warm.

Nutritional Information per Serving:
Calories 438; Total Fat 9.7 g; Saturated Fat 4.7 g; Cholesterol 181 mg; Sodium 245 mg

Beef Short Ribs

Prep Time: 10 minutes; Cooking Time: 60 minutes; Serving: 8
Ingredients
- 8 short ribs
- 1 teaspoon salt
- 1 teaspoon black pepper
- 1 cup beef broth
- 1/4 cup Worcestershire sauce
- 1 teaspoon garlic powder
- 1 teaspoon onion powder
- 1 sprig fresh rosemary

Method:
1. Whisk broth with all the spices and seasonings in a bowl.
2. Place the short ribs in a baking tray and pour the broth mixture on top.
3. Cover the ribs and marinate for at least 30 minutes in the refrigerator.

4. Press "Power Button" of Air Fry Oven and turn the dial to select the "Air Fry" mode.
5. Press the Time button and again turn the dial to set the cooking time to 60 minutes.
6. Now push the Temp button and rotate the dial to set the temperature at 350 degrees F.
7. Once preheated, place the beef baking tray in the oven and close its lid.
8. Serve warm.

Nutritional Information per Serving:
Calories 391; Total Fat 2.8 g; Saturated Fat 0.6 g; Cholesterol 330 mg; Sodium 62 mg

Garlic Braised Ribs

Prep Time: 10 minutes; Cooking Time: 1hr 30 minutes; Serving: 10
Ingredients
- 2 tablespoons vegetable oil
- 5 lbs. bone-in short ribs
- Salt and black pepper
- 2 heads garlic, halved
- 1 medium onion, chopped
- 4 ribs celery, chopped
- 2 medium carrots, chopped
- 3 tablespoons tomato paste
- ¼ cup dry red wine
- ¼ cup beef stock
- 4 sprigs thyme
- 1 cup parsley, chopped
- ½ cup chives, chopped
- 1 tablespoon lemon zest, grated

Method:
1. Toss everything in a large bowl then add short ribs.
2. Mix well to soak the ribs and marinate for 30 minutes.
3. Transfer the soaked ribs to the baking pan and add the marinade around them.
4. Press "Power Button" of Air Fry Oven and turn the dial to select the "Bake" mode.
5. Press the Time button and again turn the dial to set the cooking time to 1 hr. 30 minutes.
6. Now push the Temp button and rotate the dial to set the temperature at 400 degrees F.
7. Once preheated, place the rib's tray in the oven and close its lid.
8. Serve warm.

Nutritional Information per Serving:
Calories 453; Total Fat 2.4 g; Saturated Fat 3 g; Cholesterol 21 mg; Sodium 216 mg

BBQ Beef Roast

Prep Time: 10 minutes; Cooking Time: 15 minutes; Serving: 4
Ingredients
- 1lb. beef roast
- ½ cup BBQ sauce

Method:
1. Liberally rub the beef roast with BBQ sauce.
2. Place the saucy roast in the Air fryer basket.
3. Press "Power Button" of Air Fry Oven and turn the dial to select the "Air Fry" mode.
4. Press the Time button and again turn the dial to set the cooking time to 15 minutes.
5. Now push the Temp button and rotate the dial to set the temperature at 390 degrees F.
6. Once preheated, place the Air fryer basket in the oven and close its lid.
7. Flip the roast when cooked halfway through then resume cooking.
8. Serve warm.

Nutritional Information per Serving:
Calories 529; Total Fat 17 g; Saturated Fat 3 g; Cholesterol 65 mg; Sodium 391 mg

Rosemary Beef Roast

Prep Time: 10 minutes; Cooking Time: 15 minutes; Serving: 4
Ingredients
- 2 lb. beef roast
- 1 tablespoon olive oil

- 1 medium onion
- 1 teaspoon salt
- 2 teaspoon rosemary and thyme

Method:
1. Place beef roast in the Air fryer basket.
2. Rub it with olive oil, salt, rosemary, thyme, and onion.
3. Press "Power Button" of Air Fry Oven and turn the dial to select the "Air Fry" mode.
4. Press the Time button and again turn the dial to set the cooking time to 15 minutes.
5. Now push the Temp button and rotate the dial to set the temperature at 390 degrees F.
6. Once preheated, place the Air fryer basket in the oven and close its lid.
7. Flip the roast when cooked halfway through then resume cooking.
8. Serve warm.

Nutritional Information per Serving:
Calories 297; Total Fat 14 g; Saturated Fat 5 g; Cholesterol 99 mg; Sodium 364 mg

Beef Pesto Bake

Prep Time: 10 minutes; Cooking Time: 35 minutes; Serving: 6
Ingredients
- 25 oz. potatoes, boiled
- 14 oz. beef mince
- 23 oz. jar tomato pasta
- 12 oz. pesto
- 1 tablespoon olive oil

Method:
1. Mash the potatoes in a bowl and stir in pesto.
2. Sauté beef mince with olive oil in a frying pan until brown.
3. Layer a casserole dish with tomato pasta sauce.
4. Top the sauce with beef mince.
5. Spread the green pesto potato mash over the beef in an even layer.
6. Press "Power Button" of Air Fry Oven and turn the dial to select the "Bake" mode.
7. Press the Time button and again turn the dial to set the cooking time to 35 minutes.
8. Now push the Temp button and rotate the dial to set the temperature at 350 degrees F.
9. Once preheated, place casserole dish in the oven and close its lid.
10. Serve warm.

Nutritional Information per Serving:
Calories 352; Total Fat 14 g; Saturated Fat 2 g; Cholesterol 65 mg; Sodium 220 mg

Crusted Beef Ribs

Prep Time: 10 minutes; Cooking Time: 1hr 40 minutes; Serving: 8
Ingredients
- 8 beef short ribs, trimmed
- 1/4 cup plain flour
- 1 tablespoon olive oil
- 1 large brown onion, chopped
- 2 garlic cloves, crushed
- 3 medium carrots, peeled and diced
- 2 tablespoons tomato paste
- 2 1/2 cups beef stock
- 2 dried bay leaves
- 1 cup frozen peas
- 3 cups potato gems

Method:
1. Dust the beef ribs with flour and sear it in a pan layered with olive oil.
2. Sear the beef ribs for 4 minutes per side.
3. Transfer the ribs to a baking tray.
4. Add onion, garlic, and carrot to the same pan.
5. Sauté for 5 minutes, then stir in tomato paste, stock, and all other ingredients.
6. Stir cook for 4 minutes then pour this sauce over the ribs.

7. Press "Power Button" of Air Fry Oven and turn the dial to select the "Bake" mode.
8. Press the Time button and again turn the dial to set the cooking time to 1 hr. 30 minutes.
9. Now push the Temp button and rotate the dial to set the temperature at 350 degrees F.
10. Once preheated, place the baking pan in the oven and close its lid.
11. Serve warm.

Nutritional Information per Serving:
   Calories 388; Total Fat 8 g; Saturated Fat 1 g; Cholesterol 153mg; Sodium 339 mg

Beef Potato Meatballs

Prep Time: 10 minutes; Cooking Time: 20 minutes; Serving: 4
Ingredients
- ½ lb. minced beef
- 1 tbs parsley chopped
- 2 teaspoon curry powder
- 1 pinch salt and black pepper
- 1 lb. potato cooked, mashed
- 1 oz. cheese grated
- 1 ½ oz. potato chips crushed

Method:
1. Thoroughly mix the beef with potato and all other ingredients in a bowl.
2. Make small meatballs out of this mixture then place them in the Air fryer basket.
3. Press "Power Button" of Air Fry Oven and turn the dial to select the "Air fry" mode.
4. Press the Time button and again turn the dial to set the cooking time to 20 minutes.
5. Now push the Temp button and rotate the dial to set the temperature at 350 degrees F.
6. Once preheated, place meatballs basket in the oven and close its lid.
7. Flip the meatballs when cooked halfway through.
8. Serve warm.

Nutritional Information per Serving:
   Calories 301; Total Fat 15.8 g; Saturated Fat 2.7 g; Cholesterol 75 mg; Sodium 189 mg

Meatball Bake

Prep Time: 10 minutes; Cooking Time: 35 minutes; Serving: 6
Ingredients
- 2 tablespoons olive oil
- 2 lbs. ground beef
- 1 cup ricotta cheese
- 2 large eggs
- 1/2 cup bread crumbs
- 1/4 cup chopped fresh parsley
- 1 tablespoon oregano, chopped
- 2 teaspoons salt
- 1/4 teaspoon crushed red pepper flakes
- 1/2 teaspoon ground fennel
- 4 cups Tomato Sauce
- 1 ½ cup shredded cheddar cheese

Method:
1. Thoroughly mix the beef with all other ingredients for meatballs in a bowl.
2. Make small meatballs out of this mixture then place them in a casserole dish.
3. Pour the sauce on top and drizzle the cheese on the meatballs
4. Press "Power Button" of Air Fry Oven and turn the dial to select the "Bake" mode.
5. Press the Time button and again turn the dial to set the cooking time to 35 minutes.
6. Now push the Temp button and rotate the dial to set the temperature at 350 degrees F.
7. Once preheated, place meatballs pan in the oven and close its lid.
8. Serve warm.

Nutritional Information per Serving:
   Calories 231; Total Fat 20.1 g; Saturated Fat 2.4 g; Cholesterol 110 mg; Sodium 941 mg

Teriyaki Meatballs

Prep Time: 10 minutes; Cooking Time: 20 minutes; Serving: 6
Ingredients
Meatballs:
- 2 lbs. ground beef mince
- 3/4 cup Panko breadcrumbs
- 2 eggs
- 2 scallions or green onions, finely chopped
- 2 cloves garlic, minced
- 2 tablespoons low sodium soy sauce
- 1 tablespoon wine
- Pinch salt and pepper, to taste

Teriyaki Sauce:
- 1 teaspoon sesame oil
- 2 cloves garlic, minced
- 1/3 cup low sodium soy sauce
- 1/4 cup mirin
- 1/4 cup sake
- 1/4 cup brown sugar
- 1/2 cup water
- 1 tablespoon cornstarch
- 2 tablespoons of water
- 1 teaspoon Sriracha or more
- Sesame seeds to garnish

Method:
1. Thoroughly mix the beef with all other ingredients for meatballs in a bowl.
2. Make small meatballs out of this mixture then place them in the Air fryer basket.
3. Press "Power Button" of Air Fry Oven and turn the dial to select the "Bake" mode.
4. Press the Time button and again turn the dial to set the cooking time to 20 minutes.
5. Now push the Temp button and rotate the dial to set the temperature at 350 degrees F.
6. Once preheated, place meatballs basket in the oven and close its lid.
7. Flip the meatballs when cooked halfway through then resume cooking.
8. Meanwhile, whisk teriyaki sauce ingredients in a saucepan.
9. Stir cook for 5 minutes or more until it thickens.
10. Pour this sauce over the meatballs and garnish with sesame seeds.
11. Serve warm.

Nutritional Information per Serving:
Calories 440; Total Fat 7.9 g; Saturated Fat 1.8 g; Cholesterol 5 mg; Sodium 581 mg

Beef Pork Meatballs

Prep Time: 10 minutes; Cooking Time: 20 minutes; Serving: 6
Ingredients
- 1 lb. ground beef
- 1 lb. ground pork
- 1/2 cup Italian breadcrumbs
- 1/3 cup milk
- 1/4 cup onion, diced
- 1/2 teaspoon garlic powder
- 1 teaspoon Italian seasoning
- 1 egg
- 1/4 cup parsley chopped
- 1/4 cup shredded parmesan
- salt and pepper to taste

Method:
1. Thoroughly mix the beef with all other ingredients for meatballs in a bowl.
2. Make small meatballs out of this mixture then place them in the Air fryer basket.
3. Press "Power Button" of Air Fry Oven and turn the dial to select the "Bake" mode.
4. Press the Time button and again turn the dial to set the cooking time to 20 minutes.
5. Now push the Temp button and rotate the dial to set the temperature at 400 degrees F.
6. Once preheated, place meatballs basket in the oven and close its lid.
7. Flip the meatballs when cooked halfway through then resume cooking.
8. Serve warm.

Nutritional Information per Serving:
Calories 380; Total Fat 20 g; Saturated Fat 5 g; Cholesterol 151 mg; Sodium 686 mg

Beef Noodle Casserole

Prep Time: 10 minutes; Cooking Time: 35 minutes; Serving: 6

Ingredients

- 2 tablespoons olive oil
- 1 medium onion, chopped
- ½ lb. ground beef
- 4 fresh mushrooms, sliced
- 1 cup pasta noodles, cooked
- 2 cups marinara sauce
- 1 teaspoon butter
- 4 teaspoons flour
- 1 cup milk
- 1 egg, beaten
- 1 cup cheddar cheese, grated

Method:

1. Put a wok on moderate heat and add oil to heat.
2. Toss in onion and sauté until soft.
3. Stir in mushrooms and beef, then cook until meat is brown.
4. Add marinara sauce and cook it to a simmer.
5. Stir in pasta then spread this mixture in a casserole dish.
6. Prepare the sauce by melting butter in a saucepan over moderate heat.
7. Stir in flour and whisk well, pour in the milk.
8. Mix well and whisk ¼ cup sauce with egg then return it to the saucepan.
9. Stir cook for 1 minute then pour this sauce over the beef.
10. Drizzle cheese over the beef casserole.
11. Press "Power Button" of Air Fry Oven and turn the dial to select the "Bake" mode.
12. Press the Time button and again turn the dial to set the cooking time to 30 minutes.
13. Now push the Temp button and rotate the dial to set the temperature at 350 degrees F.
14. Once preheated, place casserole dish in the oven and close its lid.
15. Serve warm.

Nutritional Information per Serving:
Calories 361; Total Fat 16.3 g; Saturated Fat 4.9 g; Cholesterol 114 mg; Sodium 515 mg

Saucy Beef Bake

Prep Time: 10 minutes; Cooking Time: 36 minutes; Serving: 6

Ingredients

- 2 tablespoons olive oil
- 1 large onion, diced
- 2 lbs. ground beef
- 2 teaspoons salt
- 6 cloves garlic, chopped
- 1/2 cup red wine
- 6 cloves garlic, chopped
- 3 teaspoons ground cinnamon
- 2 teaspoons ground cumin
- 2 teaspoons dried oregano
- 1 teaspoon black pepper
- 1 can 28 oz. crushed tomatoes
- 1 tablespoon tomato paste

Method:

1. Put a suitable wok over moderate heat and add oil to heat.
2. Toss in onion, salt, and beef meat then stir cook for 12 minutes.
3. Stir in red wine and cook for 2 minutes.
4. Add cinnamon, garlic, oregano, cumin, and pepper, then stir cook for 2 minutes.
5. Add tomato paste and tomatoes and cook for 20 minutes on a simmer.
6. Spread this mixture in a casserole dish.
7. Press "Power Button" of Air Fry Oven and turn the dial to select the "Bake" mode.
8. Press the Time button and again turn the dial to set the cooking time to 30 minutes.

9. Now push the Temp button and rotate the dial to set the temperature at 350 degrees F.
10. Once preheated, place casserole dish in the oven and close its lid.
11. Serve warm.

Nutritional Information per Serving:
Calories 405; Total Fat 22.7 g; Saturated Fat 6.1 g; Cholesterol 4 mg; Sodium 227 mg

Parmesan Meatballs

Prep Time: 10 minutes; Cooking Time: 20 minutes; Serving: 6

Ingredients

- 2 lbs. ground beef
- 2 eggs
- 1 cup ricotta cheese
- 1/4 cup Parmesan cheese shredded
- 1/2 cup Panko breadcrumbs
- 1/4 cup basil chopped

- 1/4 cup parsley chopped
- 1 tablespoon fresh oregano chopped
- 2 teaspoon kosher salt
- 1 teaspoon ground fennel
- 1/2 teaspoon red pepper flakes
- 32 oz spaghetti sauce, to serve

Method:
1. Thoroughly mix the beef with all other ingredients for meatballs in a bowl.
2. Make small meatballs out of this mixture then place them in the Air fryer basket.
3. Press "Power Button" of Air Fry Oven and turn the dial to select the "Bake" mode.
4. Press the Time button and again turn the dial to set the cooking time to 20 minutes.
5. Now push the Temp button and rotate the dial to set the temperature at 400 degrees F.
6. Once preheated, place meatballs basket in the oven and close its lid.
7. Flip the meatballs when cooked halfway through then resume cooking.
8. Pour spaghetti sauce on top.
9. Serve warm.

Nutritional Information per Serving:
Calories 545; Total Fat 36.4 g; Saturated Fat 10.1 g; Cholesterol 200 mg; Sodium 272 mg

Tricolor Beef Skewers

Prep Time: 10 minutes; Cooking Time: 25 minutes; Serving: 4

Ingredients

- 3 garlic cloves, minced
- 4 tablespoon rapeseed oil
- 1 cup cottage cheese, cubed
- 16 cherry tomatoes

- 2 tablespoon cider vinegar
- large bunch thyme
- 1 ¼ lb. boneless beef, diced

Method:
1. Toss beef with all its thyme, oil, vinegar, and garlic.
2. Marinate the thyme beef for 2 hours in a closed container in the refrigerator.
3. Thread the marinated beef, cheese, and tomatoes on the skewers.
4. Place these skewers in an Air fryer basket.
5. Press "Power Button" of Air Fry Oven and turn the dial to select the "Air fry" mode.
6. Press the Time button and again turn the dial to set the cooking time to 25 minutes.
7. Now push the Temp button and rotate the dial to set the temperature at 350 degrees F.
8. Once preheated, place the Air fryer basket in the oven and close its lid.
9. Flip the skewers when cooked halfway through then resume cooking.
10. Serve warm.

Nutritional Information per Serving:
Calories 695; Total Fat 17.5 g; Saturated Fat 4.8 g; Cholesterol 283 mg; Sodium 355 mg

Yogurt Beef Kebabs

Prep Time: 10 minutes; Cooking Time: 25 minutes; Serving: 4

Ingredients

- ½ cup yogurt
- 1½ tablespoon mint
- 1 teaspoon ground cumin
- 1 cup eggplant, diced
- 10.5 oz. lean beef, diced
- ½ small onion, cubed

Method:

1. Whisk yogurt with mint and cumin in a suitable bowl.
2. Toss in beef cubes and mix well to coat. Marinate for 30 minutes.
3. Alternatively, thread the beef, onion, and eggplant on the skewers.
4. Place these beef skewers in the Air fry basket.
5. Press "Power Button" of Air Fry Oven and turn the dial to select the "Air fryer" mode.
6. Press the Time button and again turn the dial to set the cooking time to 25 minutes.
7. Now push the Temp button and rotate the dial to set the temperature at 370 degrees F.
8. Once preheated, place the Air fryer basket in the oven and close its lid.
9. Flip the skewers when cooked halfway through then resume cooking.
10. Serve warm.

Nutritional Information per Serving:

Calories 301; Total Fat 8.9 g; Saturated Fat 4.5 g; Cholesterol 57 mg; Sodium 340 mg

Agave Beef Kebabs

Prep Time: 10 minutes; Cooking Time: 20 minutes; Serving: 6

Ingredients

- 2 lbs. beef steaks, cubed
- 2 tablespoon jerk seasoning
- zest and juice of 1 lime
- 1 tablespoon agave syrup
- ½ teaspoon thyme leaves, chopped

Method:

1. Mix beef with jerk seasoning, lime juice, zest, agave and thyme.
2. Toss well to coat then marinate for 30 minutes.
3. Alternatively, thread the beef on the skewers.
4. Place these beef skewers in the Air fry basket.
5. Press "Power Button" of Air Fry Oven and turn the dial to select the "Air fryer" mode.
6. Press the Time button and again turn the dial to set the cooking time to 20 minutes.
7. Now push the Temp button and rotate the dial to set the temperature at 360 degrees F.
8. Once preheated, place the Air fryer basket in the oven and close its lid.
9. Flip the skewers when cooked halfway through then resume cooking.
10. Serve warm.

Nutritional Information per Serving:

Calories 548; Total Fat 22.9 g; Saturated Fat 9 g; Cholesterol 105 mg; Sodium 350 mg

Beef Skewers with Potato Salad

Prep Time: 10 minutes; Cooking Time: 25 minutes; Serving: 4

Ingredients

- juice ½ lemon
- 2 tablespoon olive oil

For the salad

- 2 potatoes, boiled, peeled and diced
- 4 large tomatoes, chopped
- 1 cucumber, chopped
- 1 garlic clove, crushed
- 1 ¼ lb. diced beef

- 1 handful black olives, chopped
- 9 oz. pack feta cheese, crumbled
- 1 bunch of mint, chopped

Method:
1. Whisk lemon juice with garlic and olive oil in a bowl.
2. Toss in beef cubes and mix well to coat. Marinate for 30 minutes.
3. Alternatively, thread the beef on the skewers.
4. Place these beef skewers in the Air fry basket.
5. Press "Power Button" of Air Fry Oven and turn the dial to select the "Air fryer" mode.
6. Press the Time button and again turn the dial to set the cooking time to 25 minutes.
7. Now push the Temp button and rotate the dial to set the temperature at 360 degrees F.
8. Once preheated, place the Air fryer basket in the oven and close its lid.
9. Flip the skewers when cooked halfway through then resume cooking.
10. Meanwhile, whisk all the salad ingredients in a salad bowl.
11. Serve the skewers with prepared salad.

Nutritional Information per Serving:
Calories 609; Total Fat 50.5 g; Saturated Fat 11.7 g; Cholesterol 58 mg; Sodium 463 mg

Classic Souvlaki Kebobs

Prep Time: 10 minutes; Cooking Time: 20 minutes; Serving: 6
Ingredients
- 2 ¼ lbs. beef shoulder fat trimmed, cut into chunks
- 1/3 cup olive oil
- ½ cup red wine
- 2 teaspoon dried oregano
- ½ cup of orange juice
- 1 teaspoon orange zest
- 2 garlic cloves, crushed

Method:
1. Whisk olive oil, red wine, oregano, oranges juice, zest, and garlic in a suitable bowl.
2. Toss in beef cubes and mix well to coat. Marinate for 30 minutes.
3. Alternatively, thread the beef, onion, and bread on the skewers.
4. Place these beef skewers in the Air fry basket.
5. Press "Power Button" of Air Fry Oven and turn the dial to select the "Air fryer" mode.
6. Press the Time button and again turn the dial to set the cooking time to 20 minutes.
7. Now push the Temp button and rotate the dial to set the temperature at 370 degrees F.
8. Once preheated, place the Air fryer basket in the oven and close its lid.
9. Flip the skewers when cooked halfway through then resume cooking.
10. Serve warm.

Nutritional Information per Serving:
Calories 537; Total Fat 19.8 g; Saturated Fat 1.4 g; Cholesterol 10 mg; Sodium 719 mg

Harissa Dipped Beef Skewers

Prep Time: 10 minutes; Cooking Time: 16 minutes; Serving: 6
Ingredients
- 1 lb. beef mince
- 4 tablespoon harissa
- 2 oz. feta cheese
- 1 large red onion, shredded
- 1 handful parsley, chopped
- 1 handful mint, chopped
- 1 tablespoon olive oil
- juice 1 lemon

Method:
1. Whisk beef mince with harissa, onion, feta, and seasoning in a bowl.
2. Make 12 sausages out of this mixture then thread them on the skewers.
3. Place these beef skewers in the Air fry basket.
4. Press "Power Button" of Air Fry Oven and turn the dial to select the "Bake" mode.
5. Press the Time button and again turn the dial to set the cooking time to 16 minutes.
6. Now push the Temp button and rotate the dial to set the temperature at 370 degrees F.

7. Once preheated, place the Air fryer basket in the oven and close its lid.
8. Flip the skewers when cooked halfway through then resume cooking.
9. Toss the remaining salad ingredients in a salad bowl.
10. Serve beef skewers with tomato salad.

Nutritional Information per Serving:
Calories 452; Total Fat 4 g; Saturated Fat 2 g; Cholesterol 65 mg; Sodium 220 mg

Onion Pepper Beef Kebobs

Prep Time: 10 minutes; Cooking Time: 20 minutes; Serving: 4

Ingredients

- 2 tablespoon pesto paste
- 2/3 lb. beefsteak, diced
- 2 red peppers, cut into chunks
- 2 red onions, cut into wedges
- 1 tablespoon olive oil

Method:
1. Toss in beef cubes with harissa and oil, then mix well to coat. Marinate for 30 minutes.
2. Alternatively, thread the beef, onion, and peppers on the skewers.
3. Place these beef skewers in the Air fry basket.
4. Press "Power Button" of Air Fry Oven and turn the dial to select the "Air fryer" mode.
5. Press the Time button and again turn the dial to set the cooking time to 20 minutes.
6. Now push the Temp button and rotate the dial to set the temperature at 370 degrees F.
7. Once preheated, place the Air fryer basket in the oven and close its lid.
8. Flip the skewers when cooked halfway through then resume cooking.
9. Serve warm.

Nutritional Information per Serving:
Calories 301; Total Fat 15.8 g; Saturated Fat 2.7 g; Cholesterol 75 mg; Sodium 389 mg

Mayo Spiced Kebobs

Prep Time: 10 minutes; Cooking Time: 10 minutes; Serving: 4

Ingredients

- 2 tablespoon cumin seed
- 2 tablespoon coriander seed
- 2 tablespoon fennel seed
- 1 tablespoon paprika
- 2 tablespoon garlic mayonnaise
- 4 garlic cloves, finely minced
- ½ teaspoon ground cinnamon
- 1 ½ lb. lean minced beef

Method:
1. Blend all the spices and seeds with garlic, cream, and cinnamon in a blender.
2. Add this cream paste to the minced beef then mix well.
3. Make 8 sausages and thread each on the skewers.
4. Place these beef skewers in the Air fry basket.
5. Press "Power Button" of Air Fry Oven and turn the dial to select the "Air fryer" mode.
6. Press the Time button and again turn the dial to set the cooking time to 10 minutes.
7. Now push the Temp button and rotate the dial to set the temperature at 370 degrees F.
8. Once preheated, place the Air fryer basket in the oven and close its lid.
9. Flip the skewers when cooked halfway through then resume cooking.
10. Serve warm.

Nutritional Information per Serving:
Calories 308; Total Fat 20.5 g; Saturated Fat 3 g; Cholesterol 42 mg; Sodium 688 mg

Beef with Orzo Salad

Prep Time: 10 minutes; Cooking Time: 27 minutes; Serving: 4
Ingredients

- 2/3 lbs. beef shoulder, cubed
- 1 teaspoon ground cumin
- ½ teaspoon cayenne pepper
- 1 teaspoon sweet smoked paprika
- 1 tablespoon olive oil
- 24 cherry tomatoes

Salad:
- ½ cup orzo, boiled
- ½ cup frozen pea
- 1 large carrot, grated
- small pack coriander, chopped
- small pack mint, chopped
- juice 1 lemon
- 2 tablespoon olive oil

Method:
1. Toss tomatoes and beef with oil, paprika, pepper, and cumin in a bowl.
2. Alternatively, thread the beef and tomatoes on the skewers.
3. Place these beef skewers in the Air fry basket.
4. Press "Power Button" of Air Fry Oven and turn the dial to select the "Air fryer" mode.
5. Press the Time button and again turn the dial to set the cooking time to 25 minutes.
6. Now push the Temp button and rotate the dial to set the temperature at 370 degrees F.
7. Once preheated, place the Air fryer basket in the oven and close its lid.
8. Flip the skewers when cooked halfway through then resume cooking.
9. Meanwhile, sauté carrots and peas with olive oil in a pan for 2 minutes.
10. Stir in mint, lemon juice, coriander, and cooked couscous.
11. Serve skewers with the couscous salad.

Nutritional Information per Serving:
Calories 231; Total Fat 20.1 g; Saturated Fat 2.4 g; Cholesterol 110 mg; Sodium 941 mg

Beef Zucchini Shashliks

Prep Time: 10 minutes; Cooking Time: 25 minutes; Serving: 4
Ingredients
- 1lb. beef, boned and diced
- 1 lime, juiced and chopped
- 3 tablespoon olive oil
- 20 garlic cloves, chopped
- 1 handful rosemary, chopped
- 3 green peppers, cubed
- 2 zucchinis, cubed
- 2 red onions, cut into wedges

Method:
1. Toss the beef with the rest of the skewer's ingredients in a bowl.
2. Thread the beef, peppers, zucchini, and onion on the skewers.
3. Place these beef skewers in the Air fry basket.
4. Press "Power Button" of Air Fry Oven and turn the dial to select the "Air fryer" mode.
5. Press the Time button and again turn the dial to set the cooking time to 25 minutes.
6. Now push the Temp button and rotate the dial to set the temperature at 370 degrees F.
7. Once preheated, place the Air fryer basket in the oven and close its lid.
8. Flip the skewers when cooked halfway through then resume cooking.
9. Serve warm.

Nutritional Information per Serving:
Calories 472; Total Fat 11.1 g; Saturated Fat 5.8 g; Cholesterol 610 mg; Sodium 749 mg

Spiced Beef Skewers

Prep Time: 10 minutes; Cooking Time: 18 minutes; Serving: 4
Ingredients
- 2 teaspoons ground cumin
- 2 teaspoons ground coriander
- 1/4 teaspoon ground cinnamon
- 1/8 teaspoon ground smoked paprika
- 2 teaspoons lime zest
- 1/2 teaspoon salt
- 1/2 teaspoon black pepper
- 1 tablespoon lemon juice

- 2 teaspoons olive oil
- 1 1/2 lbs. lean beef, cubed

Method:
1. Toss beef with the rest of the skewer's ingredients in a bowl.
2. Thread the beef and veggies on the skewers alternately.
3. Place these beef skewers in the Air fry basket.
4. Press "Power Button" of Air Fry Oven and turn the dial to select the "Air fryer" mode.
5. Press the Time button and again turn the dial to set the cooking time to 18 minutes.
6. Now push the Temp button and rotate the dial to set the temperature at 370 degrees F.
7. Once preheated, place the Air fryer basket in the oven and close its lid.
8. Flip the skewers when cooked halfway through then resume cooking.
9. Serve warm.

Nutritional Information per Serving:
Calories 327; Total Fat 3.5 g; Saturated Fat 0.5 g; Cholesterol 162 mg; Sodium 142 mg

Beef Sausage with Cucumber Sauce

Prep Time: 10 minutes; Cooking Time: 15 minutes; Serving: 6
Ingredients
Beef Kabobs
- 1 lb. ground beef
- 1/2 an onion, finely diced
- 3 garlic cloves, finely minced
- 2 teaspoons cumin
- 2 teaspoons coriander
- 1 ½ teaspoons salt
- 2 tablespoons chopped mint

Yogurt Sauce:
- 1 cup Greek yogurt
- 2 tablespoons cucumber, chopped
- 2 garlic cloves, minced
- 1/4 teaspoon salt

Method:
1. Toss beef with the rest of the kebob ingredients in a bowl.
2. Make 6 sausages out of this mince and thread them on the skewers.
3. Place these beef skewers in the Air fry basket.
4. Press "Power Button" of Air Fry Oven and turn the dial to select the "Air fryer" mode.
5. Press the Time button and again turn the dial to set the cooking time to 15 minutes.
6. Now push the Temp button and rotate the dial to set the temperature at 370 degrees F.
7. Once preheated, place the Air fryer basket in the oven and close its lid.
8. Flip the skewers when cooked halfway through then resume cooking.
9. Meanwhile, prepare the cucumber sauce by whisking all its ingredients in a bowl.
10. Serve the skewers with cucumber sauce.

Nutritional Information per Serving:
Calories 353; Total Fat 7.5 g; Saturated Fat 1.1 g; Cholesterol 20 mg; Sodium 297 mg

Beef Eggplant Medley

Prep Time: 10 minutes; Cooking Time: 20 minutes; Serving: 4
Ingredients
- 2 cloves of garlic
- 1 teaspoon dried oregano
- olive oil
- 4 beef steaks, diced
- 2 eggplant, cubed
- 8 fresh bay leaves
- 2 lemons, juiced
- a few sprigs parsley, chopped

Method:
1. Toss beef with the rest of the skewer's ingredients in a bowl.
2. Thread the beef and veggies on the skewers alternately.
3. Place these beef skewers in the Air fry basket.

4. Press "Power Button" of Air Fry Oven and turn the dial to select the "Air fryer" mode.
5. Press the Time button and again turn the dial to set the cooking time to 20 minutes.
6. Now push the Temp button and rotate the dial to set the temperature at 370 degrees F.
7. Once preheated, place the Air fryer basket in the oven and close its lid.
8. Flip the skewers when cooked halfway through then resume cooking.
9. Serve warm.

Nutritional Information per Serving:
Calories 248; Total Fat 13 g; Saturated Fat 7 g; Cholesterol 387 mg; Sodium 353 mg

Glazed Beef Kebobs

Prep Time: 10 minutes; Cooking Time: 20 minutes; Serving: 6
Ingredients
- 2 lb. beef, cubed
- 1/2 cup olive oil
- 1 lemon, juice only
- 3 cloves garlic, minced
- 1 onion, sliced
- 1 teaspoon oregano, dried
- 1/4 teaspoon dried thyme,
- 1 teaspoon salt
- 1/4 teaspoon black pepper
- 1 tablespoon parsley, chopped
- 1 cup Worcestershire sauce

Method:
1. Toss beef with the rest of the kebab ingredients in a bowl.
2. Cover the beef and marinate it for 30 minutes.
3. Thread the beef and veggies on the skewers alternately.
4. Place these beef skewers in the Air fry basket. Brush the skewers with the Worcestershire sauce.
5. Press "Power Button" of Air Fry Oven and turn the dial to select the "Air fryer" mode.
6. Press the Time button and again turn the dial to set the cooking time to 20 minutes.
7. Now push the Temp button and rotate the dial to set the temperature at 370 degrees F.
8. Once preheated, place the Air fryer basket in the oven and close its lid.
9. Flip the skewers when cooked halfway through then resume cooking.
10. Serve warm.

Nutritional Information per Serving:
Calories 457; Total Fat 19.1 g; Saturated Fat 11 g; Cholesterol 262 mg; Sodium 557 mg

Beef Kebobs with Cream Dip

Prep Time: 10 minutes; Cooking Time: 20 minutes; Serving: 6
Ingredients
- Beef Kebabs
- 2 lbs. beef, diced

For the Dressing
- 1 tablespoon mayonnaise
- 1 tablespoon olive oil
- 2 tablespoons lemon juice

- 1 large onion, squares
- Salt

- 1 teaspoon yellow mustard
- 1/4 teaspoon salt
- 1/8 teaspoon black pepper

Method:
1. Toss beef and onion with salt in a bowl to season them.
2. Thread the beef and onion on the skewers alternately.
3. Place these beef skewers in the Air fry basket.
4. Press "Power Button" of Air Fry Oven and turn the dial to select the "Air fryer" mode.
5. Press the Time button and again turn the dial to set the cooking time to 20 minutes.
6. Now push the Temp button and rotate the dial to set the temperature at 370 degrees F.
7. Once preheated, place the Air fryer basket in the oven and close its lid.

8. Flip the skewers when cooked halfway through then resume cooking.
9. Prepare the cream dip by mixing its ingredients in a bowl.
10. Serve skewers with cream dip.

Nutritional Information per Serving:
Calories 392; Total Fat 16.1 g; Saturated Fat 2.3 g; Cholesterol 231 mg; Sodium 466 mg

Asian Beef Skewers

Prep Time: 10 minutes; Cooking Time: 15 minutes; Serving: 4

Ingredients

- 3 tablespoons hoisin sauce
- 3 tablespoons sherry
- 1/4 cup soy sauce
- 1 teaspoon barbeque sauce
- 2 green onions, chopped
- 2 cloves garlic, minced
- 1 tablespoon minced fresh ginger root
- 1 1/2 lbs. flank steak, cubed

Method:
1. Toss steak cubes with sherry, all the sauces and other ingredients in a bowl.
2. Marinate the saucy spiced skewers for 30 minutes.
3. Place these beef skewers in the Air fry basket.
4. Press "Power Button" of Air Fry Oven and turn the dial to select the "Air fryer" mode.
5. Press the Time button and again turn the dial to set the cooking time to 15 minutes.
6. Now push the Temp button and rotate the dial to set the temperature at 350 degrees F.
7. Once preheated, place the Air fryer basket in the oven and close its lid.
8. Flip the skewers when cooked halfway through then resume cooking.
9. Serve warm.

Nutritional Information per Serving:
Calories 321; Total Fat 7.4 g; Saturated Fat 4.6 g; Cholesterol 105 mg; Sodium 353 mg

Korean BBQ Skewers

Prep Time: 10 minutes; Cooking Time: 15 minutes; Serving: 4

Ingredients

- 3 oz. lean sirloin steaks, cubed
- 1 small onion, finely diced
- 1/3 cup low sodium soy sauce
- 1/3 cup brown sugar
- 1 tablespoon sesame seeds
- 2 teaspoons sesame oil
- 4 cloves garlic, diced
- 1 tablespoon ginger, grated
- 1 teaspoon sriracha
- 2 tablespoons honey
- salt and pepper

Method:
1. Toss steak cubes with sauces and other ingredients in a bowl.
2. Marinate the saucy spiced skewers for 30 minutes.
3. Place these beef skewers in the Air fry basket.
4. Press "Power Button" of Air Fry Oven and turn the dial to select the "Air fryer" mode.
5. Press the Time button and again turn the dial to set the cooking time to 15 minutes.
6. Now push the Temp button and rotate the dial to set the temperature at 350 degrees F.
7. Once preheated, place the Air fryer basket in the oven and close its lid.
8. Flip the skewers when cooked halfway through then resume cooking.
9. Serve warm.

Nutritional Information per Serving:
Calories 248; Total Fat 15.7 g; Saturated Fat 2.7 g; Cholesterol 75 mg; Sodium 94 mg

Roasted Beef Brisket

Prep Time: 10 minutes; Cooking Time: 1hr 30 minutes; Serving: 12

Ingredients
- 6 lb. beef brisket, boneless

Spice rub:
- 1 cup olive oil
- juice of 1 lemon
- 1 teaspoon thyme
- 5 teaspoon minced garlic
- Salt to taste
- Black pepper to taste

- 1 stick butter, melted
- 1/2 cup olive oil
- 1 oz. soy sauce
- 1 oz. brown sugar
- 1tbs. black pepper

Method:
1. Place the beef brisket in a baking tray.
2. Whisk spice rub ingredients in a bowl
3. Liberally brush the brisket with the spice mixture.
4. Whisk the baste ingredients in a bowl and keep it aside.
5. Press "Power Button" of Air Fry Oven and turn the dial to select the "Air Roast" mode.
6. Press the Time button and again turn the dial to set the cooking time to 1 hr. 30 minutes.
7. Now push the Temp button and rotate the dial to set the temperature at 370 degrees F.
8. Once preheated, place the beef baking tray in the oven and close its lid.
9. Serve warm.

Nutritional Information per Serving:
Calories 378; Total Fat 21 g; Saturated Fat 4.3 g; Cholesterol 150 mg; Sodium 146 mg

Chapter 5: Lamb Recipes

Lamb Chops with Rosemary Sauce

Prep Time: 10 minutes; Cooking Time: 52 minutes; Serving: 8

Ingredients

- 8 lamb loin chops
- 1 small onion, peeled and chopped
- Salt and black pepper, to taste

For the sauce:

- 1 onion, peeled and chopped
- 1 tablespoon rosemary leaves
- 1 oz butter
- 1 oz plain flour
- 6 fl oz milk
- 6 fl oz vegetable stock
- 2 tablespoons cream, whipping
- Salt and black pepper, to taste

Method:

1. Place the lamb loin chops, and onion in a baking tray, then drizzle salt and black pepper on top.
2. Press "Power Button" of Air Fry Oven and turn the dial to select the "Bake" mode.
3. Press the Time button and again turn the dial to set the cooking time to 45 minutes.
4. Now push the Temp button and rotate the dial to set the temperature at 350 degrees F.
5. Once preheated, place the lamb baking tray in the oven and close its lid.
6. Prepare the white sauce by melting butter in a saucepan then stir in onions.
7. Sauté for 5 minutes, then stir flour and stir cook for 2 minutes.
8. Stir in the rest of the ingredients and mix well.
9. Pour the sauce over baked chops and serve.

Nutritional Information per Serving:
Calories 284; Total Fat 7.9 g; Saturated Fat 1.4 g; Cholesterol 36 mg; Sodium 704 mg

Roast Lamb Shoulder

Prep Time: 10 minutes; Cooking Time: 60 minutes; Serving: 2

Ingredients

- 1 lb. boneless lamb shoulder roast
- 4 cloves garlic, minced
- 1 tablespoon rosemary, chopped
- 2 teaspoon thyme leaves
- 3 tablespoon olive oil, divided
- Salt
- Black pepper
- 2 lb. baby potatoes halved

Method:

1. Toss potatoes with all the herbs, seasonings, and oil in a baking tray.
2. Press "Power Button" of Air Fry Oven and turn the dial to select the "Air Roast" mode.
3. Press the Time button and again turn the dial to set the cooking time to 60 minutes.
4. Now push the Temp button and rotate the dial to set the temperature at 370 degrees F.
5. Once preheated, place the lamb baking tray in the oven and close its lid.
6. Slice and serve warm.

Nutritional Information per Serving:
Calories 134; Total Fat 4.7 g; Saturated Fat 0.6 g; Cholesterol 124mg; Sodium 1 mg

Garlicky Lamb Chops

Prep Time: 10 minutes; Cooking Time: 45 minutes; Serving: 8

Ingredients

- 8 medium lamb chops
- 1/4 cup olive oil
- 3 thin lemon slices
- 2 garlic cloves, crushed
- 1 teaspoon dried oregano
- 1 teaspoon salt
- 1/2 teaspoon black pepper

Method:

1. Place the medium lamb chops in a baking tray and rub them with olive oil.
2. Add lemon slices, garlic, oregano, salt, and black pepper on top of the lamb chops.
3. Press "Power Button" of Air Fry Oven and turn the dial to select the "Air Roast" mode.
4. Press the Time button and again turn the dial to set the cooking time to 45 minutes.
5. Now push the Temp button and rotate the dial to set the temperature at 400 degrees F.
6. Once preheated, place the lamb baking tray in the oven and close its lid.
7. Slice and serve warm.

Nutritional Information per Serving:

Calories 387; Total Fat 6 g; Saturated Fat 9.9 g; Cholesterol 41 mg; Sodium 154 mg

New England Lamb

Prep Time: 10 minutes; Cooking Time: 60 minutes; Serving: 6

Ingredients

- 2 tablespoon canola oil
- 2 lbs. boneless leg of lamb, diced
- 1 onion, chopped
- 2 leeks white portion only, sliced
- 2 carrots, sliced
- 2 tablespoons minced fresh parsley, divided
- 1/2 teaspoon dried rosemary, crushed
- 1/2 teaspoon salt
- 1/4 teaspoon black pepper
- 1/4 teaspoon dried thyme, crushed
- 3 potatoes, peeled and sliced
- 3 tablespoons butter, melted

Method:

1. Toss the lamb cubes with all the veggies, oil, and seasonings in a baking tray.
2. Press "Power Button" of Air Fry Oven and turn the dial to select the "Air Roast" mode.
3. Press the Time button and again turn the dial to set the cooking time to 60 minutes.
4. Now push the Temp button and rotate the dial to set the temperature at 350 degrees F.
5. Once preheated, place the lamb baking tray in the oven and close its lid.
6. Slice and serve warm.

Nutritional Information per Serving:

Calories 212; Total Fat 11.8 g; Saturated Fat 2.2 g; Cholesterol 23mg; Sodium 321 mg

Onion Lamb Kebabs

Prep Time: 10 minutes; Cooking Time: 20 minutes; Serving: 4

Ingredients

- 18 oz lamb kebab
- 1 teaspoon chili powder
- 1 teaspoon cumin powder
- 1 egg
- 2 oz onion, chopped
- 2 teaspoon sesame oil

Method:

1. Whisk onion with egg, chili powder, oil, cumin powder, and salt in a bowl.
2. Add lamb to coat well then thread it on the skewers.
3. Place these lamb skewers in the Air fryer basket.
4. Press "Power Button" of Air Fry Oven and turn the dial to select the "Air Fry" mode.
5. Press the Time button and again turn the dial to set the cooking time to 20 minutes.
6. Now push the Temp button and rotate the dial to set the temperature at 395 degrees F.
7. Once preheated, place the Air fryer basket in the oven and close its lid.
8. Slice and serve warm.

Nutritional Information per Serving:

Calories 412; Total Fat 24.8 g; Saturated Fat 12.4 g; Cholesterol 3 mg; Sodium 132 mg

Zucchini Lamb Meatballs

Prep Time: 10 minutes; Cooking Time: 15 minutes; Serving: 4

Ingredients

- 1 lb. ground lamb
- avocado oil spray
- 1/2 tablespoon garlic ghee
- 1 red bell pepper diced
- 1/3 cup red onion diced
- 1/3 cup cilantro diced
- 1/3 cup zucchini diced
- 1 tablespoon gyro seasoning
- 1/2 teaspoon turmeric
- 1/2 teaspoon cumin
- 1/2 teaspoon coriander
- 2 garlic cloves minced
- Salt and black pepper to taste

Method:

1. Mix the lamb minced with all the meatball ingredients in a bowl.
2. Make small meatballs out of this mixture and place them in the Air fryer basket.
3. Press "Power Button" of Air Fry Oven and turn the dial to select the "Air Fry" mode.
4. Press the Time button and again turn the dial to set the cooking time to 15 minutes.
5. Now push the Temp button and rotate the dial to set the temperature at 370 degrees F.
6. Once preheated, place the Air fryer basket in the oven and close its lid.
7. Slice and serve warm.

Nutritional Information per Serving:

Calories 331; Total Fat 2.5 g; Saturated Fat 0.5 g; Cholesterol 35 mg; Sodium 595 mg

Mint Lamb with Roasted Hazelnuts

Prep Time: 10 minutes; Cooking Time: 25 minutes; Serving: 2

Ingredients

- ¼ cup hazelnuts, toasted
- 2/3 lb. shoulder of lamb cut into strips
- 1 tablespoon hazelnut oil
- 2 tablespoon fresh mint leaves chopped
- ½ cup frozen peas
- ¼ cup of water
- ½ cup white wine
- Salt and black pepper to taste

Method:

1. Toss lamb with hazelnuts, spices, and all the ingredients in a baking pan.
2. Press "Power Button" of Air Fry Oven and turn the dial to select the "Bake" mode.
3. Press the Time button and again turn the dial to set the cooking time to 25 minutes.
4. Now push the Temp button and rotate the dial to set the temperature at 370 degrees F.
5. Once preheated, place the baking pan in the oven and close its lid.
6. Slice and serve warm.

Nutritional Information per Serving:

Calories 322; Total Fat 11.8 g; Saturated Fat 2.2 g; Cholesterol 56 mg; Sodium 321 mg

Lamb Rack with Lemon Crust

Prep Time: 10 minutes; Cooking Time: 25 minutes; Serving: 5

Ingredients

- 1.7 lbs. frenched rack of lamb
- Salt and black pepper, to taste
- 0.13-lb. dry breadcrumbs
- 1 teaspoon grated garlic
- 1/2 teaspoon salt
- 1 teaspoon cumin seeds
- 1 teaspoon ground cumin
- 1 teaspoon oil
- ½ teaspoon Grated lemon rind
- 1 egg, beaten

Method:

1. Place the lamb rack in a baking tray and pour the whisked egg on top.
2. Whisk rest of the crusting ingredients in a bowl and spread over the lamb.
3. Press "Power Button" of Air Fry Oven and turn the dial to select the "Air Fry" mode.
4. Press the Time button and again turn the dial to set the cooking time to 25 minutes.
5. Now push the Temp button and rotate the dial to set the temperature at 350 degrees F.
6. Once preheated, place the lamb baking tray in the oven and close its lid.
7. Slice and serve warm.

Nutritional Information per Serving:
Calories 427; Total Fat 5.4 g; Saturated Fat 4.2 g; Cholesterol 168 mg; Sodium 203 mg

Braised Lamb Shanks

Prep Time: 10 minutes; Cooking Time: 20 minutes; Serving: 4

Ingredients
- 4 lamb shanks
- 1½ teaspoons salt
- ½ teaspoon black pepper
- 4 garlic cloves, crushed
- 2 tablespoons olive oil
- 4 to 6 sprigs fresh rosemary
- 3 cups beef broth, divided
- 2 tablespoons balsamic vinegar

Method:
1. Place the sham shanks in a baking pan.
2. Whisk rest of the ingredients in a bowl and pour over the shanks.
3. Place these shanks in the Air fryer basket.
4. Press "Power Button" of Air Fry Oven and turn the dial to select the "Air Fry" mode.
5. Press the Time button and again turn the dial to set the cooking time to 20 minutes.
6. Now push the Temp button and rotate the dial to set the temperature at 360 degrees F.
7. Once preheated, place the Air fryer basket in the oven and close its lid.
8. Slice and serve warm.

Nutritional Information per Serving:
Calories 336; Total Fat 9.7 g; Saturated Fat 4.7 g; Cholesterol 181 mg; Sodium 245 mg

Za'atar Lamb Chops

Prep Time: 10 minutes; Cooking Time: 10 minutes; Serving: 8

Ingredients
- 8 lamb loin chops, bone-in
- 3 garlic cloves, crushed
- 1 teaspoon olive oil
- 1/2 fresh lemon
- 1 1/4 teaspoon salt
- 1 tablespoon Za'atar
- Black pepper, to taste

Method:
1. Rub the lamb chops with oil, zaatar, salt, lemon juice, garlic, and black pepper.
2. Place these chops in the Air fryer basket.
3. Press "Power Button" of Air Fry Oven and turn the dial to select the "Air Fry" mode.
4. Press the Time button and again turn the dial to set the cooking time to 10 minutes.
5. Now push the Temp button and rotate the dial to set the temperature at 400 degrees F.
6. Once preheated, place the air fryer basket in the oven and close its lid.
7. Flip the chops when cooked halfway through then resume cooking.
8. Serve warm.

Nutritional Information per Serving:
Calories 391; Total Fat 2.8 g; Saturated Fat 0.6 g; Cholesterol 330 mg; Sodium 62 mg

Lamb Sirloin Steak

Prep Time: 10 minutes; Cooking Time: 15 minutes; Serving: 2

Ingredients

- 1/2 onion
- 4 slices ginger
- 5 cloves garlic
- 1 teaspoon garam masala
- 1 teaspoon fennel, ground
- 1 teaspoon cinnamon ground
- 1/2 teaspoon cardamom ground
- 1 teaspoon cayenne
- 1 teaspoon salt
- 1-lb. boneless lamb sirloin steaks

Method:

1. In a blender, jug add all the ingredients except the chops.
2. Rub the chops with this blended mixture and marinate for 30 minutes.
3. Transfer the chops to the Air fryer basket.
4. Press "Power Button" of Air Fry Oven and turn the dial to select the "Air Fry" mode.
5. Press the Time button and again turn the dial to set the cooking time to 15 minutes.
6. Now push the Temp button and rotate the dial to set the temperature at 330 degrees F.
7. Once preheated, place the Air fryer basket in the oven and close its lid.
8. Flip the chops when cooked halfway through then resume cooking.
9. Serve warm.

Nutritional Information per Serving:

Calories 453; Total Fat 2.4 g; Saturated Fat 3 g; Cholesterol 21 mg; Sodium 216 mg

Lemony Lamb Chops

Prep Time: 10 minutes; Cooking Time: 25 minutes; Serving: 2

Ingredients

- 2 medium lamb chops
- ¼ cup lemon juice

Method:

1. Liberally rub the lamb chops with lemon juice.
2. Place the lemony chops in the Air fryer basket.
3. Press "Power Button" of Air Fry Oven and turn the dial to select the "Air Fry" mode.
4. Press the Time button and again turn the dial to set the cooking time to 25 minutes.
5. Now push the Temp button and rotate the dial to set the temperature at 350 degrees F.
6. Once preheated, place the Air fryer basket in the oven and close its lid.
7. Flip the chops when cooked halfway through then resume cooking.
8. Serve warm.

Nutritional Information per Serving:

Calories 529; Total Fat 17 g; Saturated Fat 3 g; Cholesterol 65 mg; Sodium 391 mg

Garlicky Rosemary Lamb Chops

Prep Time: 10 minutes; Cooking Time: 12 minutes; Serving: 4

Ingredients

- 4 lamb chops
- 2 teaspoon olive oil
- 1 teaspoon fresh rosemary
- 2 garlic cloves, minced
- 2 teaspoon garlic puree
- Salt & black pepper

Method:

1. Place lamb chops in the Air fryer basket.
2. Rub them with olive oil, rosemary, garlic, garlic puree, salt, and black pepper
3. Press "Power Button" of Air Fry Oven and turn the dial to select the "Air Fry" mode.
4. Press the Time button and again turn the dial to set the cooking time to 12 minutes.
5. Now push the Temp button and rotate the dial to set the temperature at 350 degrees F.
6. Once preheated, place the Air fryer basket in the oven and close its lid.
7. Flip the chops when cooked halfway through then resume cooking.
8. Serve warm.

Calories 297; Total Fat 14 g; Saturated Fat 5 g; Cholesterol 99 mg; Sodium 364 mg

Lamb Tomato Bake

Prep Time: 10 minutes; Cooking Time: 35 minutes; Serving: 6

Ingredients

- 25 oz. potatoes, boiled
- 14 oz. lean lamb mince

Sauce

- 12 oz. white sauce

- 1 teaspoon cinnamon
- 23 oz. jar tomato pasta

- 1 tablespoon olive oil

Method:

1. Mash the potatoes in a bowl and stir in white sauce and cinnamon.
2. Sauté lamb mince with olive oil in a frying pan until brown.
3. Layer a casserole dish with tomato pasta sauce.
4. Top the sauce with lamb mince.
5. Spread the potato mash over the lamb in an even layer.
6. Press "Power Button" of Air Fry Oven and turn the dial to select the "Bake" mode.
7. Press the Time button and again turn the dial to set the cooking time to 35 minutes.
8. Now push the Temp button and rotate the dial to set the temperature at 350 degrees F.
9. Once preheated, place casserole dish in the oven and close its lid.
10. Serve warm.

Nutritional Information per Serving:
Calories 352; Total Fat 14 g; Saturated Fat 2 g; Cholesterol 65 mg; Sodium 220 mg

Lamb Baked with Tomato Topping

Prep Time: 10 minutes; Cooking Time: 1hr 40 minutes; Serving: 8

Ingredients

- 8 lamb shoulder chops, trimmed
- 1/4 cup plain flour
- 1 tablespoon olive oil
- 1 large brown onion, chopped
- 2 garlic cloves, crushed
- 3 medium carrots, peeled and diced

- 2 tablespoons tomato paste
- 2 1/2 cups beef stock
- 2 dried bay leaves
- 1 cup frozen peas
- 3 cups potato gems

Method:

1. Dust the lamb chops with flour and sear it in a pan layered with olive oil.
2. Sear the lamb chops for 4 minutes per side.
3. Transfer the chops to a baking tray.
4. Add onion, garlic, and carrot to the same pan.
5. Sauté for 5 minutes, then stir in tomato paste, stock and all other ingredients.
6. Stir cook for 4 minutes then pour this sauce over the chops.
7. Press "Power Button" of Air Fry Oven and turn the dial to select the "Bake" mode.
8. Press the Time button and again turn the dial to set the cooking time to 1 hr. 30 minutes.
9. Now push the Temp button and rotate the dial to set the temperature at 350 degrees F.
10. Once preheated, place the baking pan in the oven and close its lid.
11. Serve warm.

Nutritional Information per Serving:
Calories 388; Total Fat 8 g; Saturated Fat 1 g; Cholesterol 153mg; sodium 339 mg

Lamb Potato Chips Baked

Prep Time: 10 minutes; Cooking Time: 25 minutes; Serving: 4

Ingredients

- ½ lb. minced lamb
- 1 tbs parsley chopped
- 2 teaspoon curry powder
- 1 pinch salt and black pepper
- 1 lb. potato cooked, mashed
- 1 oz. cheese grated
- 1 ½ oz. potato chips crushed

Method:
1. Mix lamb, curry powder, seasoning and parsley.
2. Spread this lamb mixture in a casserole dish.
3. Top the lamb mixture with potato mash, cheese, and potato chips.
4. Press "Power Button" of Air Fry Oven and turn the dial to select the "Bake" mode.
5. Press the Time button and again turn the dial to set the cooking time to 20 minutes.
6. Now push the Temp button and rotate the dial to set the temperature at 350 degrees F.
7. Once preheated, place casserole dish in the oven and close its lid.
8. Serve warm.

Nutritional Information per Serving:
Calories 301; Total Fat 15.8 g; Saturated Fat 2.7 g; Cholesterol 75 mg; Sodium 189 mg

Greek Macaroni Bake

Prep Time: 10 minutes; Cooking Time: 46 minutes; Serving: 6
Ingredients

- 1 tablespoon olive oil
- 1 large onion, chopped finely
- 2 garlic cloves, minced
- 1 lb. lean lamb mince
- 1 teaspoon ground cinnamon
- 1 beef or lamb stock cube
- 2 cups tomatoes chopped
- 1 tablespoon dried oregano
- 14 oz. macaroni, boiled
- 9 0z. tub ricotta
- 2 tablespoons parmesan, grated
- 2 tablespoons milk
- bread, to serve optional

Method:
1. Sauté onion with oil in a frying pan for 10 minutes.
2. Stir in garlic and cook for 1 minute, then remove it from the heat.
3. Toss lamb mince then sauté until brown.
4. Stir in cinnamon, tomatoes, oregano, and stock cubes.
5. Cook this mixture on a simmer for 15 minutes.
6. Meanwhile, blend ricotta with parmesan, milk and garlic in a blender.
7. Spread the lamb tomatoes mixture in a casserole dish and top it with ricotta mixture.
8. Press "Power Button" of Air Fry Oven and turn the dial to select the "Bake" mode.
9. Press the Time button and again turn the dial to set the cooking time to 30 minutes.
10. Now push the Temp button and rotate the dial to set the temperature at 350 degrees F.
11. Once preheated, place casserole dish in the oven and close its lid.
12. Serve warm.

Nutritional Information per Serving:
Calories 231; Total Fat 20.1 g; Saturated Fat 2.4 g; Cholesterol 110 mg; Sodium 941 mg

Greek lamb Farfalle

Prep Time: 10 minutes; Cooking Time: 20 minutes; Serving: 4
Ingredients

- 1 tablespoon olive oil
- 1 onion, finely chopped
- 2 garlic cloves, finely chopped
- 2 teaspoon dried oregano
- 1 lb. pack lamb mince
- ¾ lb. tin chopped tomatoes
- ¼ cup pitted black olives
- ½ cup frozen spinach, defrosted

- 2 tablespoons dill, stems removed and chopped
- 9 Oz. farfalle, boiled
- 1 ball half-fat mozzarella, torn

Method:
1. Sauté onion and garlic with oil in a pan over moderate heat for 5 minutes.
2. Stir in tomatoes, spinach, dill, lamb, and olives, then stir cook for 5 minutes.
3. Spread the lamb in a casserole dish and toss in the pasta.
4. Top the pasta lamb mix with mozzarella cheese.
5. Press "Power Button" of Air Fry Oven and turn the dial to select the "Bake" mode.
6. Press the Time button and again turn the dial to set the cooking time to 10 minutes.
7. Now push the Temp button and rotate the dial to set the temperature at 350 degrees F.
8. Once preheated, place casserole dish in the oven and close its lid.
9. Serve warm.

Nutritional Information per Serving:
Calories 440; Total Fat 7.9 g; Saturated Fat 1.8 g; Cholesterol 5 mg; Sodium 581 mg

Lamb Orzo Bake

Prep Time: 10 minutes; Cooking Time: 2hr. 15 minutes; Serving: 6
Ingredients
Lamb
- 1 tablespoon olive oil
- 1 2/3 lbs. lamb shoulder, diced
- 2 onions, chopped
- 2 teaspoon dried oregano and thyme
- 1 teaspoon dried mint
- 3 bay leaves
- ½ teaspoon ground cumin
- 1 teaspoon smoked paprika

Pasta
- 14 oz. tin cherry tomatoes
- 2.6 cups vegetable stock, hot
- 10.5 oz. orzo pasta
- 2 ½ oz. peppadew peppers halved
- 2 ½ Oz. pitted kalamata olives halved
- 2 oz. sun-blushed tomatoes, chopped
- ¼ cup feta, crumbled
- Finely grated zest 1 lemon

Method:
1. Rub the lamb shoulder with all its seasonings and oil.
2. Place the lamb should in a baking tray.
3. Press "Power Button" of Air Fry Oven and turn the dial to select the "Bake" mode.
4. Press the Time button and again turn the dial to set the cooking time to 1 hr. 45 minutes.
5. Now push the Temp button and rotate the dial to set the temperature at 350 degrees F.
6. Once preheated, place the lamb baking tray in the oven and close its lid.
7. Meanwhile, cook orzo, with hot stock, peppers, tomatoes, olives, salt and black pepper in a cooking pot for 30 minutes.
8. Serve the lamb with orzo.

Nutritional Information per Serving:
Calories 380; Total Fat 20 g; Saturated Fat 5 g; Cholesterol 151 mg; Sodium 686 mg

Minced Lamb Casserole

Prep Time: 10 minutes; Cooking Time: 30 minutes; Serving: 4
Ingredients
- 2 tablespoons olive oil
- 1 medium onion, chopped
- ½ lb. ground lamb
- 4 fresh mushrooms, sliced
- 1 cup small pasta shells, cooked
- 2 cups bottled marinara sauce
- 1 teaspoon butter
- 4 teaspoons flour
- 1 cup milk
- 1 egg, beaten
- 1 cup cheddar cheese, grated

Method:

1. Put a wok on moderate heat and add oil to heat.
2. Toss in onion and sauté until soft.
3. Stir in mushrooms and lamb, then cook until meat is brown.
4. Add marinara sauce and cook it to a simmer.
5. Stir in pasta then spread this mixture in a casserole dish.
6. Prepare the sauce by melting butter in a saucepan over moderate heat.
7. Stir in flour and whisk well, pour in the milk.
8. Mix well and whisk ¼ cup sauce with egg then return it to the saucepan.
9. Stir cook for 1 minute then pour this sauce over the lamb.
10. Drizzle cheese over the lamb casserole.
11. Press "Power Button" of Air Fry Oven and turn the dial to select the "Bake" mode.
12. Press the Time button and again turn the dial to set the cooking time to 30 minutes.
13. Now push the Temp button and rotate the dial to set the temperature at 350 degrees F.
14. Once preheated, place casserole dish in the oven and close its lid.
15. Serve warm.

Nutritional Information per Serving:

Calories 361; Total Fat 16.3 g; Saturated Fat 4.9 g; Cholesterol 114 mg; Sodium 515 mg

Béchamel Baked Lamb

Prep Time: 10 minutes; Cooking Time: 60 minutes; Serving: 8

Ingredients

- 2 tablespoons olive oil
- 1 large onion, diced
- 2 lbs. ground lamb
- 2 teaspoons salt
- 6 cloves garlic, chopped
- 1/2 cup red wine
- 6 cloves garlic, chopped

- 3 teaspoons ground cinnamon
- 2 teaspoons ground cumin
- 2 teaspoons dried oregano
- 1 teaspoon black pepper
- 1 can 28 oz. crushed tomatoes
- 1 tablespoon tomato paste

Béchamel:

- 3 tablespoons olive oil
- 1/4 cup flour
- 2 ½ cups milk
- 1/2 teaspoon ground nutmeg
- ¾ teaspoon salt

- ¼ teaspoon white pepper
- 1/2 cup grated Parmesan cheese
- ½ cup plain Greek yogurt
- 2 extra-large eggs, beaten
- 3/4-lb. penne pasta, boiled

Method:

1. Put a suitable wok over moderate heat and add oil to heat.
2. Toss in onion, salt, and lamb meat then stir cook for 12 minutes.
3. Stir in red wine and cook for 2 minutes.
4. Add cinnamon, garlic, oregano, cumin, and pepper, then stir cook for 2 minutes.
5. Add tomato paste and tomatoes and cook for 20 minutes on a simmer.
6. Toss in penne pasta then spread this mixture in a casserole dish.
7. Prepare the lamb béchamel sauce in a suitable pot.
8. Add oil to heat, then stir in flour and cook for 1 minute.
9. Pour in milk and stir cook until it thickens.
10. Stir in parmesan, white pepper, nutmeg, egg, yogurt, and salt.
11. Spread this sauce over the lamb Bolognese.
12. Press "Power Button" of Air Fry Oven and turn the dial to select the "Bake" mode.
13. Press the Time button and again turn the dial to set the cooking time to 30 minutes.
14. Now push the Temp button and rotate the dial to set the temperature at 350 degrees F.

15. Once preheated, place casserole dish in the oven and close its lid.
16. Serve warm.

Nutritional Information per Serving:
Calories 405; Total Fat 22.7 g; Saturated Fat 6.1 g; Cholesterol 4 mg; Sodium 227 mg

Lamb Moussaka Bake

Prep Time: 10 minutes; Cooking Time: 50 minutes; Serving: 6
Ingredients

- ¼ cup olive oil
- 1 eggplant, diced
- 1 onion, diced
- 2 garlic cloves, crushed
- 1 lb. lamb mince
- ½ teaspoon cinnamon
- ¼ teaspoon ground cumin
- 1 teaspoon fresh rosemary
- 2 cups tomato pasta sauce
- 2 oz. butter
- ¼ cup flour
- 2 cups milk, hot
- ½ cup tasty cheese, grated
- 1 egg
- 1 pinch nutmeg
- Salt and black pepper to taste
- 7 oz. pasta, boiled

Method:
1. Put a wok on moderate heat and add oil to heat.
2. Stir in eggplant, then sauté for 5 minutes.
3. Add lamb, spices, rosemary, garlic, and onion, then stir cook for 8 minutes.
4. Stir in pasta, and tomato paste and cook on a simmer for 5 minutes.
5. Spread this lamb mixture in a casserole dish.
6. Prepare the white sauce in a suitable pot.
7. Add oil to heat, then stir in flour and cook for 1 minute.
8. Pour in milk and stir cook until it thickens.
9. Stir in cheese, egg, nutmeg, salt, and black pepper.
10. Spread this white sauce over the lamb pasta mixture.
11. Press "Power Button" of Air Fry Oven and turn the dial to select the "Bake" mode.
12. Press the Time button and again turn the dial to set the cooking time to 30 minutes.
13. Now push the Temp button and rotate the dial to set the temperature at 350 degrees F.
14. Once preheated, place casserole dish in the oven and close its lid.
15. Serve warm.

Nutritional Information per Serving:
Calories 545; Total Fat 36.4 g; Saturated Fat 10.1 g; Cholesterol 200 mg; Sodium 272 mg

Spring Lamb Skewers

Prep Time: 10 minutes; Cooking Time: 15 minutes; Serving: 4
Ingredients

- 3 garlic cloves, minced
- 4 tablespoon rapeseed oil
- 2 tablespoon cider vinegar
- large bunch thyme
- 1 ¼ lb. boneless lamb leg, diced

For the salad

- 1 cucumber, chopped
- 6 radishes, halved and sliced
- 1 fennel bulb, sliced
- 1/2 teaspoon caster sugar
- 4 tablespoon cider vinegar
- 1 handful dill sprigs

Method:
1. Toss lamb with all its thyme, oil, vinegar, and garlic.
2. Marinate the thyme lamb for 2 hours in a closed container in the refrigerator.
3. Thread the marinated lamb on the skewers.

4. Place these skewers in an Air fryer basket.
5. Press "Power Button" of Air Fry Oven and turn the dial to select the "Air fry" mode.
6. Press the Time button and again turn the dial to set the cooking time to 15 minutes.
7. Now push the Temp button and rotate the dial to set the temperature at 350 degrees F.
8. Once preheated, place the Air fryer basket in the oven and close its lid.
9. Flip the skewers when cooked halfway through then resume cooking.
10. Meanwhile, toss the salad ingredients in a salad bowl.
11. Serve the skewers with salad.

Nutritional Information per Serving:

Calories 695; Total Fat 17.5 g; Saturated Fat 4.8 g; Cholesterol 283 mg; Sodium 355 mg

Mint Lamb Kebobs

Prep Time: 10 minutes; Cooking Time: 15 minutes; Serving: 4

Ingredients

- ½ cup yogurt
- 1½ tablespoon mint
- 1 teaspoon ground cumin
- 10.5 oz. diced lean lamb
- ½ small onion, cubed
- 2 large pitta bread, cubed
- 2 handfuls lettuce, chopped

Method:

1. Whisk yogurt with mint and cumin in a suitable bowl.
2. Toss in lamb cubes and mix well to coat. Marinate for 30 minutes.
3. Alternatively, thread the lamb, onion and bread on the skewers.
4. Place these lamb skewers in the Air fry basket.
5. Press "Power Button" of Air Fry Oven and turn the dial to select the "Air fryer" mode.
6. Press the Time button and again turn the dial to set the cooking time to 15 minutes.
7. Now push the Temp button and rotate the dial to set the temperature at 370 degrees F.
8. Once preheated, place Air fryer basket in the oven and close its lid.
9. Flip the skewers when cooked halfway through then resume cooking.
10. Serve warm.

Nutritional Information per Serving:

Calories 301; Total Fat 8.9 g; Saturated Fat 4.5 g; Cholesterol 57 mg; Sodium 340 mg

Jerk Lamb Kebobs

Prep Time: 10 minutes; Cooking Time: 18 minutes; Serving: 6

Ingredients

- 2 lbs. lamb steaks
- 2 tablespoon jerk paste or marinade
- zest and juice of 1 lime
- 1 tablespoon honey
- handful thyme leaves, chopped

Method:

1. Mix lamb with jerk paste, lime juice, zest, honey and thyme.
2. Toss well to coat then marinate for 30 minutes.
3. Alternatively, thread the lamb on the skewers.
4. Place these lamb skewers in the Air fry basket.
5. Press "Power Button" of Air Fry Oven and turn the dial to select the "Air fryer" mode.
6. Press the Time button and again turn the dial to set the cooking time to 18 minutes.
7. Now push the Temp button and rotate the dial to set the temperature at 360 degrees F.
8. Once preheated, place Air fryer basket in the oven and close its lid.
9. Flip the skewers when cooked halfway through then resume cooking.
10. Serve warm.

Nutritional Information per Serving:

Calories 548; Total Fat 22.9 g; Saturated Fat 9 g; Cholesterol 105 mg; Sodium 350 mg

Lamb Skewers with Greek Salad

Prep Time: 10 minutes; Cooking Time: 20 minutes; Serving: 4

Ingredients
- juice ½ lemon
- 2 tablespoon olive oil

For the salad
- 4 large tomatoes, chopped
- 1 cucumber, chopped
- 1 handful black olives, chopped
- 1 garlic clove, crushed
- 1 ¼ lb. diced lamb

- 9 oz. pack feta cheese, crumbled
- 1 bunch of mint, chopped

Method:
1. Whisk lemon juice with garlic and olive oil in a bowl.
2. Toss in lamb cubes and mix well to coat. Marinate for 30 minutes.
3. Alternatively, thread the lamb on the skewers.
4. Place these lamb skewers in the Air fry basket.
5. Press "Power Button" of Air Fry Oven and turn the dial to select the "Air fryer" mode.
6. Press the Time button and again turn the dial to set the cooking time to 20 minutes.
7. Now push the Temp button and rotate the dial to set the temperature at 360 degrees F.
8. Once preheated, place Air fryer basket in the oven and close its lid.
9. Flip the skewers when cooked halfway through then resume cooking.
10. Meanwhile, whisk all the salad ingredients in a salad bowl.
11. Serve the skewers with prepared salad.

Nutritional Information per Serving:
Calories 451; Total Fat 10.5 g; Saturated Fat 11.7 g; Cholesterol 58 mg; Sodium 463 mg

Lamb Souvlaki Kebobs

Prep Time: 10 minutes; Cooking Time: 20 minutes; Serving: 6

Ingredients
- 2 ¼ lbs. lamb shoulder fat trimmed, cut into chunks
- 1/3 cup olive oil
- ½ cup red wine
- 2 teaspoon dried oregano
- zest and juice 2 lemons
- 2 garlic cloves, crushed

Method:
1. Whisk olive oil, red wine, oregano, lemon juice, zest, and garlic in a suitable bowl.
2. Toss in lamb cubes and mix well to coat. Marinate for 30 minutes.
3. Alternatively, thread the lamb, onion and bread on the skewers.
4. Place these lamb skewers in the Air fry basket.
5. Press "Power Button" of Air Fry Oven and turn the dial to select the "Air fryer" mode.
6. Press the Time button and again turn the dial to set the cooking time to 20 minutes.
7. Now push the Temp button and rotate the dial to set the temperature at 370 degrees F.
8. Once preheated, place Air fryer basket in the oven and close its lid.
9. Flip the skewers when cooked halfway through then resume cooking.
10. Serve warm.

Nutritional Information per Serving:
Calories 537; Total Fat 19.8 g; Saturated Fat 1.4 g; Cholesterol 10 mg; Sodium 719 mg

Lamb Skewers with Brown Rice

Prep Time: 10 minutes; Cooking Time: 16 minutes; Serving: 6

Ingredients

- 10.5 oz. brown basmati rice
- 1 lb. lamb mince
- 1 tablespoon harissa
- 2 oz. feta cheese
- 1 large red onion, (½ sliced, ½ shredded)
- 1 handful parsley, chopped
- 1 handful mint, chopped
- ¼ cup pitted black kalamata olive, quartered
- 1 cucumber, diced
- 10.5 cherry tomato, halved
- 1 tablespoon olive oil
- juice 1 lemon

Method:
1. Whisk lamb mince with harissa, onion, feta, and seasoning in a bowl.
2. Make 12 sausages out of this mixture then thread them on the skewers.
3. Place these lamb skewers in the Air fry basket.
4. Press "Power Button" of Air Fry Oven and turn the dial to select the "Bake" mode.
5. Press the Time button and again turn the dial to set the cooking time to 16 minutes.
6. Now push the Temp button and rotate the dial to set the temperature at 370 degrees F.
7. Once preheated, place Air fryer basket in the oven and close its lid.
8. Flip the skewers when cooked halfway through then resume cooking.
9. Toss the remaining salad ingredients in a salad bowl.
10. Serve lamb skewers with tomato salad.

Nutritional Information per Serving:
Calories 452; Total Fat 4 g; Saturated Fat 2 g; Cholesterol 65 mg; Sodium 220 mg

Harissa Lamb Kebobs

Prep Time: 10 minutes; Cooking Time: 20 minutes; Serving: 4
Ingredients
- 2 tablespoon harissa paste
- 2/3 lb. lamb steak, diced
- 2 red peppers, cut into chunks
- 2 red onions, cut into wedges
- 9 ½ oz. couscous, plain
- 1 tablespoon olive oil

Method:
1. Toss in lamb cubes with harissa and oil, then mix well to coat. Marinate for 30 minutes.
2. Alternatively, thread the lamb, onion and peppers on the skewers.
3. Place these lamb skewers in the Air fry basket.
4. Press "Power Button" of Air Fry Oven and turn the dial to select the "Air fryer" mode.
5. Press the Time button and again turn the dial to set the cooking time to 20 minutes.
6. Now push the Temp button and rotate the dial to set the temperature at 370 degrees F.
7. Once preheated, place Air fryer basket in the oven and close its lid.
8. Flip the skewers when cooked halfway through then resume cooking.
9. Serve warm.

Nutritional Information per Serving:
Calories 356; Total Fat 15.8 g; Saturated Fat 2.7 g; Cholesterol 75 mg; Sodium 389 mg

Merguez Kebobs

Prep Time: 10 minutes; Cooking Time: 10 minutes; Serving: 8
Ingredients
- 2 tablespoon cumin seed
- 2 tablespoon coriander seed
- 2 tablespoon fennel seed
- 1 tablespoon paprika
- 2 tablespoon harissa
- 4 garlic cloves, finely minced
- ½ teaspoon ground cinnamon
- 1 ½ lb. lean minced lamb

For the yogurt
- 3 carrots, grated
- 2 teaspoon cumin seed, toasted
- 9 Oz. Greek yogurt
- small handful chopped the coriander

- a small handful of chopped mint

Method:
1. Blend all the spices and seeds with garlic, harissa, and cinnamon in a blender.
2. Add this harissa paste to the minced lamb then mix well.
3. Make 8 sausages and thread each on the skewers.
4. Place these lamb skewers in the Air fry basket.
5. Press "Power Button" of Air Fry Oven and turn the dial to select the "Air fryer" mode.
6. Press the Time button and again turn the dial to set the cooking time to 10 minutes.
7. Now push the Temp button and rotate the dial to set the temperature at 370 degrees F.
8. Once preheated, place Air fryer basket in the oven and close its lid.
9. Flip the skewers when cooked halfway through then resume cooking.
10. Prepare the yogurt ingredients in a bowl.
11. Serve skewers with the yogurt mixture.

Nutritional Information per Serving:
Calories 328; Total Fat 20.5 g; Saturated Fat 3 g; Cholesterol 42 mg; Sodium 688 mg

Lamb with Pea Couscous

Prep Time: 10 minutes; Cooking Time: 12 minutes; Serving: 4

Ingredients
- 2/3 lbs. lean lamb shoulder, cubed
- 1 teaspoon ground cumin
- ½ teaspoon cayenne pepper
- 1 teaspoon sweet smoked paprika
- 1 tablespoon olive oil
- 24 cherry tomatoes

Salad:
- ½ cup couscous, boiled
- ½ cup frozen pea
- 1 large carrot, grated
- small pack coriander, chopped
- small pack mint, chopped
- juice 1 lemon
- 2 tablespoon olive oil

Method:
1. Toss tomatoes and lamb with oil, paprika, pepper, and cumin in a bowl.
2. Alternatively, thread the lamb and tomatoes on the skewers.
3. Place these lamb skewers in the Air fry basket.
4. Press "Power Button" of Air Fry Oven and turn the dial to select the "Air fryer" mode.
5. Press the Time button and again turn the dial to set the cooking time to 10 minutes.
6. Now push the Temp button and rotate the dial to set the temperature at 370 degrees F.
7. Once preheated, place Air fryer basket in the oven and close its lid.
8. Flip the skewers when cooked halfway through then resume cooking.
9. Meanwhile, sauté carrots and peas with olive oil in a pan for 2 minutes.
10. Stir in mint, lemon juice, coriander, and cooked couscous.
11. Serve skewers with the couscous salad.

Nutritional Information per Serving:
Calories 231; Total Fat 20.1 g; Saturated Fat 2.4 g; Cholesterol 110 mg; Sodium 941 mg

Lamb Shashlik with Garlic

Prep Time: 10 minutes; Cooking Time: 20 minutes; Serving: 4

Ingredients
- 1 small leg of lamb, boned and diced
- 1 lemon, juiced and chopped
- 3 tablespoon olive oil
- 20 garlic cloves, chopped
- 1 handful rosemary, chopped
- 3 green peppers, cubed
- 2 red onions, cut into wedges

Method:

1. Toss the lamb with the rest of the skewer's ingredients in a bowl.
2. Thread the lamb, peppers, and onion on the skewers.
3. Place these lamb skewers in the Air fry basket.
4. Press "Power Button" of Air Fry Oven and turn the dial to select the "Air fryer" mode.
5. Press the Time button and again turn the dial to set the cooking time to 20 minutes.
6. Now push the Temp button and rotate the dial to set the temperature at 370 degrees F.
7. Once preheated, place Air fryer basket in the oven and close its lid.
8. Flip the skewers when cooked halfway through then resume cooking.
9. Serve warm.

Nutritional Information per Serving:
Calories 472; Total Fat 11.1 g; Saturated Fat 5.8 g; Cholesterol 610 mg; Sodium 749 mg

Spiced Lamb Skewers

Prep Time: 10 minutes; Cooking Time: 20 minutes; Serving: 4
Ingredients

- 2 teaspoons ground cumin
- 2 teaspoons ground coriander
- 1/4 teaspoon ground cinnamon
- 1/8 teaspoon ground smoked paprika
- 2 teaspoons lemon zest
- 1/2 teaspoon salt
- 1/2 teaspoon black pepper
- 1 tablespoon lemon juice
- 2 teaspoons olive oil
- 1 1/2 lbs. lean lamb, cubed
- 1/2 yellow bell pepper, sliced into squares
- 1 onion, cut into pieces

Method:
1. Toss lamb with the rest of the skewer's ingredients in a bowl.
2. Thread the lamb and veggies on the skewers alternately.
3. Place these lamb skewers in the Air fry basket.
4. Press "Power Button" of Air Fry Oven and turn the dial to select the "Air fryer" mode.
5. Press the Time button and again turn the dial to set the cooking time to 20 minutes.
6. Now push the Temp button and rotate the dial to set the temperature at 370 degrees F.
7. Once preheated, place Air fryer basket in the oven and close its lid.
8. Flip the skewers when cooked halfway through then resume cooking.
9. Serve warm.

Nutritional Information per Serving:
Calories 327; Total Fat 3.5 g; Saturated Fat 0.5 g; Cholesterol 162 mg; Sodium 142 mg

Lamb Kebobs with Yogurt Sacue

Prep Time: 10 minutes; Cooking Time: 16 minutes; Serving: 6
Ingredients
Lamb Kabobs

- 1 lb. ground lamb
- 1/2 an onion, finely diced
- 3 garlic cloves, finely minced
- 2 teaspoons cumin
- 2 teaspoons coriander
- 2 teaspoons sumac
- 1 teaspoon Aleppo Chili flakes
- 1 ½ teaspoons salt
- 2 tablespoons chopped mint

Yogurt Sauce:

- 1 cup greek yogurt
- 2 tablespoons dill, chopped
- 2 garlic cloves, minced
- 1/4 teaspoon salt

Method:
1. Toss lamb with the rest of the kebob ingredients in a bowl.
2. Make 6 sausages out of this mince and thread them on the skewers.

3. Place these lamb skewers in the Air fry basket.
4. Press "Power Button" of Air Fry Oven and turn the dial to select the "Air fryer" mode.
5. Press the Time button and again turn the dial to set the cooking time to 16 minutes.
6. Now push the Temp button and rotate the dial to set the temperature at 370 degrees F.
7. Once preheated, place Air fryer basket in the oven and close its lid.
8. Flip the skewers when cooked halfway through then resume cooking.
9. Meanwhile, prepare the yogurt sauce by whisking all its ingredients in a bowl.
10. Serve the skewers with yogurt sauce.

Nutritional Information per Serving:
Calories 353; Total Fat 7.5 g; Saturated Fat 1.1 g; Cholesterol 20 mg; Sodium 297 mg

Red Pepper Lamb

Prep Time: 10 minutes; Cooking Time: 20 minutes; Serving: 4
Ingredients

- 2 cloves of garlic
- 1 teaspoon dried oregano
- olive oil
- 4 lamb steaks, diced
- 2 red peppers, cubed
- 8 fresh bay leaves
- 2 lemons, juiced
- a few sprigs parsley, chopped

Method:
1. Toss lamb with the rest of the skewer's ingredients in a bowl.
2. Thread the lamb and veggies on the skewers alternately.
3. Place these lamb skewers in the Air fry basket.
4. Press "Power Button" of Air Fry Oven and turn the dial to select the "Air fryer" mode.
5. Press the Time button and again turn the dial to set the cooking time to 20 minutes.
6. Now push the Temp button and rotate the dial to set the temperature at 370 degrees F.
7. Once preheated, place Air fryer basket in the oven and close its lid.
8. Flip the skewers when cooked halfway through then resume cooking.
9. Serve warm.

Nutritional Information per Serving:
Calories 248; Total Fat 13 g; Saturated Fat 7 g; Cholesterol 387 mg; Sodium 353 mg

Herbed Lamb Kebobs

Prep Time: 10 minutes; Cooking Time: 20 minutes; Serving: 6
Ingredients

- For the marinade:
- 2 lb. leg of lamb, cubed
- 1/2 cup olive oil
- 1 lemon, juice only
- 3 cloves garlic, minced
- 1 onion, sliced
- 1 teaspoon oregano, dried
- 1/4 teaspoon dried thyme,
- 1 teaspoon salt
- 1/4 teaspoon black pepper
- 1 tablespoon parsley, chopped
- 2 red pepper, cut into square
- 1 onion, cut into chunks

Method:
1. Toss lamb with the rest of the kebab ingredients in a bowl.
2. Cover the lamb and marinate it for 30 minutes.
3. Thread the lamb and veggies on the skewers alternately.
4. Place these lamb skewers in the Air fry basket.
5. Press "Power Button" of Air Fry Oven and turn the dial to select the "Air fryer" mode.
6. Press the Time button and again turn the dial to set the cooking time to 20 minutes.
7. Now push the Temp button and rotate the dial to set the temperature at 370 degrees F.
8. Once preheated, place Air fryer basket in the oven and close its lid.

9. Flip the skewers when cooked halfway through then resume cooking.
10. Serve warm.

Nutritional Information per Serving:
Calories 457; Total Fat 19.1 g; Saturated Fat 11 g; Cholesterol 262 mg; Sodium 557 mg

Lamb kebobs with Creamy Dressing

Prep Time: 10 minutes; Cooking Time: 20 minutes; Serving: 6

Ingredients

Lamb Kebabs
- 2 lbs. lamb loin chops, diced
- 1 large onion, squares
- sea salt

For the Wrap
- 6 tortillas
- 1/4 cup onions, sliced
- 1/2 cup tomatoes, sliced
- 1 1/2 cups romaine lettuce, chopped
- 1 teaspoon sumac

For the Dressing
- 1 tablespoon mayonnaise
- 1 tablespoon olive oil
- 2 tablespoons lemon juice
- 1 teaspoon yellow mustard
- 1/4 teaspoon salt
- 1/8 teaspoon black pepper
- 1/4 teaspoon sumac

Method:
1. Toss lamb and onion with salt in a bowl to season them.
2. Thread the lamb and onion on the skewers alternately.
3. Place these lamb skewers in the Air fry basket.
4. Press "Power Button" of Air Fry Oven and turn the dial to select the "Air fryer" mode.
5. Press the Time button and again turn the dial to set the cooking time to 20 minutes.
6. Now push the Temp button and rotate the dial to set the temperature at 370 degrees F.
7. Once preheated, place Air fryer basket in the oven and close its lid.
8. Flip the skewers when cooked halfway through then resume cooking.
9. Prepare the dressing by mixing its ingredients in a bowl.
10. Place the warm tortillas on the serving plates.
11. Divide the tortilla ingredients on the tortillas and top them with lamb kebabs.
12. Pour the prepared dressing on top then roll the tortillas.
13. Serve warm.

Nutritional Information per Serving:
Calories 392; Total Fat 16.1 g; Saturated Fat 2.3 g; Cholesterol 231 mg; Sodium 466 mg

Indian Lamb Skewers

Prep Time: 10 minutes; Cooking Time: 15 minutes; Serving: 4

Ingredients
- 1-lb. boneless lamb sirloin steaks, diced
- 1/2 onion
- 4 slices ginger
- 5 cloves garlic
- 1 teaspoon garam masala
- 1 teaspoon fennel, ground
- 1 teaspoon cinnamon, ground
- 1/2 teaspoon cardamom, ground
- 1 teaspoon cayenne
- 1 teaspoon salt

Method:
1. Blend all the spices, ginger, garlic, and onion in a blender.
2. Toss the lamb with prepared spice mixture then thread them over the skewers.
3. Marinate the spiced skewers for 30 minutes.
4. Place these lamb skewers in the Air fry basket.

5. Press "Power Button" of Air Fry Oven and turn the dial to select the "Air fryer" mode.
6. Press the Time button and again turn the dial to set the cooking time to 15 minutes.
7. Now push the Temp button and rotate the dial to set the temperature at 350 degrees F.
8. Once preheated, place Air fryer basket in the oven and close its lid.
9. Flip the skewers when cooked halfway through then resume cooking.
10. Serve warm.

Nutritional Information per Serving:
Calories 321; Total Fat 7.4 g; Saturated Fat 4.6 g; Cholesterol 105 mg; Sodium 353 mg

Shawarma Skewers

Prep Time: 10 minutes; Cooking Time: 18 minutes; Serving: 4
Ingredients
- ¾ lb. ground lamb
- 1 teaspoon cumin
- 1 teaspoon paprika
- 1 teaspoon garlic powder
- 1 teaspoon onion powder
- ½ teaspoon cinnamon
- ½ teaspoon turmeric
- ½ teaspoon fennel seeds
- ½ teaspoon coriander seed, ground
- ½ teaspoon salt
- 4 bamboo skewers

Method:
1. Mix lamb mince with all the spices and kebab ingredients in a bowl.
2. Make 4 sausages out of this mixture and thread them on the skewers.
3. Refrigerate the lamb skewers for 10 minutes to marinate.
4. Place these lamb skewers in the Air fry basket.
5. Press "Power Button" of Air Fry Oven and turn the dial to select the "Air fryer" mode.
6. Press the Time button and again turn the dial to set the cooking time to 8 minutes.
7. Now push the Temp button and rotate the dial to set the temperature at 350 degrees F.
8. Once preheated, place Air fryer basket in the oven and close its lid.
9. Flip the skewers when cooked halfway through then resume cooking.
10. Serve warm.

Nutritional Information per Serving:
Calories 248; Total Fat 15.7 g; Saturated Fat 2.7 g; Cholesterol 75 mg; Sodium 94 mg

Roasted Lamb Leg

Prep Time: 10 minutes; Cooking Time: 45 minutes; Serving: 12
Ingredients
- 6 lb. leg of lamb, boneless
- 1/2-gallon milk

Spice rub:
- 1 cup olive oil
- juice of 1 lemon
- 1 teaspoon thyme
- 5 teaspoon minced garlic
- Salt to taste
- Black pepper to taste

Stuffing ingredients:
- ¼ cup feta cheese, crumbled
- ¼ cup spinach

Baste ingredients:
- 1 stick butter
- 1/2 cup olive oil
- 1 oz. soy sauce
- 1 oz. brown sugar
- 1 tbs. black pepper

Method:
1. Soak the lamb leg in the milk in a pot and cover to marinate.
2. Refrigerate the lamb leg for 8 hours then remove it from the milk.
3. Place the lamb leg in a baking tray.

4. Whisk spice rub ingredients in a bowl, mix stuffing ingredients in another bowl.
5. Carve few slits in the lamb then add the stuffing in these slits.
6. Whisk the baste ingredients in a bowl and keep it aside.
7. Press "Power Button" of Air Fry Oven and turn the dial to select the "Air Roast" mode.
8. Press the Time button and again turn the dial to set the cooking time to 45 minutes.
9. Now push the Temp button and rotate the dial to set the temperature at 370 degrees F.
10. Once preheated, place the lamb baking tray in the oven and close its lid.
11. Baste the lamb leg with the basting mixture every 10 minutes.
12. Serve warm.

Nutritional Information per Serving:

Calories 378; Total Fat 21 g; Saturated Fat 4.3 g; Cholesterol 150 mg; Sodium 146 mg

Chapter 6: Pork Recipes

Pork Chops with Cashew Sauce

Prep Time: 10 minutes; Cooking Time: 52 minutes; Serving: 8

Ingredients

- 8 pork loin chops
- 1 small onion, peeled and chopped
- Salt and black pepper, to taste

For the sauce:

- ¼ cup cashews, finely chopped
- 1 cup cashew butter
- 1 oz wheat flour
- 6 fl oz milk
- 6 fl oz beef stock
- 2 tablespoons coconut cream, whipping
- Salt and black pepper, to taste

Method:

1. Place the pork loin chops and onion in a baking tray, then drizzle salt and black pepper on top.
2. Press "Power Button" of Air Fry Oven and turn the dial to select the "Bake" mode.
3. Press the Time button and again turn the dial to set the cooking time to 45 minutes.
4. Now push the Temp button and rotate the dial to set the temperature at 350 degrees F.
5. Once preheated, place the pork baking tray in the oven and close its lid.
6. Prepare the white sauce by first melting butter in a saucepan then stir in cashews.
7. Sauté for 5 minutes, then stir flour and stir cook for 2 minutes.
8. Stir in the rest of the sauce ingredients and mix well.
9. Pour the sauce over baked chops and serve.

Nutritional Information per Serving:

Calories 284; Total Fat 7.9 g; Saturated Fat 1.4 g; Cholesterol 36 mg; Sodium 704 mg

Roast Pork Shoulder

Prep Time: 10 minutes; Cooking Time: 60 minutes; Serving: 2

Ingredients

- 1 lb. boneless pork shoulder roast
- 4 cloves garlic, minced
- 1 tablespoon rosemary, chopped
- 2 teaspoon thyme leaves
- 3 tablespoon olive oil, divided
- Salt
- Black pepper
- 2 lb. baby potatoes halved

Method:

1. Toss potatoes with all the herbs, seasonings, and oil in a baking tray.
2. Press "Power Button" of Air Fry Oven and turn the dial to select the "Air Roast" mode.
3. Press the Time button and again turn the dial to set the cooking time to 60 minutes.
4. Now push the Temp button and rotate the dial to set the temperature at 370 degrees F.
5. Once preheated, place the pork baking tray in the oven and close its lid.
6. Slice and serve warm.

Nutritional Information per Serving:

Calories 334; Total Fat 4.7 g; Saturated Fat 0.6 g; Cholesterol 124mg; Sodium 1 mg

Garlicky Pork Chops

Prep Time: 10 minutes; Cooking Time: 45 minutes; Serving: 8

Ingredients

- 8 medium pork chops
- 1/4 cup olive oil
- 3 thin lemon slices
- 2 garlic cloves, crushed
- 1 teaspoon dried oregano
- 1 teaspoon salt
- 1/2 teaspoon black pepper

Method:

1. Place the medium pork chops in a baking tray and rub them with olive oil.
2. Add lemon slices, garlic, oregano, salt, and black pepper on top of the pork chops.
3. Press "Power Button" of Air Fry Oven and turn the dial to select the "Air Roast" mode.
4. Press the Time button and again turn the dial to set the cooking time to 45 minutes.
5. Now push the Temp button and rotate the dial to set the temperature at 400 degrees F.
6. Once preheated, place the pork baking tray in the oven and close its lid.
7. Slice and serve warm.

Nutritional Information per Serving:

Calories 387; Total Fat 6 g; Saturated Fat 9.9 g; Cholesterol 41 mg; Sodium 154 mg

Potato Pork Satay

Prep Time: 10 minutes; Cooking Time: 60 minutes; Serving: 6

Ingredients

- 2 tablespoon canola oil
- 2 lbs. boneless pork, diced
- 1 onion, chopped
- 2 leeks white portion only, sliced
- 2 carrots, sliced
- 2 tablespoons minced fresh parsley, divided
- 1/2 teaspoon dried rosemary, crushed
- 1/2 teaspoon salt
- 1/4 teaspoon ground black pepper
- 1/4 teaspoon dried thyme, crushed
- 3 potatoes, peeled and sliced
- 3 tablespoons butter, melted

Method:

1. Toss the pork cubes with all the veggies, oil, and seasonings in a baking tray.
2. Press "Power Button" of Air Fry Oven and turn the dial to select the "Air Roast" mode.
3. Press the Time button and again turn the dial to set the cooking time to 60 minutes.
4. Now push the Temp button and rotate the dial to set the temperature at 350 degrees F.
5. Once preheated, place the pork baking tray in the oven and close its lid.
6. Slice and serve warm.

Nutritional Information per Serving:

Calories 212; Total Fat 11.8 g; Saturated Fat 2.2 g; Cholesterol 23mg; Sodium 321 mg

Chili Pork Kebobs

Prep Time: 10 minutes; Cooking Time: 20 minutes; Serving: 4

Ingredients

- ½ lb. pork cubes
- 1 teaspoon chili powder
- 1 teaspoon cumin powder
- 1 teaspoon salt
- 1 teaspoon black pepper
- 1 egg, whisked
- 2 oz shallots, finely chopped
- 2 teaspoon avocado oil

Method:

1. Whisk onion with egg, chili powder, shallot, black pepper, oil, cumin powder, and salt in a bowl.
2. Add pork to coat well then thread it on the skewers.
3. Place these pork skewers in the Air fryer basket.
4. Press "Power Button" of Air Fry Oven and turn the dial to select the "Air Fry" mode.
5. Press the Time button and again turn the dial to set the cooking time to 20 minutes.
6. Now push the Temp button and rotate the dial to set the temperature at 395 degrees F.
7. Once preheated, place the Air fryer basket in the oven and close its lid.
8. Slice and serve warm.

Nutritional Information per Serving:

Calories 412; Total Fat 24.8 g; Saturated Fat 12.4 g; Cholesterol 3 mg; Sodium 132 mg

Pork Vegetable Meatballs

Prep Time: 10 minutes; Cooking Time: 15 minutes; Serving: 4

Ingredients

- 1 lb. ground pork
- Cooking oil spray
- 1/2 tablespoon ghee
- 1 red bell pepper finely chopped
- 1/3 cup red onion finely chopped
- 1/3 cup cilantro finely chopped
- 1/3 cup zucchini finely chopped
- 1 tablespoon herb seasoning
- 1/2 teaspoon turmeric
- 1/2 teaspoon cumin
- 1/2 teaspoon coriander
- 2 garlic cloves minced
- Salt and black pepper to taste

Method:

1. Mix the pork minced with all the meatball ingredients in a bowl.
2. Make small meatballs out of this mixture and place them in the Air fryer basket.
3. Press "Power Button" of Air Fry Oven and turn the dial to select the "Air Fry" mode.
4. Press the Time button and again turn the dial to set the cooking time to 15 minutes.
5. Now push the Temp button and rotate the dial to set the temperature at 370 degrees F.
6. Once preheated, place the Air fryer basket in the oven and close its lid.
7. Slice and serve warm.

Nutritional Information per Serving:

Calories 331; Total Fat 2.5 g; Saturated Fat 0.5 g; Cholesterol 35 mg; Sodium 595 mg

Mint Pork Strips

Prep Time: 10 minutes; Cooking Time: 25 minutes; Serving: 2

Ingredients

- ¼ cup pine nuts, toasted
- 2/3 lb. shoulder of pork cut into strips
- 1 tablespoon avocado oil
- 2 tablespoon fresh mint leaves chopped
- ½ cup frozen peas
- ¼ cup of water
- ½ cup red wine
- Salt and black pepper to taste

Method:

1. Toss pork with pine nuts, spices, and all the ingredients in a baking pan.
2. Press "Power Button" of Air Fry Oven and turn the dial to select the "Bake" mode.
3. Press the Time button and again turn the dial to set the cooking time to 25 minutes.
4. Now push the Temp button and rotate the dial to set the temperature at 370 degrees F.
5. Once preheated, place the baking pan in the oven and close its lid.
6. Slice and serve warm.

Nutritional Information per Serving:

Calories 322; Total Fat 11.8 g; Saturated Fat 2.2 g; Cholesterol 56 mg; Sodium 321 mg

Pork Chops with Crust

Prep Time: 10 minutes; Cooking Time: 25 minutes; Serving: 5

Ingredients

- 5 pork chops
- Salt and black pepper, to taste
- 1 cup breadcrumbs
- 1 teaspoon grated garlic
- 1/2 teaspoon salt
- 1 teaspoon cumin seeds
- 1 teaspoon ground cumin
- 1 teaspoon oil
- ½ teaspoon Grated lemon rind
- 1 egg, beaten

Method:

1. Place the pork chops in a baking tray and pour the whisked egg on top.

2. Whisk rest of the crusting ingredients in a bowl and spread over the pork.
3. Press "Power Button" of Air Fry Oven and turn the dial to select the "Air Fry" mode.
4. Press the Time button and again turn the dial to set the cooking time to 25 minutes.
5. Now push the Temp button and rotate the dial to set the temperature at 350 degrees F.
6. Once preheated, place the pork baking tray in the oven and close its lid.
7. Slice and serve warm.

Nutritional Information per Serving:
Calories 279; Total Fat 15.4 g; Saturated Fat 4.2 g; Cholesterol 168 mg; Sodium 203 mg

Basic Pork Shanks

Prep Time: 10 minutes; Cooking Time: 20 minutes; Serving: 4
Ingredients

- 4 pork shanks
- 1½ teaspoons salt
- ½ teaspoon black pepper
- 4 garlic cloves, crushed
- 2 tablespoons olive oil
- 4 to 6 sprigs fresh rosemary
- 3 cups beef broth, divided
- 2 tablespoons balsamic vinegar

Method:
1. Place the pork shanks in a baking pan.
2. Whisk rest of the ingredients in a bowl and pour over the shanks.
3. Place these shanks in the Air fryer basket.
4. Press "Power Button" of Air Fry Oven and turn the dial to select the "Air Fry" mode.
5. Press the Time button and again turn the dial to set the cooking time to 20 minutes.
6. Now push the Temp button and rotate the dial to set the temperature at 360 degrees F.
7. Once preheated, place the Air fryer basket in the oven and close its lid.
8. Slice and serve warm.

Nutritional Information per Serving:
Calories 388; Total Fat 9.7 g; Saturated Fat 4.7 g; Cholesterol 181 mg; Sodium 245 mg

Bone-in Za'atar Chops

Prep Time: 10 minutes; Cooking Time: 10 minutes; Serving: 8
Ingredients

- 8 pork loin chops, bone-in
- 1 tablespoon Za'atar
- 3 garlic cloves, crushed
- 1 teaspoon avocado oil
- 2 tablespoons lemon juice
- 1 1/4 teaspoon salt
- Black pepper, to taste

Method:
1. Rub the pork chops with oil, za'atar, salt, lemon juice, garlic, and black pepper.
2. Place these chops in the Air fryer basket.
3. Press "Power Button" of Air Fry Oven and turn the dial to select the "Air Fry" mode.
4. Press the Time button and again turn the dial to set the cooking time to 10 minutes.
5. Now push the Temp button and rotate the dial to set the temperature at 400 degrees F.
6. Once preheated, place the air fryer basket in the oven and close its lid.
7. Flip the chops when cooked halfway through then resume cooking.
8. Serve warm.

Nutritional Information per Serving:
Calories 391; Total Fat 2.8 g; Saturated Fat 0.6 g; Cholesterol 330 mg; Sodium 62 mg

Pork Sirloin Steak

Prep Time: 10 minutes; Cooking Time: 15 minutes; Serving: 2
Ingredients

- 1/2 onion
- 4 slices ginger
- 5 cloves garlic
- 1 teaspoon allspice powder
- 1 teaspoon fennel, ground
- 1 teaspoon cinnamon ground
- 1 teaspoon cayenne pepper
- 1 teaspoon salt
- 1-lb. boneless pork sirloin steaks

Method:
1. In a blender, jug add all the ingredients except the chops.
2. Rub the chops with this blended mixture and marinate for 30 minutes.
3. Transfer the chops to the Air fryer basket.
4. Press "Power Button" of Air Fry Oven and turn the dial to select the "Air Fry" mode.
5. Press the Time button and again turn the dial to set the cooking time to 15 minutes.
6. Now push the Temp button and rotate the dial to set the temperature at 330 degrees F.
7. Once preheated, place the Air fryer basket in the oven and close its lid.
8. Flip the chops when cooked halfway through then resume cooking.
9. Serve warm.

Nutritional Information per Serving:
Calories 453; Total Fat 2.4 g; Saturated Fat 3 g; Cholesterol 21 mg; Sodium 216 mg

Lime Glazed Pork Chops

Prep Time: 10 minutes; Cooking Time: 25 minutes; Serving: 2
Ingredients
- 2 medium pork chops
- ¼ cup lime juice
- Salt, to taste
- Black pepper, to taste

Method:
1. Liberally rub the pork chops with lime juice, salt, and black pepper.
2. Place the lime chops in the Air fryer basket.
3. Press "Power Button" of Air Fry Oven and turn the dial to select the "Air Fry" mode.
4. Press the Time button and again turn the dial to set the cooking time to 25 minutes.
5. Now push the Temp button and rotate the dial to set the temperature at 350 degrees F.
6. Once preheated, place the Air fryer basket in the oven and close its lid.
7. Flip the chops when cooked halfway through then resume cooking.
8. Serve warm.

Nutritional Information per Serving:
Calories 529; Total Fat 17 g; Saturated Fat 3 g; Cholesterol 65 mg; Sodium 391 mg

Garlic Pork Chops

Prep Time: 10 minutes; Cooking Time: 12 minutes; Serving: 4
Ingredients
- 4 pork loin chops
- 2 teaspoon olive oil
- 4 garlic cloves, minced
- Salt & black pepper, to taste

Method:
1. Place pork loin chops in the Air fryer basket.
2. Rub them with olive oil, rosemary, garlic, salt, and black pepper
3. Press "Power Button" of Air Fry Oven and turn the dial to select the "Air Fry" mode.
4. Press the Time button and again turn the dial to set the cooking time to 12 minutes.
5. Now push the Temp button and rotate the dial to set the temperature at 350 degrees F.
6. Once preheated, place the Air fryer basket in the oven and close its lid.
7. Flip the chops when cooked halfway through then resume cooking.
8. Serve warm.

Nutritional Information per Serving:

Calories 297; Total Fat 14 g; Saturated Fat 5 g; Cholesterol 99 mg; Sodium 364 mg

Pork Sweet Potato Bake

Prep Time: 10 minutes; Cooking Time: 35 minutes; Serving: 6
Ingredients
- 25 oz. sweet potatoes, boiled
- 23 oz. jar tomato pasta
- 14 oz. pork mince
- 1 teaspoon cinnamon
- 12 oz. white sauce
- 1 tablespoon olive oil

Method:
1. Mash the boiled sweet potatoes in a bowl and stir in white sauce and cinnamon.
2. Sauté pork mince with olive oil in a frying pan until brown.
3. Layer a casserole dish with tomato pasta sauce.
4. Top the sauce with pork mince.
5. Spread the potato mash over the pork in an even layer.
6. Press "Power Button" of Air Fry Oven and turn the dial to select the "Bake" mode.
7. Press the Time button and again turn the dial to set the cooking time to 35 minutes.
8. Now push the Temp button and rotate the dial to set the temperature at 350 degrees F.
9. Once preheated, place casserole dish in the oven and close its lid.
10. Serve warm.

Nutritional Information per Serving:
Calories 352; Total Fat 14 g; Saturated Fat 2 g; Cholesterol 65 mg; Sodium 220 mg

Pork Au Gratin

Prep Time: 10 minutes; Cooking Time: 1hr 40 minutes; Serving: 8
Ingredients
- 8 pork loin chops, trimmed
- 1/4 cup white flour
- 1 tablespoon olive oil
- 1 large onion, chopped
- 2 garlic cloves, crushed
- 3 carrots, peeled and diced
- 2 tablespoons tomato paste
- 2 1/2 cups beef stock
- 2 dried bay leaves
- 3 cups tater tots

Method:
1. Dust the pork chops with flour and sear it in a pan layered with olive oil.
2. Sear the pork loin chops for 4 minutes per side.
3. Transfer the chops to a baking tray.
4. Add onion, garlic, and carrot to the same pan.
5. Sauté for 5 minutes, then stir in tomato paste, stock, and all other ingredients.
6. Stir cook for 4 minutes then pour this sauce over the chops.
7. Press "Power Button" of Air Fry Oven and turn the dial to select the "Bake" mode.
8. Press the Time button and again turn the dial to set the cooking time to 1 hr. 30 minutes.
9. Now push the Temp button and rotate the dial to set the temperature at 350 degrees F.
10. Once preheated, place the baking pan in the oven and close its lid.
11. Serve warm.

Nutritional Information per Serving:
Calories 388; Total Fat 8 g; Saturated Fat 1 g; Cholesterol 153mg; Sodium 339 mg

Crispy Pork Casserole

Prep Time: 10 minutes; Cooking Time: 25 minutes; Serving: 4
Ingredients
- ½ lb. minced pork
- 1 tbs parsley chopped
- 2 teaspoon curry powder
- 1 pinch salt and black pepper

- 1 lb. sweet potato cooked, mashed
- 1 oz. cheese grated
- 1 ½ oz. tortilla chips crushed

Method:
1. Mix pork, curry powder, seasoning, and parsley.
2. Spread this pork mixture in a casserole dish.
3. Top the pork mixture with sweet potato mash, cheese, and tortilla chips.
4. Press "Power Button" of Air Fry Oven and turn the dial to select the "Bake" mode.
5. Press the Time button and again turn the dial to set the cooking time to 20 minutes.
6. Now push the Temp button and rotate the dial to set the temperature at 350 degrees F.
7. Once preheated, place casserole dish in the oven and close its lid.
8. Serve warm.

Nutritional Information per Serving:
Calories 351; Total Fat 15.8 g; Saturated Fat 2.7 g; Cholesterol 75 mg; Sodium 189 mg

Greek Pork Pie

Prep Time: 10 minutes; Cooking Time: 46 minutes; Serving: 6
Ingredients
- 1 tablespoon olive oil
- 1 shallot, chopped
- 2 garlic cloves, crushed
- 1 lb. pork mince
- 1 teaspoon ground cinnamon
- 2 cups tomatoes chopped
- 1 tablespoon dried oregano
- 14 oz. macaroni, boiled
- 2 tablespoons almond milk
- 9 Oz. ricotta
- 2 tablespoons mozzarella cheese, grated

Method:
1. Sauté onion with oil in a frying pan for 10 minutes.
2. Stir in garlic and cook for 1 minute, then remove it from the heat.
3. Toss pork mince then sauté until brown.
4. Stir in cinnamon, tomatoes, and oregano.
5. Cook this mixture on a simmer for 15 minutes.
6. Meanwhile, blend ricotta with garlic, cheese, and milk in a blender.
7. Spread the pork tomatoes mixture in a casserole dish and top it with ricotta mixture.
8. Press "Power Button" of Air Fry Oven and turn the dial to select the "Bake" mode.
9. Press the Time button and again turn the dial to set the cooking time to 30 minutes.
10. Now push the Temp button and rotate the dial to set the temperature at 350 degrees F.
11. Once preheated, place casserole dish in the oven and close its lid.
12. Serve warm.

Nutritional Information per Serving:
Calories 231; Total Fat 20.1 g; Saturated Fat 2.4 g; Cholesterol 110 mg; Sodium 941 mg

Kale Pork Pasta

Prep Time: 10 minutes; Cooking Time: 20 minutes; Serving: 4
Ingredients
- 1 tablespoon olive oil
- 1 onion, finely chopped
- 2 garlic cloves, finely chopped
- 2 teaspoon dried oregano
- 1 lb. pork mince
- ¾ lb. tin chopped tomatoes
- ¼ cup pitted black olives
- ½ cup kale, chopped
- 2 tablespoons dill, stems removed and chopped
- 9 Oz. bow tie pasta, boiled
- 1 ball half-fat mozzarella cheese, torn

Method:
1. Sauté onion and garlic with oil in a pan over moderate heat for 5 minutes.

2. Stir in tomatoes, kale, pork, and olives, then stir cook for 5 minutes.
3. Spread the pork in a casserole dish and toss in the pasta.
4. Top the pasta pork mix with mozzarella cheese.
5. Press "Power Button" of Air Fry Oven and turn the dial to select the "Bake" mode.
6. Press the Time button and again turn the dial to set the cooking time to 10 minutes.
7. Now push the Temp button and rotate the dial to set the temperature at 350 degrees F.
8. Once preheated, place casserole dish in the oven and close its lid.
9. Serve warm.

Nutritional Information per Serving:
Calories 440; Total Fat 7.9 g; Saturated Fat 1.8 g; Cholesterol 5 mg; Sodium 581 mg

Pork Orzo Bake

Prep Time: 10 minutes; Cooking Time: 2hr. 15 minutes; Serving: 6
Ingredients
Pork
- 1 tablespoon olive oil
- 1 2/3 lbs. pork shoulder, diced
- 2 onions, chopped
- 2 teaspoon dried thyme
- 1 teaspoon dried mint
- ½ teaspoon ground cumin
- 1 teaspoon paprika

Pasta
- 14 oz. tin cherry tomatoes
- 2.6 cups vegetable stock, hot
- 10.5 oz. orzo pasta
- ¼ cup feta, crumbled
- Finely grated zest 1 lemon

Method:
1. Rub the pork shoulder with all its seasonings and oil.
2. Place the pork should in a baking tray.
3. Press "Power Button" of Air Fry Oven and turn the dial to select the "Bake" mode.
4. Press the Time button and again turn the dial to set the cooking time to 1 hr. 45 minutes.
5. Now push the Temp button and rotate the dial to set the temperature at 350 degrees F.
6. Once preheated, place the pork baking tray in the oven and close its lid.
7. Meanwhile, cook orzo, with hot stock, tomatoes, lemon zest, salt, and black pepper in a cooking pot for 30 minutes.
8. Serve the pork with orzo.

Nutritional Information per Serving:
Calories 380; Total Fat 20 g; Saturated Fat 5 g; Cholesterol 151 mg; Sodium 686 mg

Pork Mushroom Bake

Prep Time: 10 minutes; Cooking Time: 30 minutes; Serving: 4
Ingredients
- 2 tablespoons olive oil
- 1 onion, chopped
- ½ lb. ground pork
- 4 fresh mushrooms, sliced
- 2 cups marinara sauce
- 1 teaspoon butter
- 4 teaspoons flour
- 1 cup milk
- 1 egg, beaten
- 1 cup cheddar cheese, grated

Method:
1. Put a wok on moderate heat and add oil to heat.
2. Toss in onion and sauté until soft.
3. Stir in mushrooms and pork, then cook until meat is brown.
4. Add marinara sauce and cook it to a simmer.
5. Spread this mixture in a casserole dish.

6. Prepare the white sauce by melting butter in a saucepan over moderate heat.
7. Stir in flour and whisk well, pour in the milk.
8. Mix well and whisk ¼ cup sauce with egg then return it to the saucepan.
9. Stir cook for 1 minute then pour this sauce over the pork.
10. Drizzle cheese over the pork casserole.
11. Press "Power Button" of Air Fry Oven and turn the dial to select the "Bake" mode.
12. Press the Time button and again turn the dial to set the cooking time to 30 minutes.
13. Now push the Temp button and rotate the dial to set the temperature at 350 degrees F.
14. Once preheated, place casserole dish in the oven and close its lid.
15. Serve warm.

Nutritional Information per Serving:
Calories 361; Total Fat 16.3 g; Saturated Fat 4.9 g; Cholesterol 114 mg; Sodium 515 mg

Saucy Pork Mince

Prep Time: 10 minutes; Cooking Time: 60 minutes; Serving: 8

Ingredients
- 2 tablespoons olive oil
- 1 large onion, diced
- 2 lbs. ground pork
- 2 teaspoons salt
- 6 cloves garlic, chopped
- 1/2 cup red wine
- 6 cloves garlic, chopped
- 3 teaspoons ground cinnamon
- 2 teaspoons ground cumin
- 2 teaspoons dried oregano
- 1 teaspoon black pepper
- 1 can 28 oz. crushed tomatoes
- 1 tablespoon tomato passata

Method:
1. Put a suitable wok over moderate heat and add oil to heat.
2. Toss in onion, salt, and pork meat then stir cook for 12 minutes.
3. Stir in red wine and cook for 2 minutes.
4. Add cinnamon, garlic, oregano, cumin, and pepper, then stir cook for 2 minutes.
5. Add tomato passata and tomatoes and cook for 20 minutes on a simmer.
6. Spread this mixture in a casserole dish.
7. Press "Power Button" of Air Fry Oven and turn the dial to select the "Bake" mode.
8. Press the Time button and again turn the dial to set the cooking time to 20 minutes.
9. Now push the Temp button and rotate the dial to set the temperature at 350 degrees F.
10. Once preheated, place casserole dish in the oven and close its lid.
11. Serve warm.

Nutritional Information per Serving:
Calories 405; Total Fat 22.7 g; Saturated Fat 6.1 g; Cholesterol 4 mg; Sodium 227 mg

Pork Squash Bake

Prep Time: 10 minutes; Cooking Time: 50 minutes; Serving: 6

Ingredients
- ¼ cup olive oil
- 1 yellow squash, peeled and chopped
- 1 onion, diced
- 2 garlic cloves, crushed
- 1 lb. pork mince
- ½ teaspoon cinnamon
- ¼ teaspoon ground cumin
- 1 teaspoon fresh rosemary
- 2 cups tomato passata
- 2 oz. butter
- ¼ cup flour
- 2 cups almond milk
- ½ cup tasty cheese, grated
- 1 egg
- Salt and black pepper to taste

Method:

1. Put a wok on moderate heat and add oil to heat.
2. Stir in squash, then sauté for 5 minutes.
3. Add pork, spices, rosemary, garlic, and onion, then stir cook for 8 minutes.
4. Stir in pasta, and tomato paste and cook on a simmer for 5 minutes.
5. Spread this pork mixture in a casserole dish.
6. Prepare the white sauce in a suitable pot.
7. Add oil to heat, then stir in flour and cook for 1 minute.
8. Pour in milk and stir cook until it thickens.
9. Stir in cheese, egg, salt, and black pepper.
10. Spread this white sauce over the pork pasta mixture.
11. Press "Power Button" of Air Fry Oven and turn the dial to select the "Bake" mode.
12. Press the Time button and again turn the dial to set the cooking time to 30 minutes.
13. Now push the Temp button and rotate the dial to set the temperature at 350 degrees F.
14. Once preheated, place casserole dish in the oven and close its lid.
15. Serve warm.

Nutritional Information per Serving:
Calories 545; Total Fat 36.4 g; Saturated Fat 10.1 g; Cholesterol 200 mg; Sodium 272 mg

Cider Pork Skewers

Prep Time: 10 minutes; Cooking Time: 15 minutes; Serving: 4
Ingredients
- 3 garlic cloves, minced
- 4 tablespoon rapeseed oil
- 2 tablespoon cider vinegar
- large bunch thyme
- 1 ¼ lb. boneless pork, diced

Method:
1. Toss pork with all its thyme, oil, vinegar, and garlic.
2. Marinate the thyme pork for 2 hours in a closed container in the refrigerator.
3. Thread the marinated pork on the skewers.
4. Place these skewers in an Air fryer basket.
5. Press "Power Button" of Air Fry Oven and turn the dial to select the "Air fry" mode.
6. Press the Time button and again turn the dial to set the cooking time to 15 minutes.
7. Now push the Temp button and rotate the dial to set the temperature at 350 degrees F.
8. Once preheated, place the Air fryer basket in the oven and close its lid.
9. Flip the skewers when cooked halfway through then resume cooking.
10. Serve the skewers with salad.

Nutritional Information per Serving:
Calories 395; Total Fat 17.5 g; Saturated Fat 4.8 g; Cholesterol 283 mg; Sodium 355 mg

Mint Pork Kebobs

Prep Time: 10 minutes; Cooking Time: 15 minutes; Serving: 4
Ingredients
- ½ cup cream
- 1½ tablespoon mint
- 1 teaspoon ground cumin
- 10.5 oz. diced pork
- ½ small onion, cubed
- 1 cup cottage cheese, cubed

Method:
1. Whisk the cream with mint and cumin in a suitable bowl.
2. Toss in pork cubes and mix well to coat. Marinate for 30 minutes.
3. Alternatively, thread the pork, onion and cottage cheese on the skewers.
4. Place these pork skewers in the Air fry basket.
5. Press "Power Button" of Air Fry Oven and turn the dial to select the "Air fryer" mode.

6. Press the Time button and again turn the dial to set the cooking time to 15 minutes.
7. Now push the Temp button and rotate the dial to set the temperature at 370 degrees F.
8. Once preheated, place the Air fryer basket in the oven and close its lid.
9. Flip the skewers when cooked halfway through then resume cooking.
10. Serve warm.

Nutritional Information per Serving:
Calories 311; Total Fat 8.9 g; Saturated Fat 4.5 g; Cholesterol 57 mg; Sodium 340 mg

Tahini Pork Kebobs

Prep Time: 10 minutes; Cooking Time: 18 minutes; Serving: 6
Ingredients

- 2 lbs. pork steaks
- 2 tablespoon tahini
- zest and juice of 1 lemon
- 1 tablespoon maple syrup
- handful thyme leaves, chopped

Method:
1. Mix pork with tahini paste, lemon juice, zest, maple syrup and thyme.
2. Toss well to coat then marinate for 30 minutes.
3. Alternatively, thread the pork on the skewers.
4. Place these pork skewers in the Air fry basket.
5. Press "Power Button" of Air Fry Oven and turn the dial to select the "Air fryer" mode.
6. Press the Time button and again turn the dial to set the cooking time to 18 minutes.
7. Now push the Temp button and rotate the dial to set the temperature at 360 degrees F.
8. Once preheated, place the Air fryer basket in the oven and close its lid.
9. Flip the skewers when cooked halfway through then resume cooking.
10. Serve warm.

Nutritional Information per Serving:
Calories 548; Total Fat 22.9 g; Saturated Fat 9 g; Cholesterol 105 mg; Sodium 350 mg

Pork Skewers with Garden Salad

Prep Time: 10 minutes; Cooking Time: 20 minutes; Serving: 4
Ingredients

- 1 ¼ lb. boneless pork, diced
- 2 teaspoons balsamic vinegar

For the salad
- 4 large tomatoes, chopped
- 1 cucumber, chopped
- 1 handful black olives, chopped
- 2 tablespoons olive oil
- 1 garlic clove, crushed

- 9 oz. pack feta cheese, crumbled
- 1 bunch of parsley, chopped

Method:
1. Whisk balsamic vinegar with garlic and olive oil in a bowl.
2. Toss in pork cubes and mix well to coat. Marinate for 30 minutes.
3. Alternatively, thread the pork on the skewers.
4. Place these pork skewers in the Air fry basket.
5. Press "Power Button" of Air Fry Oven and turn the dial to select the "Air fryer" mode.
6. Press the Time button and again turn the dial to set the cooking time to 20 minutes.
7. Now push the Temp button and rotate the dial to set the temperature at 360 degrees F.
8. Once preheated, place the Air fryer basket in the oven and close its lid.
9. Flip the skewers when cooked halfway through then resume cooking.
10. Meanwhile, whisk all the salad ingredients in a salad bowl.
11. Serve the skewers with prepared salad.

Nutritional Information per Serving:

Calories 289; Total Fat 50.5 g; Saturated Fat 11.7 g; Cholesterol 58 mg; Sodium 463 mg

Wine Soaked Pork Kebobs

Prep Time: 10 minutes; Cooking Time: 20 minutes; Serving: 6

Ingredients
- 2 ¼ lbs. pork shoulder, diced
- 1/3 cup avocado oil
- ½ cup red wine
- 2 teaspoon dried oregano
- zest and juice 2 limes
- 2 garlic cloves, crushed

Method:
1. Whisk avocado oil, red wine, oregano, lime juice, zest, and garlic in a suitable bowl.
2. Toss in pork cubes and mix well to coat. Marinate for 30 minutes.
3. Alternatively, thread the pork, onion, and bread on the skewers.
4. Place these pork skewers in the Air fry basket.
5. Press "Power Button" of Air Fry Oven and turn the dial to select the "Air fryer" mode.
6. Press the Time button and again turn the dial to set the cooking time to 20 minutes.
7. Now push the Temp button and rotate the dial to set the temperature at 370 degrees F.
8. Once preheated, place the Air fryer basket in the oven and close its lid.
9. Flip the skewers when cooked halfway through then resume cooking.
10. Serve warm.

Nutritional Information per Serving:
Calories 237; Total Fat 19.8 g; Saturated Fat 1.4 g; Cholesterol 10 mg; Sodium 719 mg

Pork Sausages

Prep Time: 10 minutes; Cooking Time: 16 minutes; Serving: 6

Ingredients
- 1 lb. pork mince
- 2 oz. feta cheese
- 1 large red onion, chopped
- ¼ cup parsley, chopped
- ¼ cup mint, chopped
- 1 tablespoon olive oil
- juice 1 lemon

Method:
1. Whisk pork mince with onion, feta, and everything in a bowl.
2. Make 12 sausages out of this mixture then thread them on the skewers.
3. Place these pork skewers in the Air fry basket.
4. Press "Power Button" of Air Fry Oven and turn the dial to select the "Bake" mode.
5. Press the Time button and again turn the dial to set the cooking time to 16 minutes.
6. Now push the Temp button and rotate the dial to set the temperature at 370 degrees F.
7. Once preheated, place the Air fryer basket in the oven and close its lid.
8. Flip the skewers when cooked halfway through then resume cooking.
9. Serve warm.

Nutritional Information per Serving:
Calories 452; Total Fat 4 g; Saturated Fat 2 g; Cholesterol 65 mg; Sodium 220 mg

Pest Pork Kebobs

Prep Time: 10 minutes; Cooking Time: 20 minutes; Serving: 4

Ingredients
- 9 ½ oz. couscous, boiled
- 2 tablespoon pesto paste
- 2/3 lb. pork steak, diced
- 2 red peppers, cut into chunks
- 2 red onions, cut into chunks
- 1 tablespoon olive oil

Method:
1. Toss in pork cubes with pesto and oil, then mix well to coat. Marinate for 30 minutes.

2. Alternatively, thread the pork, onion, and peppers on the skewers.
3. Place these pork skewers in the Air fry basket.
4. Press "Power Button" of Air Fry Oven and turn the dial to select the "Air fryer" mode.
5. Press the Time button and again turn the dial to set the cooking time to 20 minutes.
6. Now push the Temp button and rotate the dial to set the temperature at 370 degrees F.
7. Once preheated, place the Air fryer basket in the oven and close its lid.
8. Flip the skewers when cooked halfway through then resume cooking.
9. Serve warm with couscous.

Nutritional Information per Serving:
Calories 331; Total Fat 15.8 g; Saturated Fat 2.7 g; Cholesterol 75 mg; Sodium 389 mg

Pork Sausage with Yogurt Dip

Prep Time: 10 minutes; Cooking Time: 10 minutes; Serving: 8
Ingredients
- 2 tablespoon cumin seed
- 2 tablespoon coriander seed
- 2 tablespoon fennel seed
- 1 tablespoon paprika

- 4 garlic cloves, minced
- ½ teaspoon ground cinnamon
- 1 ½ lb. lean minced pork

For the yogurt
- 3 zucchinis, grated
- 2 teaspoon cumin seed, toasted
- 9 Oz. Greek yogurt

- small handful chopped the coriander
- a small handful of chopped mint

Method:
1. Blend all the spices and seeds with garlic and cinnamon in a blender.
2. Add this spice paste to the minced pork then mix well.
3. Make 8 sausages and thread each on the skewers.
4. Place these pork skewers in the Air fry basket.
5. Press "Power Button" of Air Fry Oven and turn the dial to select the "Air fryer" mode.
6. Press the Time button and again turn the dial to set the cooking time to 10 minutes.
7. Now push the Temp button and rotate the dial to set the temperature at 370 degrees F.
8. Once preheated, place the Air fryer basket in the oven and close its lid.
9. Flip the skewers when cooked halfway through then resume cooking.
10. Prepare the yogurt ingredients in a bowl.
11. Serve skewers with the yogurt mixture.

Nutritional Information per Serving:
Calories 341; Total Fat 20.5 g; Saturated Fat 3 g; Cholesterol 42 mg; Sodium 688 mg

Pork with Quinoa Salad

Prep Time: 10 minutes; Cooking Time: 12 minutes; Serving: 4
Ingredients
- 2/3 lbs. lean pork shoulder, cubed
- 1 teaspoon ground cumin
- ½ teaspoon cayenne pepper

- 1 teaspoon sweet smoked paprika
- 1 tablespoon olive oil
- 24 cherry tomatoes

Salad:
- ½ cup quinoa, boiled
- ½ cup frozen pea
- 1 large carrot, grated
- small pack coriander, chopped

- small pack mint, chopped
- juice 1 lemon
- 2 tablespoon olive oil

Method:
1. Toss pork with oil, paprika, pepper, and cumin in a bowl.

2. Alternatively, thread the pork on the skewers.
3. Place these pork skewers in the Air fry basket.
4. Press "Power Button" of Air Fry Oven and turn the dial to select the "Air fryer" mode.
5. Press the Time button and again turn the dial to set the cooking time to 10 minutes.
6. Now push the Temp button and rotate the dial to set the temperature at 370 degrees F.
7. Once preheated, place the Air fryer basket in the oven and close its lid.
8. Flip the skewers when cooked halfway through then resume cooking.
9. Meanwhile, sauté carrots and peas with olive oil in a pan for 2 minutes.
10. Stir in mint, lemon juice, coriander, and cooked quinoa.
11. Serve skewers with the couscous salad.

Nutritional Information per Serving:

Calories 331; Total Fat 20.1 g; Saturated Fat 2.4 g; Cholesterol 110 mg; Sodium 941 mg

Pork Garlic Skewers

Prep Time: 10 minutes; Cooking Time: 20 minutes; Serving: 4

Ingredients

- 1 lb. pork, boned and diced
- 1 lemon, juiced and chopped
- 3 tablespoon olive oil
- 20 garlic cloves, chopped
- 1 handful rosemary, chopped
- 3 green peppers, cubed
- 2 red onions, cut into wedges

Method:

1. Toss the pork with the rest of the skewer's ingredients in a bowl.
2. Thread the pork, peppers, garlic, and onion on the skewers, alternately.
3. Place these pork skewers in the Air fry basket.
4. Press "Power Button" of Air Fry Oven and turn the dial to select the "Air fryer" mode.
5. Press the Time button and again turn the dial to set the cooking time to 20 minutes.
6. Now push the Temp button and rotate the dial to set the temperature at 370 degrees F.
7. Once preheated, place the Air fryer basket in the oven and close its lid.
8. Flip the skewers when cooked halfway through then resume cooking.
9. Serve warm.

Nutritional Information per Serving:

Calories 472; Total Fat 11.1 g; Saturated Fat 5.8 g; Cholesterol 610 mg; Sodium 749 mg

Zesty Pork Skewers

Prep Time: 10 minutes; Cooking Time: 20 minutes; Serving: 4

Ingredients

- 2 teaspoons ground cumin
- 2 teaspoons ground coriander
- 1 onion, cut into pieces
- 1/4 teaspoon ground cinnamon
- 1/8 teaspoon ground smoked paprika
- 2 teaspoons orange zest
- 1/2 yellow bell pepper, sliced into squares
- 1/2 teaspoon salt
- 1/2 teaspoon black pepper
- 1 tablespoon lemon juice
- 2 teaspoons olive oil
- 1 1/2 lbs. pork, cubed

Method:

1. Toss pork with the rest of the skewer's ingredients in a bowl.
2. Thread the pork and veggies on the skewers alternately.
3. Place these pork skewers in the Air fry basket.
4. Press "Power Button" of Air Fry Oven and turn the dial to select the "Air fryer" mode.
5. Press the Time button and again turn the dial to set the cooking time to 20 minutes.
6. Now push the Temp button and rotate the dial to set the temperature at 370 degrees F.

7. Once preheated, place the Air fryer basket in the oven and close its lid.
8. Flip the skewers when cooked halfway through then resume cooking.
9. Serve warm.

Nutritional Information per Serving:

Calories 327; Total Fat 3.5 g; Saturated Fat 0.5 g; Cholesterol 162 mg; Sodium 142 mg

Alepo Pork Kebobs

Prep Time: 10 minutes; Cooking Time: 16 minutes; Serving: 6

Ingredients

Pork Kabobs

- 1 lb. ground pork
- 1/2 an onion, finely diced
- 3 garlic cloves, finely minced
- 2 teaspoons cumin
- 2 teaspoons coriander
- 2 teaspoons sumac
- 1 teaspoon Aleppo Chili flakes
- 1 ½ teaspoons salt
- 2 tablespoons chopped mint

Method:

1. Toss pork with the rest of the kebob ingredients in a bowl.
2. Make 6 sausages out of this mince and thread them on the skewers.
3. Place these pork skewers in the Air fry basket.
4. Press "Power Button" of Air Fry Oven and turn the dial to select the "Air fryer" mode.
5. Press the Time button and again turn the dial to set the cooking time to 16 minutes.
6. Now push the Temp button and rotate the dial to set the temperature at 370 degrees F.
7. Once preheated, place the Air fryer basket in the oven and close its lid.
8. Flip the skewers when cooked halfway through then resume cooking.
9. Serve the skewers with yogurt sauce.

Nutritional Information per Serving:

Calories 353; Total Fat 7.5 g; Saturated Fat 1.1 g; Cholesterol 20 mg; Sodium 297 mg

Zucchini Pork Kebobs

Prep Time: 10 minutes; Cooking Time: 20 minutes; Serving: 4

Ingredients

- 2 garlic cloves
- 1 teaspoon dried oregano
- olive oil
- 4 pork steaks, diced
- 2 zucchinis, cubed
- 8 fresh bay leaves
- 2 lime, juiced
- a few sprigs parsley, chopped

Method:

1. Toss pork with the rest of the skewer's ingredients in a bowl.
2. Thread the pork and veggies on the skewers alternately.
3. Place these pork skewers in the Air fry basket.
4. Press "Power Button" of Air Fry Oven and turn the dial to select the "Air fryer" mode.
5. Press the Time button and again turn the dial to set the cooking time to 20 minutes.
6. Now push the Temp button and rotate the dial to set the temperature at 370 degrees F.
7. Once preheated, place the Air fryer basket in the oven and close its lid.
8. Flip the skewers when cooked halfway through then resume cooking.
9. Serve warm.

Nutritional Information per Serving:

Calories 248; Total Fat 13 g; Saturated Fat 7 g; Cholesterol 387 mg; Sodium 353 mg

Lime Glazed Pork Kebobs

Prep Time: 10 minutes; Cooking Time: 20 minutes; Serving: 6

Ingredients

- 2 lb. pork, cubed
- 1/2 cup olive oil
- 1 lime juice
- 3 cloves garlic, minced
- 1 onion, sliced
- 1 teaspoon oregano, dried
- 1/4 teaspoon dried thyme,
- 1 teaspoon salt
- 1/4 teaspoon black pepper
- 1 tablespoon parsley, chopped
- 2 red pepper, cut into square
- 1 onion, cut into chunks

Method:

1. Toss pork with the rest of the kebab ingredients in a bowl.
2. Cover the pork and marinate it for 30 minutes.
3. Thread the pork and veggies on the skewers alternately.
4. Place these pork skewers in the Air fry basket.
5. Press "Power Button" of Air Fry Oven and turn the dial to select the "Air fryer" mode.
6. Press the Time button and again turn the dial to set the cooking time to 20 minutes.
7. Now push the Temp button and rotate the dial to set the temperature at 370 degrees F.
8. Once preheated, place the Air fryer basket in the oven and close its lid.
9. Flip the skewers when cooked halfway through then resume cooking.
10. Serve warm.

Nutritional Information per Serving:

Calories 457; Total Fat 19.1 g; Saturated Fat 11 g; Cholesterol 262 mg; Sodium 557 mg

Pork Kebab Tacos

Prep Time: 10 minutes; Cooking Time: 20 minutes; Serving: 6

Ingredients

- Pork Kebabs
- 2 lbs. pork loin chops, diced
- 1 large onion, squares
- Salt, to taste

For the Wrap

- 6 burrito wraps
- 1/4 cup onions, sliced
- 1/2 cup tomatoes, sliced
- 1 1/2 cups romaine lettuce, chopped

Method:

1. Toss pork and onion with salt in a bowl to season them.
2. Thread the pork and onion on the skewers alternately.
3. Place these pork skewers in the Air fry basket.
4. Press "Power Button" of Air Fry Oven and turn the dial to select the "Air fryer" mode.
5. Press the Time button and again turn the dial to set the cooking time to 20 minutes.
6. Now push the Temp button and rotate the dial to set the temperature at 370 degrees F.
7. Once preheated, place the Air fryer basket in the oven and close its lid.
8. Flip the skewers when cooked halfway through then resume cooking.
9. Place the warm burrito wrap on the serving plates.
10. Divide the tortilla ingredients on the tortillas and top them with pork kebabs.
11. Serve warm.

Nutritional Information per Serving:

Calories 392; Total Fat 16.1 g; Saturated Fat 2.3 g; Cholesterol 231 mg; Sodium 466 mg

Rainbow Pork Skewers

Prep Time: 10 minutes; Cooking Time: 15 minutes; Serving: 4

Ingredients

- 1-lb. boneless pork steaks, diced
- 1 eggplant, diced

- 1 yellow squash, diced
- 1 zucchini, diced
- 1/2 onion
- 4 slices ginger
- 5 cloves garlic
- 1 teaspoon cinnamon, ground
- 1 teaspoon cayenne
- 1 teaspoon salt

Method:
1. Blend all the spices, ginger, garlic, and onion in a blender.
2. Toss the pork and veggies with prepared spice mixture then thread them over the skewers.
3. Marinate the spiced skewers for 30 minutes.
4. Place these pork skewers in the Air fry basket.
5. Press "Power Button" of Air Fry Oven and turn the dial to select the "Air fryer" mode.
6. Press the Time button and again turn the dial to set the cooking time to 15 minutes.
7. Now push the Temp button and rotate the dial to set the temperature at 350 degrees F.
8. Once preheated, place the Air fryer basket in the oven and close its lid.
9. Flip the skewers when cooked halfway through then resume cooking.
10. Serve warm.

Nutritional Information per Serving:
Calories 321; Total Fat 7.4 g; Saturated Fat 4.6 g; Cholesterol 105 mg; Sodium 353 mg

Tangy Pork Sausages

Prep Time: 10 minutes; Cooking Time: 18 minutes; Serving: 4

Ingredients
- ¾ lb. ground pork
- ¼ cup breadcrumbs
- ½ cup egg, beaten
- 1 teaspoon cumin
- 1 teaspoon paprika
- 1 teaspoon garlic powder
- 1 teaspoon onion powder
- ½ teaspoon cinnamon
- ½ teaspoon turmeric
- ½ teaspoon fennel seeds
- ½ teaspoon coriander seed, ground
- ½ teaspoon salt

Method:
1. Mix pork mince with all the spices and kebab ingredients in a bowl.
2. Make 4 sausages out of this mixture and thread them on the skewers.
3. Refrigerate the pork skewers for 10 minutes to marinate.
4. Place these pork skewers in the Air fry basket.
5. Press "Power Button" of Air Fry Oven and turn the dial to select the "Air fryer" mode.
6. Press the Time button and again turn the dial to set the cooking time to 8 minutes.
7. Now push the Temp button and rotate the dial to set the temperature at 350 degrees F.
8. Once preheated, place the Air fryer basket in the oven and close its lid.
9. Flip the skewers when cooked halfway through then resume cooking.
10. Serve warm.

Nutritional Information per Serving:
Calories 248; Total Fat 15.7 g; Saturated Fat 2.7 g; Cholesterol 75 mg; Sodium 94 mg

Roasted Pork Shoulder

Prep Time: 10 minutes; Cooking Time: 1hr 30 minutes; Serving: 12

Ingredients
- 6 lb. pork shoulder, boneless

Spice rub:
- 1 cup olive oil
- juice of 1 lemon
- 1 teaspoon thyme
- 8 cups buttermilk

- 5 teaspoon minced garlic
- Salt to taste
- Black pepper to taste

Method:

1. Soak the pork shoulder in the buttermilk in a pot and cover to marinate.
2. Refrigerate the pork leg for 8 hours then remove it from the milk.
3. Place the pork shoulder in a baking tray.
4. Whisk spice rub ingredients in a bowl and brush over the pork liberally.
5. Press "Power Button" of Air Fry Oven and turn the dial to select the "Air Roast" mode.
6. Press the Time button and again turn the dial to set the cooking time to 1 hr. 30 minutes.
7. Now push the Temp button and rotate the dial to set the temperature at 370 degrees F.
8. Once preheated, place the pork baking tray in the oven and close its lid.
9. Serve warm.

Nutritional Information per Serving:

Calories 378; Total Fat 21 g; Saturated Fat 4.3 g; Cholesterol 150 mg; Sodium 146 mg

Chapter 7: Fish & Seafood Recipes

Simple Salmon

Preparation Time: 10 minutes; Cooking Time: 12 minutes; Servings: 4

Ingredients:
- 4 (6-oz.) salmon fillets
- Salt and ground black pepper, as required

Method:
1. Season the salmon fillets with salt and black pepper evenly.
2. Press "Power Button" of Air Fry Oven and turn the dial to select the "Air Broil" mode.
3. Press the Time button and again turn the dial to set the cooking time to 12 minutes.
4. Press "Start/Pause" button to start.
5. When the unit beeps to show that it is preheated, open the lid.
6. Arrange the fish fillets over the greased "Wire Rack" and insert in the oven.
7. Serve hot.

Nutritional Information per Serving:

Calories 225; Total Fat 10.5 g; Saturated Fat 1.5 g; Cholesterol 75 mg; Sodium 114 mg

Buttered Salmon

Preparation Time: 10 minutes; Cooking Time: 10 minutes; Servings: 2

Ingredients:
- 2 (6-oz.) salmon fillets
- Salt and ground black pepper, as required
- 1 tablespoon butter, melted

Method:
1. Season each salmon fillet with salt and black pepper and then, coat with the butter.
2. Press "Power Button" of Air Fry Oven and turn the dial to select the "Air Fry" mode.
3. Press the Time button and again turn the dial to set the cooking time to 10 minutes.
4. Now push the Temp button and rotate the dial to set the temperature at 360 degrees F.
5. Press "Start/Pause" button to start.
6. When the unit beeps to show that it is preheated, open the lid.
7. Arrange the salmon fillets in greased "Air Fry Basket" and insert in the oven.
8. Serve hot.

Nutritional Information per Serving:

Calories 276; Total Fat 16.3 g; Saturated Fat 5.2 g; Cholesterol 90 mg; Sodium 193 mg

Cajun Salmon

Preparation Time: 10 minutes; Cooking Time: 7 minutes; Servings: 2

Ingredients:
- 2 (7-oz.) (¾-inch thick) salmon fillets
- 1 tablespoon Cajun seasoning
- ½ teaspoon sugar
- 1 tablespoon fresh lemon juice

Method:
1. Sprinkle the salmon fillets with Cajun seasoning and sugar evenly.
2. Press "Power Button" of Air Fry Oven and turn the dial to select the "Air Fry" mode.
3. Press the Time button and again turn the dial to set the cooking time to 7 minutes.
4. Now push the Temp button and rotate the dial to set the temperature at 356 degrees F.
5. Press "Start/Pause" button to start.
6. When the unit beeps to show that it is preheated, open the lid.
7. Arrange the salmon fillets, skin-side up in greased "Air Fry Basket" and insert in the oven.
8. Drizzle with the lemon juice and serve hot.

Spicy Salmon

Preparation Time: 10 minutes; Cooking Time: 11 minutes; Servings: 2

Ingredients:

- 1 teaspoon smoked paprika
- 1 teaspoon cayenne pepper
- 1 teaspoon onion powder
- 1 teaspoon garlic powder
- Salt and ground black pepper, as required
- 2 (6-oz.) (1½-inch thick) salmon fillets
- 2 teaspoons olive oil

Method:

1. Add the spices in a bowl and mix well.
2. Drizzle the salmon fillets with oil and then, rub with the spice mixture.
3. Press "Power Button" of Air Fry Oven and turn the dial to select the "Air Fry" mode.
4. Press the Time button and again turn the dial to set the cooking time to 11 minutes.
5. Now push the Temp button and rotate the dial to set the temperature at 390 degrees F.
6. Press "Start/Pause" button to start.
7. When the unit beeps to show that it is preheated, open the lid.
8. Arrange the salmon fillets in greased "Air Fry Basket" and insert in the oven.
9. Serve hot.

Nutritional Information per Serving:
  Calories 280; Total Fat 15.5 g; Saturated Fat 2.2 g; Cholesterol 75 mg; Sodium 154 mg

Lemony Salmon

Preparation Time: 10 minutes; Cooking Time: 8 minutes; Servings: 3

Ingredients:

- 1½ lbs. salmon
- ½ teaspoon red chili powder
- Salt and ground black pepper, as required
- 1 lemon, cut into slices
- 1 tablespoon fresh dill, chopped

Method:

1. Season the salmon with chili powder, salt, and black pepper.
2. Press "Power Button" of Air Fry Oven and turn the dial to select the "Air Fry" mode.
3. Press the Time button and again turn the dial to set the cooking time to 8 minutes.
4. Now push the Temp button and rotate the dial to set the temperature at 375 degrees F.
5. Press "Start/Pause" button to start.
6. When the unit beeps to show that it is preheated, open the lid.
7. Arrange the salmon fillets in greased "Air Fry Basket" and insert in the oven.
8. Garnish with fresh dill and serve hot.

Nutritional Information per Serving:
  Calories 305; Total Fat 14.1 g; Saturated Fat 2 g; Cholesterol 100 mg; Sodium 157 mg

Honey Glazed Salmon

Preparation Time: 10 minutes; Cooking Time: 8 minutes; Servings: 2

Ingredients:

- 2 (6-oz.) salmon fillets
- Salt, as required
- 2 tablespoons honey

Method:

1. Sprinkle the salmon fillets with salt and then, coat with honey.
2. Press "Power Button" of Air Fry Oven and turn the dial to select the "Air Fry" mode.

3. Press the Time button and again turn the dial to set the cooking time to 8 minutes.
4. Now push the Temp button and rotate the dial to set the temperature at 355 degrees F.
5. Press "Start/Pause" button to start.
6. When the unit beeps to show that it is preheated, open the lid.
7. Arrange the salmon fillets in greased "Air Fry Basket" and insert in the oven.
8. Serve hot.

Nutritional Information per Serving:
Calories 289; Total Fat 10.5 g; Saturated Fat 1.5 g; Cholesterol 75 mg; Sodium 153 mg

Sweet & Sour Glazed Salmon

Preparation Time: 12 minutes; Cooking Time: 20 minutes; Servings: 2
Ingredients:
- 1/3 cup soy sauce
- 1/3 cup honey
- 3 teaspoons rice wine vinegar
- 1 teaspoon water
- 4 (3½-oz.) salmon fillets

Method:
1. In a small bowl, mix together the soy sauce, honey, vinegar, and water.
2. In another small bowl, reserve about half of the mixture.
3. Add salmon fillets in the remaining mixture and coat well.
4. Cover the bowl and refrigerate to marinate for about 2 hours.
5. Press "Power Button" of Air Fry Oven and turn the dial to select the "Air Fry" mode.
6. Press the Time button and again turn the dial to set the cooking time to 12 minutes.
7. Now push the Temp button and rotate the dial to set the temperature at 355 degrees F.
8. Press "Start/Pause" button to start.
9. When the unit beeps to show that it is preheated, open the lid.
10. Arrange the salmon fillets in greased "Air Fry Basket" and insert in the oven.
11. Flip the salmon fillets once halfway through and coat with the reserved marinade after every 3 minutes.
12. Serve hot.

Nutritional Information per Serving:
Calories 462; Total Fat 12.3 g; Saturated Fat 1.8 g; Cholesterol 88 mg; Sodium 2400 mg

Salmon Parcel

Preparation Time: 15 minutes; Cooking Time: 23 minutes; Servings: 2
Ingredients:
- 2 (4-oz.) salmon fillets
- 6 asparagus stalks
- ¼ cup white sauce
- 1 teaspoon oil
- ¼ cup champagne
- Salt and ground black pepper, as required

Method:
1. In a bowl, mix together all the ingredients.
2. Divide the salmon mixture over 2 pieces of foil evenly.
3. Seal the foil around the salmon mixture to form the packet.
4. Press "Power Button" of Air Fry Oven and turn the dial to select the "Air Fry" mode.
5. Press the Time button and again turn the dial to set the cooking time to 13 minutes.
6. Now push the Temp button and rotate the dial to set the temperature at 355 degrees F.
7. Press "Start/Pause" button to start.
8. When the unit beeps to show that it is preheated, open the lid.
9. Arrange the salmon parcels in "Air Fry Basket" and insert in the oven.
10. Serve hot.

Nutritional Information per Serving:
    Calories 243; Total Fat 12.7 g; Saturated Fat 2.2 g; Cholesterol 52 mg; Sodium 240 mg

Salmon with Broccoli

Preparation Time: 15 minutes; Cooking Time: 12 minutes; Servings: 2
Ingredients:

- 1½ cups small broccoli florets
- 2 tablespoons vegetable oil, divided
- Salt and ground black pepper, as required
- 1 (½-inch) piece fresh ginger, grated
- 1 tablespoon soy sauce
- 1 teaspoon rice vinegar
- 1 teaspoon light brown sugar
- ¼ teaspoon cornstarch
- 2 (6-oz.) skin-on salmon fillets
- 1 scallion, thinly sliced

Method:

1. In a bowl, mix together the broccoli, 1 tablespoon of oil, salt, and black pepper.
2. In another bowl, mix well the ginger, soy sauce, vinegar, sugar, and cornstarch.
3. Coat the salmon fillets with remaining oil and then with the ginger mixture.
4. Press "Power Button" of Air Fry Oven and turn the dial to select the "Air Fry" mode.
5. Press the Time button and again turn the dial to set the cooking time to 12 minutes.
6. Now push the Temp button and rotate the dial to set the temperature at 375 degrees F.
7. Press "Start/Pause" button to start.
8. When the unit beeps to show that it is preheated, open the lid.
9. Arrange the broccoli florets in greased "Air Fry Basket" and top with the salmon fillets.
10. Insert the basket in the oven.
11. Serve hot.

Nutritional Information per Serving:
    Calories 385; Total Fat 24.4 g; Saturated Fat 4.2 g; Cholesterol 75 mg; Sodium 550 mg

Salmon with Prawns & Pasta

Preparation Time: 20 minutes; Cooking Time: 18 minutes; Servings: 4
Ingredients:

- 14 oz. pasta (of your choice)
- 4 tablespoons pesto, divided
- 4 (4-oz.) salmon steaks
- 2 tablespoons olive oil
- ½ lb. cherry tomatoes, chopped
- 8 large prawns, peeled and deveined
- 2 tablespoons fresh lemon juice
- 2 tablespoons fresh thyme, chopped

Method:

1. In a large pan of salted boiling water, add the pasta and cook for about 8-10 minutes or until desired doneness.
2. Meanwhile, in the bottom of a baking pan, spread 1 tablespoon of pesto.
3. Place salmon steaks and tomatoes over pesto in a single layer and drizzle with the oil.
4. Arrange the prawns on top in a single layer.
5. Drizzle with lemon juice and sprinkle with thyme.
6. Press "Power Button" of Air Fry Oven and turn the dial to select the "Air Fry" mode.
7. Press the Time button and again turn the dial to set the cooking time to 8 minutes.
8. Now push the Temp button and rotate the dial to set the temperature at 390 degrees F.
9. Press "Start/Pause" button to start.
10. When the unit beeps to show that it is preheated, open the lid.
11. Arrange the baking pan in "Air Fry Basket" and insert in the oven.
12. .Drain the pasta and transfer into a large bowl.
13. Add the remaining pesto and toss to coat well.
14. Divide the pasta onto serving plate and top with salmon mixture.

15. Serve immediately.

Nutritional Information per Serving:

Calories 592; Total Fat 23.2 g; Saturated Fat 3.8 g; Cholesterol 149 mg; Sodium 203 mg

Salmon Burgers

Preparation Time: 20 minutes; Cooking Time: 22 minutes; Servings: 6

Ingredients:

- 3 large russet potatoes, peeled and cubed
- 1 (6-oz.) cooked salmon fillet
- 1 egg
- ¾ cup frozen vegetables (of your choice), parboiled and drained
- 2 tablespoons fresh parsley, chopped
- 1 teaspoon fresh dill, chopped
- Salt and ground black pepper, as required
- 1 cup breadcrumbs
- ¼ cup olive oil

Method:

1. In a pan of the boiling water, cook the potatoes for about 10 minutes.
2. Drain the potatoes well.
3. Transfer the potatoes into a bowl and mash with a potato masher.
4. Set aside to cool completely.
5. In another bowl, add the salmon and flake with a fork.
6. Add the cooked potatoes, egg, parboiled vegetables, parsley, dill, salt and black pepper and mix until well combined.
7. Make 6 equal-sized patties from the mixture.
8. Coat patties with breadcrumb evenly and then drizzle with the oil evenly.
9. Press "Power Button" of Air Fry Oven and turn the dial to select the "Air Fry" mode.
10. Press the Time button and again turn the dial to set the cooking time to 12 minutes.
11. Now push the Temp button and rotate the dial to set the temperature at 355 degrees F.
12. Press "Start/Pause" button to start.
13. When the unit beeps to show that it is preheated, open the lid.
14. Arrange the patties in greased "Air Fry Basket" and insert in the oven.
15. Flip the patties once halfway through.
16. Serve hot.

Nutritional Information per Serving:

Calories 334; Total Fat 12.1 g; Saturated Fat 2 g; Cholesterol 40 mg; Sodium 175 mg

Ranch Tilapia

Preparation Time: 15 minutes; Cooking Time: 13 minutes; Servings: 4

Ingredients:

- ¾ cup cornflakes, crushed
- 1 (1-oz.) packet dry ranch-style dressing mix
- 2½ tablespoons vegetable oil
- 2 eggs
- 4 (6-oz.) tilapia fillets

Method:

1. In a shallow bowl, beat the eggs.
2. In another bowl, add the cornflakes, ranch dressing, and oil and mix until a crumbly mixture forms.
3. Dip the fish fillets into egg and then, coat with the breadcrumbs mixture.
4. Press "Power Button" of Air Fry Oven and turn the dial to select the "Air Fry" mode.
5. Press the Time button and again turn the dial to set the cooking time to 13 minutes.
6. Now push the Temp button and rotate the dial to set the temperature at 356 degrees F.
7. Press "Start/Pause" button to start.
8. When the unit beeps to show that it is preheated, open the lid.

9. Arrange the tilapia fillets in greased "Air Fry Basket" and insert in the oven.
10. Serve hot.

Nutritional Information per Serving:

Calories 267; Total Fat 12.2 g; Saturated Fat 3 g; Cholesterol 1685 mg; Sodium 168 mg

Chinese Cod

Preparation Time: 15 minutes; Cooking Time: 15 minutes; Servings: 2

Ingredients:

- 2 (7-oz.) cod fillets
- Salt and ground black pepper, as required
- ¼ teaspoon sesame oil
- 1 cup water
- 5 little squares rock sugar
- 5 tablespoons light soy sauce
- 1 teaspoon dark soy sauce
- 2 scallions (green part), sliced
- ¼ cup fresh cilantro, chopped
- 3 tablespoons olive oil
- 5 ginger slices

Method:

1. Season each cod fillet evenly with salt, and black pepper and drizzle with sesame oil.
2. Set aside at room temperature for about 15-20 minutes.
3. Dip the fish fillets into egg and then, coat with the breadcrumbs mixture.
4. Press "Power Button" of Air Fry Oven and turn the dial to select the "Air Fry" mode.
5. Press the Time button and again turn the dial to set the cooking time to 12 minutes.
6. Now push the Temp button and rotate the dial to set the temperature at 355 degrees F.
7. Press "Start/Pause" button to start.
8. When the unit beeps to show that it is preheated, open the lid.
9. Arrange the cod fillets in greased "Air Fry Basket" and insert in the oven.
10. Meanwhile, in a small pan, add the water and bring it to a boil.
11. Add the rock sugar and both soy sauces and cook until sugar is dissolved, stirring continuously.
12. Remove from the heat and set aside.
13. Remove the cod fillets from oven and transfer onto serving plates.
14. Top each fillet with scallion and cilantro.
15. In a small frying pan, heat the olive oil over medium heat and sauté the ginger slices for about 2-3 minutes.
16. Remove the frying pan from heat and discard the ginger slices.
17. Carefully, pour the hot oil evenly over cod fillets.
18. Top with the sauce mixture and serve.

Nutritional Information per Serving:

Calories 380; Total Fat 23.4 g; Saturated Fat 3.1 g; Cholesterol 97 mg; Sodium 2400 mg

Cod Parcel

Preparation Time: 20 minutes; Cooking Time: 15 minutes; Servings: 2

Ingredients:

- 2 tablespoons butter, melted
- 1 tablespoon fresh lemon juice
- ½ teaspoon dried tarragon
- Salt and ground black pepper, as required
- ½ cup red bell peppers, seeded and thinly sliced
- ½ cup carrots, peeled and julienned
- ½ cup fennel bulbs, julienned
- 2 (5-oz.) frozen cod fillets, thawed
- 1 tablespoon olive oil

Method:

1. In a large bowl, mix together the butter, lemon juice, tarragon, salt, and black pepper.
2. Add the bell pepper, carrot, and fennel bulb and generously coat with the mixture.

3. Arrange 2 large parchment squares onto a smooth surface.
4. Coat the cod fillets with oil and then, sprinkle evenly with salt and black pepper.
5. Arrange 1 cod fillet onto each parchment square and top each evenly with the vegetables.
6. Top with any remaining sauce from the bowl.
7. Fold the parchment paper and crimp the sides to secure fish and vegetables.
8. Press "Power Button" of Air Fry Oven and turn the dial to select the "Air Fry" mode.
9. Press the Time button and again turn the dial to set the cooking time to 15 minutes.
10. Now push the Temp button and rotate the dial to set the temperature at 350 degrees F.
11. Press "Start/Pause" button to start.
12. When the unit beeps to show that it is preheated, open the lid.
13. Arrange the cod parcels in "Air Fry Basket" and insert in the oven.
14. Serve hot.

Nutritional Information per Serving:
Calories 306; Total Fat 20 g; Saturated Fat 8.4 g; Cholesterol 100 mg; Sodium 281 mg

Cod Burgers

Preparation Time: 15 minutes; Cooking Time: 7 minutes; Servings: 6
Ingredients:
- ½ lb. cod fillets
- ½ teaspoon fresh lime zest, grated finely
- ½ egg
- ½ teaspoon red chili paste
- Salt, to taste
- ½ tablespoon fresh lime juice
- 3 tablespoons coconut, grated and divided
- 1 small scallion, chopped finely
- 1 tablespoon fresh parsley, chopped

Method:
1. In a food processor, add cod filets, lime zest, egg, chili paste, salt and lime juice and pulse until smooth.
2. Transfer the cod mixture into a bowl.
3. Add 1½ tablespoons coconut, scallion and parsley and mix until well combined.
4. Make 6 equal-sized patties from the mixture.
5. In a shallow dish, place the remaining coconut.
6. Coat the patties in coconut evenly.
7. Press "Power Button" of Air Fry Oven and turn the dial to select the "Air Fry" mode.
8. Press the Time button and again turn the dial to set the cooking time to 7 minutes.
9. Now push the Temp button and rotate the dial to set the temperature at 375 degrees F.
10. Press "Start/Pause" button to start.
11. When the unit beeps to show that it is preheated, open the lid.
12. Arrange the patties in greased "Air Fry Basket" and insert in the oven.
13. Serve hot.

Nutritional Information per Serving:
Calories 56; Total Fat 1.6 g; Saturated Fat 0.9 g; Cholesterol 35 mg; Sodium 68 mg

Spicy Catfish

Preparation Time: 15 minutes; Cooking Time: 13 minutes; Servings: 2
Ingredients:
- 2 tablespoons almond flour
- 1 teaspoon red chili powder
- ½ teaspoon paprika
- ½ teaspoon garlic powder
- Salt, as required
- 2 (6-oz.) catfish fillets
- 1 tablespoon olive oil

Method:

1. In a bowl, mix together the flour, paprika, garlic powder and salt.
2. Add the catfish fillets and coat with the mixture evenly.
3. Now, coat each fillet with oil.
4. Press "Power Button" of Air Fry Oven and turn the dial to select the "Air Fry" mode.
5. Press the Time button and again turn the dial to set the cooking time to 13 minutes.
6. Now push the Temp button and rotate the dial to set the temperature at 400 degrees F.
7. Press "Start/Pause" button to start.
8. When the unit beeps to show that it is preheated, open the lid.
9. Arrange the fish fillets in greased "Air Fry Basket" and insert in the oven.
10. Flip the fish fillets once halfway through.
11. Serve hot.

Nutritional Information per Serving:
Calories 340; Total Fat 23.5 g; Saturated Fat 3.7 g; Cholesterol 80 mg; Sodium 184 mg

Seasoned Catfish

Preparation Time: 15 minutes; Cooking Time: 23 minutes; Servings: 4
Ingredients:
- 4 (4-oz.) catfish fillets
- 2 tablespoons Italian seasoning
- Salt and ground black pepper, as required
- 1 tablespoon olive oil
- 1 tablespoon fresh parsley, chopped

Method:
1. Rub the fish fillets with seasoning, salt and black pepper generously and then, coat with oil.
2. Press "Power Button" of Air Fry Oven and turn the dial to select the "Air Fry" mode.
3. Press the Time button and again turn the dial to set the cooking time to 20 minutes.
4. Now push the Temp button and rotate the dial to set the temperature at 400 degrees F.
5. Press "Start/Pause" button to start.
6. When the unit beeps to show that it is preheated, open the lid.
7. Arrange the fish fillets in greased "Air Fry Basket" and insert in the oven.
8. Flip the fish fillets once halfway through.
9. Serve hot with the garnishing of parsley.

Nutritional Information per Serving:
Calories 205; Total Fat 14.2 g; Saturated Fat 2.4 g; Cholesterol 58 mg; Sodium 102 mg

Crispy Catfish

Preparation Time: 15 minutes; Cooking Time: 15 minutes; Servings: 5
Ingredients:
- 5 (6-oz.) catfish fillets
- 1 cup milk
- 2 teaspoons fresh lemon juice
- ½ cup yellow mustard
- ½ cup cornmeal
- ¼ cup all-purpose flour
- 2 tablespoons dried parsley flakes
- ¼ teaspoon red chili powder
- ¼ teaspoon cayenne pepper
- ¼ teaspoon onion powder
- ¼ teaspoon garlic powder
- Salt and ground black pepper, as required
- Olive oil cooking spray

Method:
1. In a large bowl, place the catfish, milk, and lemon juice and refrigerate for about 15 minutes.
2. In a shallow bowl, add the mustard.
3. In another bowl, mix together the cornmeal, flour, parsley flakes, and spices.

4. Remove the catfish fillets from milk mixture and with paper towels, pat them dry.
5. Coat each fish fillet with mustard and then, roll into cornmeal mixture.
6. Then, spray each fillet with the cooking spray.
7. Press "Power Button" of Air Fry Oven and turn the dial to select the "Air Fry" mode.
8. Press the Time button and again turn the dial to set the cooking time to 15 minutes.
9. Now push the Temp button and rotate the dial to set the temperature at 400 degrees F.
10. Press "Start/Pause" button to start.
11. When the unit beeps to show that it is preheated, open the lid.
12. Arrange the catfish fillets in greased "Air Fry Basket" and insert in the oven.
13. After 10 minutes of cooking, flip the fillets and spray with the cooking spray.
14. Serve hot.

Nutritional Information per Serving:
Calories 340; Total Fat 15.5 g; Saturated Fat 3.1 g; Cholesterol 84 mg; Sodium 435 mg

Cornmeal Coated Catfish

Preparation Time: 15 minutes; Cooking Time: 14 minutes; Servings: 4
Ingredients:
- 2 tablespoons cornmeal
- 2 teaspoons Cajun seasoning
- ½ teaspoon paprika
- ½ teaspoon garlic powder
- Salt, as required
- 2 (6-oz.) catfish fillets
- 1 tablespoon olive oil

Method:
1. In a bowl, mix together the cornmeal, Cajun seasoning, paprika, garlic powder, and salt.
2. Add the catfish fillets and coat with the mixture.
3. Now, coat each fillet with oil.
4. Press "Power Button" of Air Fry Oven and turn the dial to select the "Air Fry" mode.
5. Press the Time button and again turn the dial to set the cooking time to 14 minutes.
6. Now push the Temp button and rotate the dial to set the temperature at 400 degrees F.
7. Press "Start/Pause" button to start.
8. When the unit beeps to show that it is preheated, open the lid.
9. Arrange the catfish fillets in greased "Air Fry Basket" and insert in the oven.
10. After 10 minutes of cooking, flip the fillets and spray with the cooking spray.
11. Serve hot

Nutritional Information per Serving:
Calories 161; Total Fat 10.1 g; Saturated Fat 1.7 g; Cholesterol 40 mg; Sodium 110 mg

Breaded Flounder

Preparation Time: 15 minutes; Cooking Time: 12 minutes; Servings: 3
Ingredients:
- 1 egg
- 1 cup dry breadcrumbs
- ¼ cup vegetable oil
- 3 (6-oz.) flounder fillets
- 1 lemon, sliced

Method:
1. In a shallow bowl, beat the egg
2. In another bowl, add the breadcrumbs and oil and mix until crumbly mixture is formed.
3. Dip flounder fillets into the beaten egg and then, coat with the breadcrumb mixture.
4. Press "Power Button" of Air Fry Oven and turn the dial to select the "Air Fry" mode.
5. Press the Time button and again turn the dial to set the cooking time to 12 minutes.
6. Now push the Temp button and rotate the dial to set the temperature at 356 degrees F.
7. Press "Start/Pause" button to start.

8. When the unit beeps to show that it is preheated, open the lid.
9. Arrange the flounder fillets in greased "Air Fry Basket" and insert in the oven.
10. Garnish with the lemon slices and serve hot.

Nutritional Information per Serving:
Calories 524; Total Fat 24.2 g; Saturated Fat 5.1 g; Cholesterol 170 mg; Sodium 463 mg

Glazed Haddock

Preparation Time: 15 minutes; Cooking Time: 15 minutes; Servings: 4

Ingredients:
- 1 garlic clove, minced
- ¼ teaspoon fresh ginger, grated finely
- ½ cup low-sodium soy sauce
- ¼ cup fresh orange juice
- 2 tablespoons fresh lime juice
- ½ cup cooking wine
- ¼ cup sugar
- ¼ teaspoon red pepper flakes, crushed
- 1 lb. haddock steaks

Method:
1. In a pan, add all the ingredients except haddock steaks and bring to a boil.
2. Cook for about 3-4 minutes, stirring continuously.
3. Remove from the heat and set aside to cool.
4. In a reseal able bag, add half of marinade and haddock steaks.
5. Seal the bag and shake to coat well.
6. Refrigerate for about 30 minutes.
7. Remove the fish steaks from bag, reserving the remaining marinade.
8. Press "Power Button" of Air Fry Oven and turn the dial to select the "Air Fry" mode.
9. Press the Time button and again turn the dial to set the cooking time to 11 minutes.
10. Now push the Temp button and rotate the dial to set the temperature at 390 degrees F.
11. Press "Start/Pause" button to start.
12. When the unit beeps to show that it is preheated, open the lid.
13. Arrange the haddock steaks in greased "Air Fry Basket" and insert in the oven.
14. Transfer the haddock steak onto a serving platter and immediately, coat with the remaining glaze.
15. Serve immediately.

Nutritional Information per Serving:
Calories 218; Total Fat 1.1 g; Saturated Fat 0.2 g; Cholesterol 84 mg; Sodium 1860 mg

Simple Haddock

Preparation Time: 15 minutes; Cooking Time: 8 minutes; Servings: 2

Ingredients:
- 2 (6-oz.) haddock fillets
- 1 tablespoon olive oil
- Salt and ground black pepper, as required

Method:
1. Coat the fish fillets with oil and then, sprinkle with salt and black pepper.
2. Press "Power Button" of Air Fry Oven and turn the dial to select the "Air Fry" mode.
3. Press the Time button and again turn the dial to set the cooking time to 8 minutes.
4. Now push the Temp button and rotate the dial to set the temperature at 355 degrees F.
5. Press "Start/Pause" button to start.
6. When the unit beeps to show that it is preheated, open the lid.
7. Arrange the haddock fillets in greased "Air Fry Basket" and insert in the oven.
8. Serve hot.

Nutritional Information per Serving:
Calories 251; Total Fat 8.6 g; Saturated Fat 1.3 g; Cholesterol 126 mg; Sodium 226 mg

Buttered Halibut

Preparation Time: 15 minutes; Cooking Time: 30 minutes; Servings: 4

Ingredients:

- 1 lb. halibut fillets
- 1 tablespoon ginger paste
- 1 tablespoon garlic paste
- Salt and ground black pepper, as required
- 3 jalapeño peppers, chopped
- ¾ cup butter, chopped

Method:

1. Coat the halibut fillets with ginger-garlic paste and then, season with salt and black pepper.
2. Press "Power Button" of Air Fry Oven and turn the dial to select the "Air Fry" mode.
3. Press the Time button and again turn the dial to set the cooking time to 30 minutes.
4. Now push the Temp button and rotate the dial to set the temperature at 380 degrees F.
5. Press "Start/Pause" button to start.
6. When the unit beeps to show that it is preheated, open the lid.
7. Arrange the halibut fillets in greased "Air Fry Basket" and top with green chilies, followed by the butter.
8. Insert the basket in the oven.
9. Serve hot.

Nutritional Information per Serving:

Calories 443; Total Fat 37.4 g; Saturated Fat 22.2 g; Cholesterol 128 mg; Sodium 620 mg

Breaded Hake

Preparation Time: 15 minutes; Cooking Time: 12 minutes; Servings: 4

Ingredients:

- 1 egg
- 4 oz. breadcrumbs
- 2 tablespoons vegetable oil
- 4 (6-oz.) hake fillets
- 1 lemon, cut into wedges

Method:

1. In a shallow bowl, whisk the egg.
2. In another bowl, add the breadcrumbs, and oil and mix until a crumbly mixture forms.
3. Dip fish fillets into the egg and then, coat with the breadcrumbs mixture.
4. Press "Power Button" of Air Fry Oven and turn the dial to select the "Air Fry" mode.
5. Press the Time button and again turn the dial to set the cooking time to 12 minutes.
6. Now push the Temp button and rotate the dial to set the temperature at 350 degrees F.
7. Press "Start/Pause" button to start.
8. When the unit beeps to show that it is preheated, open the lid.
9. Arrange the hake fillets in greased "Air Fry Basket" and insert in the oven.
10. Serve hot.

Nutritional Information per Serving:

Calories 297; Total Fat 10.6 g; Saturated Fat 2 g; Cholesterol 89 mg; Sodium 439 mg

Sesame Seeds Coated Tuna

Preparation Time: 15 minutes; Cooking Time: 6 minutes; Servings: 2

Ingredients:

- 1 egg white
- ¼ cup white sesame seeds
- 1 tablespoon black sesame seeds
- Salt and ground black pepper, as required
- 2 (6-oz.) tuna steaks

Method:

1. In a shallow bowl, beat the egg white.
2. In another bowl, mix together the sesame seeds, salt, and black pepper.
3. Dip the tuna steaks into egg white and then, coat with the sesame seeds mixture.
4. Press "Power Button" of Air Fry Oven and turn the dial to select the "Air Fry" mode.
5. Press the Time button and again turn the dial to set the cooking time to 6 minutes.
6. Now push the Temp button and rotate the dial to set the temperature at 400 degrees F.
7. Press "Start/Pause" button to start.
8. When the unit beeps to show that it is preheated, open the lid.
9. Arrange the tuna steaks in greased "Air Fry Basket" and insert in the oven.
10. Flip the tuna steaks once halfway through.
11. Serve hot.

Nutritional Information per Serving:
Calories 450; Total Fat 21.9 g; Saturated Fat 4.3 g; Cholesterol 83 mg; Sodium 182 mg

Tuna Burgers

Preparation Time: 15 minutes; Cooking Time: 10 minutes; Servings: 8
Ingredients:
- 2 (6-oz.) cans tuna, drained
- ½ cup panko breadcrumbs
- 1 egg
- 2 teaspoons Dijon mustard
- 2 tablespoons fresh parsley, chopped
- Dash of Tabasco sauce
- Salt and ground black pepper, as required
- 1 tablespoon fresh lemon juice
- 1 tablespoon olive oil

Method:
1. In a large bowl, add all ingredients and mix until well combined.
2. Make equal sized patties from the mixture and arrange onto a foil-lined tray.
3. Refrigerate overnight.
4. Press "Power Button" of Air Fry Oven and turn the dial to select the "Air Fry" mode.
5. Press the Time button and again turn the dial to set the cooking time to 10 minutes.
6. Now push the Temp button and rotate the dial to set the temperature at 355 degrees F.
7. Press "Start/Pause" button to start.
8. When the unit beeps to show that it is preheated, open the lid.
9. Arrange the patties in greased "Air Fry Basket" and insert in the oven.
10. Serve hot.

Nutritional Information per Serving:
Calories 512; Total Fat 25.1 g; Saturated Fat 5.3 g; Cholesterol 135 mg; Sodium 178 mg

Garlic Shrimp

Prep Time: 10 minutes; Cooking Time: 14 minutes; Serving: 4
Ingredients
- 1 lb. shrimp, peeled and deveined,
- 1 tablespoon cooking oil
- 1/4 teaspoon garlic powder
- Salt, to taste
- Black pepper, to taste
- 2 lemon wedges
- 1 teaspoon minced parsley

Method:
1. Toss the shrimp with oil and all other ingredients in a bowl.
2. Spread the seasoned shrimp in the Air fryer Basket.
3. Press "Power Button" of Air Fry Oven and turn the dial to select the "Air Fry" mode.
4. Press the Time button and again turn the dial to set the cooking time to 14 minutes.
5. Now push the Temp button and rotate the dial to set the temperature at 400 degrees F.
6. Once preheated, place the Air fryer basket in the oven and close its lid.

7. Toss and flip the shrimp when cooked halfway through.
8. Serve warm.

Nutritional Information per Serving:
Calories 135; Total Fat 1.9g; Saturated Fat 0.6g; Cholesterol 239mg; Sodium 277mg

Lemon Pepper Shrimp

Prep Time: 10 minutes; Cooking Time: 8 minutes; Serving: 4

Ingredients

- 1 tablespoon olive oil
- 1 lemon, juiced
- 1 teaspoon lemon pepper
- 1/4 teaspoon paprika
- 1/4 teaspoon garlic powder
- 12 oz. medium shrimp, peeled and deveined
- 1 lemon, sliced

Method:
1. Toss the shrimp with oil and all other ingredients in a bowl.
2. Spread the seasoned shrimp in the Air fryer Basket.
3. Press "Power Button" of Air Fry Oven and turn the dial to select the "Air Roast" mode.
4. Press the Time button and again turn the dial to set the cooking time to 8 minutes.
5. Now push the Temp button and rotate the dial to set the temperature at 400 degrees F.
6. Once preheated, place the Air fryer basket in the oven and close its lid.
7. Toss and flip the shrimp when cooked halfway through.
8. Serve warm.

Nutritional Information per Serving:
Calories 118; Total Fat 4.6g; Saturated Fat 0.5g; Cholesterol 167mg; Sodium 193mg

Coconut Shrimp

Prep Time: 10 minutes; Cooking Time: 12 minutes; Serving: 4

Ingredients

Shrimp
- 1/2 cup flour
- Salt
- Black pepper
- 1 cup panko bread crumbs
- 1/2 cup sweetened coconut shredded
- 2 large eggs, beaten
- 1 lb. large shrimp, peeled and deveined

Dipping Sauce
- 1/2 cup mayonnaise
- 1 tablespoon Sriracha
- 1 tablespoon Thai sweet chili sauce

Method:
1. Mix flour with black pepper and salt in a bowl and dredge the shrimp through it.
2. Dip the shrimp in the egg and coat well with the breadcrumbs.
3. Place the crusted shrimp in the Air fryer basket.
4. Press "Power Button" of Air Fry Oven and turn the dial to select the "Air Roast" mode.
5. Press the Time button and again turn the dial to set the cooking time to 12 minutes.
6. Now push the Temp button and rotate the dial to set the temperature at 400 degrees F.
7. Once preheated, place the Air fryer basket in the oven and close its lid.
8. Toss and flip the shrimp when cooked halfway through.
9. Whisk mayonnaise with sriracha and chili sauce in a bowl.
10. Serve shrimp with mayo sauce.

Nutritional Information per Serving:
Calories 301; Total Fat 11.5g; Saturated Fat 3.7g; Cholesterol 175mg; Sodium 452mg

Garlic Parmesan Shrimp

Prep Time: 10 minutes; Cooking Time: 10 minutes; Serving: 4

Ingredients

- 1lb shrimp, deveined and peeled
- 1 tablespoon olive oil
- 1 teaspoon salt
- 1 teaspoon fresh cracked pepper
- 1 tablespoon lemon juice
- 6 cloves garlic, diced
- 1/2 cup grated parmesan cheese
- 1/4 cup diced cilantro

Method:

1. Toss the shrimp with oil and all other ingredients in a bowl.
2. Spread the seasoned shrimp in the Air fryer Basket.
3. Press "Power Button" of Air Fry Oven and turn the dial to select the "Air Roast" mode.
4. Press the Time button and again turn the dial to set the cooking time to 10 minutes.
5. Now push the Temp button and rotate the dial to set the temperature at 350 degrees F.
6. Once preheated, place the Air fryer basket in the oven and close its lid.
7. Toss and flip the shrimp when cooked halfway through.
8. Serve warm.

Nutritional Information per Serving:

Calories 184; Total Fat 6.2g; Saturated Fat 1.6g; Cholesterol 241mg; Sodium 893mg

Bang Bang Breaded Shrimp

Prep Time: 10 minutes; Cooking Time: 14 minutes; Serving: 4

Ingredients

- 1 lb. raw shrimp peeled and deveined
- 1 egg white
- 1/2 cup flour
- 3/4 cup panko bread crumbs

Bang Bang Sauce
- 1/3 cup Greek yogurt
- 2 tablespoon Sriracha

- 1 teaspoon paprika
- Montreal Seasoning to taste
- salt and pepper to taste
- cooking spray

- 1/4 cup sweet chili sauce

Method:

1. Mix flour with salt, black pepper, paprika, and Montreal seasoning in a bowl.
2. Dredge the shrimp the flour then dip in the egg.
3. Coat the shrimp with the breadcrumbs and place them in an Air fryer basket.
4. Press "Power Button" of Air Fry Oven and turn the dial to select the "Air Roast" mode.
5. Press the Time button and again turn the dial to set the cooking time to 14 minutes.
6. Now push the Temp button and rotate the dial to set the temperature at 400 degrees F.
7. Once preheated, place the Air fryer basket in the oven and close its lid.
8. Toss and flip the shrimp when cooked halfway through.
9. Serve warm.

Nutritional Information per Serving:

Calories 200; Total Fat 2.7g; Saturated Fat 0.5g; Cholesterol 100mg; Sodium 663mg

Taco Fried Shrimp

Prep Time: 10 minutes; Cooking Time: 5 minutes; Serving: 6

Ingredients

- 17 shrimp, defrosted, peeled, and deveined
- 1 cup bread crumbs Italian
- 1 tablespoon taco seasoning
- 1 tablespoon garlic salt
- 4 tablespoon butter melted
- olive oil spray

Method:
1. Toss the shrimp with oil and all other ingredients in a bowl.
2. Spread the seasoned shrimp in the Air fryer Basket.
3. Press "Power Button" of Air Fry Oven and turn the dial to select the "Air Roast" mode.
4. Press the Time button and again turn the dial to set the cooking time to 5 minutes.
5. Now push the Temp button and rotate the dial to set the temperature at 400 degrees F.
6. Once preheated, place the Air fryer basket in the oven and close its lid.
7. Toss and flip the shrimp when cooked halfway through.
8. Serve warm.

Nutritional Information per Serving:
Calories 350; Total Fat 17.6g; Saturated Fat 10.1g; Cholesterol 235mg; Sodium 760mg

Garlic Mussels

Prep Time: 10 minutes; Cooking Time: 6 minutes; Serving: 4

Ingredients
- 1 lb. mussels
- 1 tablespoon butter
- 1 cup of water
- 2 teaspoons minced garlic
- 1 teaspoon chives
- 1 teaspoon basil
- 1 teaspoon parsley

Method:
1. Toss the mussels with oil and all other ingredients in a bowl.
2. Spread the seasoned shrimp in the oven baking tray.
3. Press "Power Button" of Air Fry Oven and turn the dial to select the "Air Roast" mode.
4. Press the Time button and again turn the dial to set the cooking time to 6 minutes.
5. Now push the Temp button and rotate the dial to set the temperature at 390 degrees F.
6. Once preheated, place the mussel's tray in the oven and close its lid.
7. Serve warm.

Nutritional Information per Serving:
Calories 125; Total Fat 5.4g; Saturated Fat 2.3g; Cholesterol 39mg; Sodium 347mg

Mussels with Saffron Sauce

Prep Time: 10 minutes; Cooking Time: 8 minutes; Serving: 4

Ingredients
- 1 tablespoon unsalted butter
- 1 tablespoon minced garlic
- 1 tablespoon minced shallot
- 1/4 cup dry white wine
- 3 tablespoons heavy cream
- 4 threads saffron
- 1 lb. fresh mussels

Method:
1. Whisk cream with saffron, shallots, white wine, and butter in a bowl.
2. Place the mussels in the oven baking tray and pour the cream sauce on top.
3. Press "Power Button" of Air Fry Oven and turn the dial to select the "Bake" mode.
4. Press the Time button and again turn the dial to set the cooking time to 8 minutes.
5. Now push the Temp button and rotate the dial to set the temperature at 370 degrees F.
6. Once preheated, place the mussel's baking tray in the oven and close its lid.
7. Serve warm.

Nutritional Information per Serving:
Calories 374; Total Fat 14.7g; Saturated Fat 5.9g; Cholesterol 118mg; Sodium 999mg

Cajun Shrimp Bake

Prep Time: 10 minutes; Cooking Time: 40 minutes; Serving: 8

Ingredients

- 4 andouille sausages, chopped
- 1 lb. shrimp, peeled and deveined
- 4 red potatoes, quartered
- 2 pieces corn, quartered

Cajun Spice Mix

- 2 teaspoons garlic powder
- 2 ½ teaspoons paprika
- 1 ¼ teaspoons dried oregano
- 1 teaspoon onion powder
- 1 ¼ teaspoons dried thyme

- 2 tablespoons oil, divided
- 1 tablespoon butter, cubed
- 4 cloves garlic, minced

- ½ teaspoon red pepper flakes
- 1 teaspoon cayenne pepper
- 2 teaspoons salt
- 1 teaspoon pepper

Method:

1. Mix Cajun mix spices in a bowl and then toss in all the veggies and seafood.
2. Stir in sausage, corn, oil, and butter then mix well.
3. Spread potatoes, corn, and garlic in the oven baking tray.
4. Press "Power Button" of Air Fry Oven and turn the dial to select the "Bake" mode.
5. Press the Time button and again turn the dial to set the cooking time to 25 minutes.
6. Now push the Temp button and rotate the dial to set the temperature at 375 degrees F.
7. Once preheated, place the potato's baking tray in the oven and close its lid.
8. When potatoes are done, add shrimp and sausage to the potatoes.
9. Return the baking tray to the oven and bake for 15 minutes.
10. Serve warm.

Nutritional Information per Serving:

Calories 363; Total Fat 17.7g; Saturated Fat 5.7g; Cholesterol 147mg; Sodium 662mg

Shrimp with Garlic Sauce

Prep Time: 10 minutes; Cooking Time: 13 minutes; Serving: 4

Ingredients

- 1 1/4 lbs. shrimp, peeled and deveined
- 1/4 cup butter
- 1 tablespoon minced garlic

- 2 tablespoon fresh lemon juice
- Salt and pepper
- 1/8 teaspoon Red pepper flakes
- 2 tablespoon minced fresh parsley

Method:

1. Toss the shrimp with oil and all other ingredients in a bowl.
2. Spread the seasoned shrimp in the baking pan.
3. Press "Power Button" of Air Fry Oven and turn the dial to select the "Bake" mode.
4. Press the Time button and again turn the dial to set the cooking time to 13 minutes.
5. Now push the Temp button and rotate the dial to set the temperature at 350 degrees F.
6. Once preheated, place the baking pan in the oven and close its lid.
7. Serve warm.

Nutritional Information per Serving:

Calories 207; Total Fat 14.1g; Saturated Fat 7.4g; Cholesterol 212mg; Sodium 885mg

Shrimp Scampi

Prep Time: 10 minutes; Cooking Time: 13 minutes; Serving: 8

Ingredients

- 2 lbs. jumbo shrimp, deveined and peeled
- 3 tablespoons olive oil
- 4 tablespoons lemon juice

- 2 teaspoons salt
- 1/2 teaspoon black pepper
- 1/4 cup butter
- 4 cloves garlic, minced

- 1 small shallot, minced
- 2 tablespoons minced fresh parsley
- 1/2 teaspoon dried oregano
- 1/4 teaspoon crushed red pepper flakes
- 1 egg yolk
- 2/3 cup panko bread crumbs

Method:
1. Toss shrimp with egg, spices, seasonings, oil, herbs, butter, and shallots in a bowl.
2. Mix well, then add breadcrumbs to coat well.
3. Spread the shrimp in a baking tray in a single layer.
4. Press "Power Button" of Air Fry Oven and turn the dial to select the "Bake" mode.
5. Press the Time button and again turn the dial to set the cooking time to 13 minutes.
6. Now push the Temp button and rotate the dial to set the temperature at 425 degrees F.
7. Once preheated, place the shrimp's baking tray in the oven and close its lid.
8. Toss and flip the shrimp when cooked halfway through.
9. Serve warm.

Nutritional Information per Serving:
Calories 220; Total Fat 13.2g; Saturated Fat 5g; Cholesterol 181mg; Sodium 270mg

Shrimp Parmesan Bake

Prep Time: 10 minutes; Cooking Time: 8 minutes; Serving: 4
Ingredients
- 1 1/2 lb. large raw shrimp, peeled and deveined
- 1/4 cup melted butter
- 1 teaspoon coarse salt
- 1/4 teaspoon black pepper
- 1 teaspoon garlic powder
- 1/2 teaspoon crushed red pepper
- 1/4 cup Parmesan cheese, grated

Method:
1. Toss the shrimp with oil and all other ingredients in a bowl.
2. Spread the seasoned shrimp in the Baking tray.
3. Press "Power Button" of Air Fry Oven and turn the dial to select the "Bake" mode.
4. Press the Time button and again turn the dial to set the cooking time to 8 minutes.
5. Now push the Temp button and rotate the dial to set the temperature at 400 degrees F.
6. Once preheated, place the lobster's baking tray in the oven and close its lid.
7. Switch the Air fryer oven to broil mode and cook for 1 minute.
8. Serve warm.

Nutritional Information per Serving:
Calories 231; Total Fat 14.9g; Saturated Fat 7.6g; Cholesterol 249mg; Sodium 1058mg

Shrimp in Lemon Sauce

Prep Time: 10 minutes; Cooking Time: 8 minutes; Serving: 4
Ingredients
- 1 1/4 lbs. large shrimp, peeled and deveined
- Cooking spray
- 1/4 cup fresh lemon juice
- 2 tablespoons light butter, melted
- 3 garlic cloves, minced
- 1 teaspoon Worcestershire sauce
- 3/4 teaspoon lemon-pepper seasoning
- 1/4 teaspoon ground red pepper
- 2 tablespoons chopped fresh parsley

Method:
1. Toss the shrimp with oil and all other ingredients in a bowl.
2. Spread the seasoned shrimp in the baking tray.
3. Press "Power Button" of Air Fry Oven and turn the dial to select the "Air Roast" mode.
4. Press the Time button and again turn the dial to set the cooking time to 8 minutes.
5. Now push the Temp button and rotate the dial to set the temperature at 425 degrees F.

6. Once preheated, place the shrimp's baking tray in the oven and close its lid.
7. Serve warm.

Nutritional Information per Serving:

Calories 176; Total Fat 6.1g; Saturated Fat 3.8g; Cholesterol 218mg; Sodium 237mg

Garlic Shrimp Skewers

Prep Time: 10 minutes; Cooking Time: 8 minutes; Serving: 8

Ingredients

- 1 lb. prawns, peeled and deveined
- 2 tablespoons olive oil
- Salt, to taste
- 3 tablespoons butter
- 3 garlic cloves, minced
- 1/4 teaspoon salt
- 1 teaspoon minced chives for garnish

Method:

1. Toss the shrimp with oil and all other ingredients in a bowl.
2. Spread the seasoned shrimp in the baking tray.
3. Press "Power Button" of Air Fry Oven and turn the dial to select the "Air Roast" mode.
4. Press the Time button and again turn the dial to set the cooking time to 8 minutes.
5. Now push the Temp button and rotate the dial to set the temperature at 425 degrees F.
6. Once preheated, place the shrimp's baking tray in the oven and close its lid.
7. Serve warm.

Nutritional Information per Serving:

Calories 105; Total Fat 6.1g; Saturated Fat 3g; Cholesterol 116mg; Sodium 520mg

Shrimp Skewers with Pineapple

Prep Time: 10 minutes; Cooking Time: 6 minutes; Serving: 4

Ingredients

- 1/2 cup coconut milk
- 4 teaspoons Tabasco Sauce
- 2 teaspoons soy sauce
- 1/4 cup orange juice
- 1/4 cup lime juice
- 1 lb. shrimp, peeled and deveined
- 3/4 lb. pineapple chunks, diced

Method:

1. Toss the shrimp and pineapple with all other ingredients in a bowl.
2. Thread shrimp and pineapple on the skewers.
3. Place the shrimp pineapple skewers in the Air fryer Basket.
4. Press "Power Button" of Air Fry Oven and turn the dial to select the "Air fry" mode.
5. Press the Time button and again turn the dial to set the cooking time to 6 minutes.
6. Now push the Temp button and rotate the dial to set the temperature at 350 degrees F.
7. Once preheated, place the Air fryer basket in the oven and close its lid.
8. Toss and flip the shrimp when cooked halfway through.
9. Serve warm.

Nutritional Information per Serving:

Calories 212; Total Fat 7.3g; Saturated Fat 6.4g; Cholesterol 162mg; Sodium 327mg

Teriyaki Shrimp Skewer

Prep Time: 10 minutes; Cooking Time: 6 minutes; Serving: 4

Ingredients

Shrimp Skewers:

- 1 lb. shrimp, peeled and deveined
- 1 pineapple, peeled, and cut into chunks
- 2 zucchinis, cut into thick slices
- 3 red and orange bell peppers, cut into 2-inch chunks

- Bamboo or metal skewers

Teriyaki BBQ Sauce:
- 1/2 cup teriyaki sauce
- 2 tablespoon fish sauce
- 2 tablespoon chili garlic sauce

Method:
1. Toss the shrimp and veggies with all other ingredients in a bowl.
2. Thread shrimp and veggies on the skewers alternately.
3. Place the shrimp vegetable skewers in the Air fryer Basket.
4. Mix the teriyaki sauce ingredients in a bowl and pour over the skewers.
5. Press "Power Button" of Air Fry Oven and turn the dial to select the "Air fry" mode.
6. Press the Time button and again turn the dial to set the cooking time to 6 minutes.
7. Now push the Temp button and rotate the dial to set the temperature at 350 degrees F.
8. Once preheated, place the Air fryer basket in the oven and close its lid.
9. Toss and flip the shrimp when cooked halfway through.
10. Serve warm.

Nutritional Information per Serving:
Calories 181; Total Fat 1.4g; Saturated Fat 0.2g; Cholesterol 233mg; Sodium 2366mg

Cajun Shrimp Skewers

Prep Time: 10 minutes; Cooking Time: 6 minutes; Serving: 8
Ingredients
- 1/2 cup 8 tablespoon butter
- 4 cloves of garlic pressed or minced
- 1 tablespoon Cajun spice
- 1/2 teaspoon salt
- 1 tablespoon lemon juice
- 2 lbs. shrimp, peeled and deveined

Method:
1. Toss the shrimp and garlic with all other ingredients in a bowl.
2. Thread shrimp on the skewers.
3. Place the shrimp skewers in the Air fryer Basket.
4. Press "Power Button" of Air Fry Oven and turn the dial to select the "Air fry" mode.
5. Press the Time button and again turn the dial to set the cooking time to 6 minutes.
6. Now push the Temp button and rotate the dial to set the temperature at 350 degrees F.
7. Once preheated, place the Air fryer basket in the oven and close its lid.
8. Toss and flip the shrimp when cooked halfway through.
9. Serve warm.

Nutritional Information per Serving:
Calories 105; Total Fat 11g; Saturated Fat 7g; Cholesterol 34mg; Sodium 5mg

Italian Shrimp Skewers

Prep Time: 10 minutes; Cooking Time: 6 minutes; Serving: 4
Ingredients
- 1 lb. large shrimp peeled and deveined
- 1/4 cup olive oil
- 2 tablespoons lemon juice
- 3/4 teaspoon salt
- 1/4 teaspoon pepper
- 1 teaspoon Italian seasoning
- 2 teaspoons garlic minced
- 1 tablespoon parsley chopped
- lemon wedges for serving

Method:
1. Toss the shrimp with all other ingredients in a bowl.
2. Thread shrimp on the skewers.
3. Place the shrimp skewers in the Air fryer Basket.
4. Press "Power Button" of Air Fry Oven and turn the dial to select the "Air fry" mode.

5. Press the Time button and again turn the dial to set the cooking time to 6 minutes.
6. Now push the Temp button and rotate the dial to set the temperature at 350 degrees F.
7. Once preheated, place the Air fryer basket in the oven and close its lid.
8. Toss and flip the shrimp when cooked halfway through.
9. Serve warm.

Nutritional Information per Serving:
Calories 336; Total Fat 17g; Saturated Fat 1.9g; Cholesterol 321mg; Sodium 761mg

Prawn Burgers

Preparation Time: 15 minutes; Cooking Time: 6 minutes; Servings: 2

Ingredients:
- ½ cup prawns, peeled, deveined and chopped very finely
- ½ cup breadcrumbs
- 2-3 tablespoons onion, chopped finely
- ½ teaspoon ginger, minced
- ½ teaspoon garlic, minced
- ½ teaspoon red chili powder
- ½ teaspoon ground cumin
- ¼ teaspoon ground turmeric
- Salt and ground black pepper, as required

Method:
1. In a bowl, add all ingredients and mix until well combined.
2. Make small sized patties from mixture.
3. Press "Power Button" of Air Fry Oven and turn the dial to select the "Air Fry" mode.
4. Press the Time button and again turn the dial to set the cooking time to 6 minutes.
5. Now push the Temp button and rotate the dial to set the temperature at 355 degrees F.
6. Press "Start/Pause" button to start.
7. When the unit beeps to show that it is preheated, open the lid.
8. Arrange the patties in greased "Air Fry Basket" and insert in the oven.
9. Serve hot.

Nutritional Information per Serving:
Calories 186; Total Fat 2.7 g; Saturated Fat 0.7 g; Cholesterol 119 mg; Sodium 422 mg

Chapter 8: Vgetables Recipes

Basil Tomatoes

Preparation Time: 10 minutes; Cooking Time: 10 minutes; Servings: 2
Ingredients:

- 3 tomatoes, halved
- Olive oil cooking spray
- Salt and ground black pepper, as required
- 1 tablespoon fresh basil, chopped

Method:

1. IDrizzle cut sides of the tomato halves with cooking spray evenly.
2. Sprinkle with salt, black pepper and basil.
3. Press "Power Button" of Air Fry Oven and turn the dial to select the "Air Fry" mode.
4. Press the Time button and again turn the dial to set the cooking time to 10 minutes.
5. Now push the Temp button and rotate the dial to set the temperature at 320 degrees F.
6. Press "Start/Pause" button to start.
7. When the unit beeps to show that it is preheated, open the lid.
8. Arrange the tomatoes in "Air Fry Basket" and insert in the oven.
9. Serve warm.

Nutritional Information per Serving:
Calories 34; Total Fat 0.4 g; Saturated Fat 0.1 g; Cholesterol 0 mg; Sodium 87 mg

Pesto Tomatoes

Preparation Time: 15 minutes; Cooking Time: 14 minutes; Servings: 4
Ingredients:

- 3 large heirloom tomatoes, cut into ½ inch thick slices.
- 1 cup pesto
- 8 oz. feta cheese, cut into ½ inch thick slices.
- ½ cup red onions, sliced thinly
- 1 tablespoon olive oil

Method:

1. Spread some pesto on each slice of tomato.
2. Top each tomato slice with a feta slice and onion and drizzle with oil.
3. Press "Power Button" of Air Fry Oven and turn the dial to select the "Air Fry" mode.
4. Press the Time button and again turn the dial to set the cooking time to 14 minutes.
5. Now push the Temp button and rotate the dial to set the temperature at 390 degrees F.
6. Press "Start/Pause" button to start.
7. When the unit beeps to show that it is preheated, open the lid.
8. Arrange the tomatoes in greased "Air Fry Basket" and insert in the oven.
9. Serve warm.

Nutritional Information per Serving:
Calories 480; Total Fat 41.9 g; Saturated Fat 14 g; Cholesterol 65 mg; Sodium 1000 mg

Stuffed Tomatoes

Preparation Time: 15 minutes; Cooking Time: 15 minutes; Servings: 2
Ingredients:

- 2 large tomatoes
- ½ cup broccoli, chopped finely
- ½ cup Cheddar cheese, shredded
- Salt and ground black pepper, as required
- 1 tablespoon unsalted butter, melted
- ½ teaspoon dried thyme, crushed

Method:

1. Carefully, cut the top of each tomato and scoop out pulp and seeds.

2. In a bowl, mix together chopped broccoli, cheese, salt and black pepper.
3. Stuff each tomato with broccoli mixture evenly.
4. Press "Power Button" of Air Fry Oven and turn the dial to select the "Air Fry" mode.
5. Press the Time button and again turn the dial to set the cooking time to 15 minutes.
6. Now push the Temp button and rotate the dial to set the temperature at 355 degrees F.
7. Press "Start/Pause" button to start.
8. When the unit beeps to show that it is preheated, open the lid.
9. Arrange the tomatoes in greased "Air Fry Basket" and insert in the oven.
10. Serve warm with the garnishing of thyme.

Nutritional Information per Serving:
Calories 206; Total Fat 15.6 g; Saturated Fat 9.7 g; Cholesterol 45 mg; Sodium 310 mg

Parmesan Asparagus

Preparation Time: 10 minutes; Cooking Time: 10 minutes; Servings: 3
Ingredients:
- 1 lb. fresh asparagus, trimmed
- 1 tablespoon Parmesan cheese, grated
- 1 tablespoon butter, melted
- 1 teaspoon garlic powder
- Salt and ground black pepper, as required

Method:
1. In a bowl, mix together the asparagus, cheese, butter, garlic powder, salt, and black pepper.
2. Press "Power Button" of Air Fry Oven and turn the dial to select the "Air Fry" mode.
3. Press the Time button and again turn the dial to set the cooking time to 10 minutes.
4. Now push the Temp button and rotate the dial to set the temperature at 400 degrees F.
5. Press "Start/Pause" button to start.
6. When the unit beeps to show that it is preheated, open the lid.
7. Arrange the veggie mixture in greased "Air Fry Basket" and insert in the oven.
8. Serve hot.

Nutritional Information per Serving:
Calories 73; Total Fat 4.4 g; Saturated Fat 2.7 g; Cholesterol 12 mg; Sodium 95 mg

Almond Asparagus

Preparation Time: 15 minutes; Cooking Time: 6 minutes; Servings: 3
Ingredients:
- 1 lb. asparagus
- 2 tablespoons olive oil
- 2 tablespoons balsamic vinegar
- Salt and ground black pepper, as required
- 1/3 cup almonds, sliced

Method:
1. In a bowl, mix together the asparagus, oil, vinegar, salt, and black pepper.
2. Press "Power Button" of Air Fry Oven and turn the dial to select the "Air Fry" mode.
3. Press the Time button and again turn the dial to set the cooking time to 6minutes.
4. Now push the Temp button and rotate the dial to set the temperature at 400 degrees F.
5. Press "Start/Pause" button to start.
6. When the unit beeps to show that it is preheated, open the lid.
7. Arrange the veggie mixture in greased "Air Fry Basket" and insert in the oven.
8. Serve hot.

Nutritional Information per Serving:
Calories 173; Total Fat 14.8 g; Saturated Fat 1.8 g; Cholesterol 0 mg; Sodium 54 mg

Spicy Butternut Squash

Preparation Time: 15 minutes; Cooking Time: 20 minutes; Servings: 4

Ingredients:
- 1 medium butternut squash, peeled, seeded and cut into chunk
- 2 teaspoons cumin seeds
- 1/8 teaspoon garlic powder
- 1/8 teaspoon chili flakes, crushed
- Salt and ground black pepper, as required
- 1 tablespoon olive oil
- 2 tablespoons pine nuts
- 2 tablespoons fresh cilantro, chopped

Method:
1. In a bowl, mix together the squash, spices, and oil.
2. Press "Power Button" of Air Fry Oven and turn the dial to select the "Air Fry" mode.
3. Press the Time button and again turn the dial to set the cooking time to 20 minutes.
4. Now push the Temp button and rotate the dial to set the temperature at 375 degrees F.
5. Press "Start/Pause" button to start.
6. When the unit beeps to show that it is preheated, open the lid.
7. Arrange the squash chunks in greased "Air Fry Basket" and insert in the oven.
8. Serve hot with the garnishing of pine nuts and cilantro.

Nutritional Information per Serving:
Calories 191; Total Fat 7 g; Saturated Fat 0.8 g; Cholesterol 0 mg; Sodium 52 mg

Sweet & Spicy Parsnips

Preparation Time: 15 minutes; Cooking Time: 44 minutes; Servings: 5

Ingredients:
- 1½ lbs. parsnip, peeled and cut into 1-inch chunks
- 1 tablespoon butter, melted
- 2 tablespoons honey
- 1 tablespoon dried parsley flakes, crushed
- ¼ teaspoon red pepper flakes, crushed
- Salt and ground black pepper, as required

Method:
1. In a large bowl, mix together the parsnips and butter.
2. Press "Power Button" of Air Fry Oven and turn the dial to select the "Air Fry" mode.
3. Press the Time button and again turn the dial to set the cooking time to 44 minutes.
4. Now push the Temp button and rotate the dial to set the temperature at 355 degrees F.
5. Press "Start/Pause" button to start.
6. When the unit beeps to show that it is preheated, open the lid.
7. Arrange the squash chunks in greased "Air Fry Basket" and insert in the oven.
8. Meanwhile, in another large bowl, mix together the remaining ingredients.
9. After 40 minutes of cooking, press "Start/Pause" button to pause the unit.
10. Transfer the parsnips chunks into the bowl of honey mixture and toss to coat well.
11. Again, arrange the parsnip chunks in "Air Fry Basket" and insert in the oven.
12. Serve hot.

Nutritional Information per Serving:
Calories 149; Total Fat 2.7 g; Saturated Fat 1.5 g; Cholesterol 6 mg; Sodium 62 mg

Caramelized Baby Carrots

Preparation Time: 10 minutes; Cooking Time: 15 minutes; Servings: 4

Ingredients:
- ½ cup butter, melted
- ½ cup brown sugar
- 1 lb. bag baby carrots

Method:
1. In a bowl, mix together the butter, brown sugar and carrots.
2. Press "Power Button" of Air Fry Oven and turn the dial to select the "Air Fry" mode.
3. Press the Time button and again turn the dial to set the cooking time to 15 minutes.
4. Now push the Temp button and rotate the dial to set the temperature at 400 degrees F.
5. Press "Start/Pause" button to start.
6. When the unit beeps to show that it is preheated, open the lid.
7. Arrange the carrots in greased "Air Fry Basket" and insert in the oven.
8. Serve warm.

Nutritional Information per Serving:
Calories 312; Total Fat 23.2 g; Saturated Fat 14.5 g; Cholesterol 61 mg; Sodium 257 mg

Carrot with Spinach

Preparation Time: 15 minutes; Cooking Time: 35 minutes; Servings: 4

Ingredients:
- 4 teaspoons butter, melted and divided
- ¼ lb. carrots, peeled and sliced
- 1 lb. zucchinis, sliced
- 1 tablespoon fresh basil, chopped
- Salt and ground black pepper, as required

Method:
1. In a bowl, mix together 2 teaspoons of the butter and carrots.
2. Press "Power Button" of Air Fry Oven and turn the dial to select the "Air Fry" mode.
3. Press the Time button and again turn the dial to set the cooking time to 35 minutes.
4. Now push the Temp button and rotate the dial to set the temperature at 400 degrees F.
5. Press "Start/Pause" button to start.
6. When the unit beeps to show that it is preheated, open the lid.
7. Arrange the carrots in greased "Air Fry Basket" and insert in the oven.
8. Meanwhile, in a large bowl, mix together remaining butter, zucchini, basil, salt and black pepper.
9. After 5 minutes of cooking, place the zucchini mixture into the basket with carrots.
10. Toss the vegetable mixture 2-3 times during the cooking.
11. Serve hot.

Nutritional Information per Serving:
Calories 64; Total Fat 4 g; Saturated Fat 2.5 g; Cholesterol 10 mg; Sodium 97 mg

Broccoli with Sweet Potatoes

Preparation Time: 15 minutes; Cooking Time: 20 minutes; Servings: 4

Ingredients:
- 2 medium sweet potatoes, peeled and cut in 1-inch cubes
- 1 head broccoli, cut in 1-inch florets
- 2 tablespoons vegetable oil
- Salt and ground black pepper, as required

Method:
1. In a large bowl, add all the ingredients and toss to coat well.
2. Press "Power Button" of Air Fry Oven and turn the dial to select the "Air Roast" mode.
3. Press the Time button and again turn the dial to set the cooking time to 20 minutes.
4. Now push the Temp button and rotate the dial to set the temperature at 415 degrees F.
5. Press "Start/Pause" button to start.
6. When the unit beeps to show that it is preheated, open the lid.
7. Arrange the carrots in greased "Air Fry Basket" and insert in the oven.

8. Meanwhile, in a large bowl, mix together remaining butter, zucchini, basil, salt and black pepper.
9. After 5 minutes of cooking, place the zucchini mixture into the basket with carrots.
10. Serve hot.

Nutritional Information per Serving:

Calories 170; Total Fat 7.1 g; Saturated Fat 1.4 g; Cholesterol 0 mg; Sodium 67 mg

Broccoli with Olives

Preparation Time: 15 minutes; Cooking Time: 15 minutes; Servings: 6

Ingredients:

- 1½ lbs. broccoli head, stemmed and cut into 1-inch florets
- 2 tablespoons olive oil
- Salt and ground black pepper, as required
- 1/3 cup Kalamata olives, halved and pitted
- 2 teaspoons fresh lemon zest, grated
- ¼ cup Parmesan cheese, grated

Method:

1. In a pan of the boiling water, add the broccoli and cook for about 3-4 minutes.
2. Drain the broccoli well.
3. In a bowl, place the broccoli, oil, salt, and black pepper and toss to coat well.
4. Press "Power Button" of Air Fry Oven and turn the dial to select the "Air Fry" mode.
5. Press the Time button and again turn the dial to set the cooking time to 15 minutes.
6. Now push the Temp button and rotate the dial to set the temperature at 355 degrees F.
7. Press "Start/Pause" button to start.
8. When the unit beeps to show that it is preheated, open the lid.
9. Arrange the broccoli in greased "Air Fry Basket" and insert in the oven.
10. After 8 minutes of cooking, toss the broccoli florets.
11. Transfer the broccoli into a large bowl and immediately, stir in the olives, lemon zest and cheese.
12. Serve immediately.

Nutritional Information per Serving:

Calories 100; Total Fat 6.6 g; Saturated Fat 1.2 g; Cholesterol 3 mg; Sodium 158 mg

Broccoli with Cauliflower

Preparation Time: 15 minutes; Cooking Time: 20 minutes; Servings: 4

Ingredients:

- 1½ cups broccoli, cut into 1-inch pieces
- 1½ cups cauliflower, cut into 1-inch pieces
- 1 tablespoon olive oil
- Salt, as required

Method:

1. In a bowl, add the vegetables, oil, and salt and toss to coat well.
2. Press "Power Button" of Air Fry Oven and turn the dial to select the "Air Fry" mode.
3. Press the Time button and again turn the dial to set the cooking time to 20 minutes.
4. Now push the Temp button and rotate the dial to set the temperature at 375 degrees F.
5. Press "Start/Pause" button to start.
6. When the unit beeps to show that it is preheated, open the lid.
7. Arrange the veggie mixture in greased "Air Fry Basket" and insert in the oven.
8. Serve hot.

Nutritional Information per Serving:

Calories 51; Total Fat 3.7 g; Saturated Fat 0.5 g; Cholesterol 0 mg; Sodium 61 mg

Cauliflower in Buffalo Sauce

Preparation Time: 13 minutes; Cooking Time: 12 minutes; Servings: 4
Ingredients:

- 1 large head cauliflower, cut into bite-size florets
- 1 tablespoon olive oil
- 2 teaspoons garlic powder
- Salt and ground black pepper, as required
- 1 tablespoon butter, melted
- 2/3 cup warm buffalo sauce

Method:

1. In a large bowl, add cauliflower florets, olive oil, garlic powder, salt and pepper and toss to coat.
2. Press "Power Button" of Air Fry Oven and turn the dial to select the "Air Fry" mode.
3. Press the Time button and again turn the dial to set the cooking time to 12 minutes.
4. Now push the Temp button and rotate the dial to set the temperature at 375 degrees F.
5. Press "Start/Pause" button to start.
6. When the unit beeps to show that it is preheated, open the lid.
7. Arrange the cauliflower florets in "Air Fry Basket" and insert in the oven.
8. After 7 minutes of cooking, coat the cauliflower florets with buffalo sauce.
9. Serve hot.

Nutritional Information per Serving:
Calories 183; Total Fat 17.1 g; Saturated Fat 4.3 g; Cholesterol 8 mg; Sodium 826 mg

Curried Cauliflower

Preparation Time: 15 minutes; Cooking Time: 10 minutes; Servings: 4
Ingredients:

- 2 tablespoons golden raisins
- ½ head cauliflower, cored and cut into 1-inch pieces
- ½ cup olive oil, divided
- ½ tablespoon curry powder
- Salt, to taste
- 2 tablespoons pine nuts, toasted

Method:

1. Soak the raisins in boiling water and set aside.
2. In a bowl, mix together the cauliflower, oil, curry powder and salt.
3. Press "Power Button" of Air Fry Oven and turn the dial to select the "Air Fry" mode.
4. Press the Time button and again turn the dial to set the cooking time to 10 minutes.
5. Now push the Temp button and rotate the dial to set the temperature at 390 degrees F.
6. Press "Start/Pause" button to start.
7. When the unit beeps to show that it is preheated, open the lid.
8. Arrange the cauliflower florets in "Air Fry Basket" and insert in the oven.
9. Drain the golden raisins into a strainer.
10. In a bowl, add cauliflower, raisins and pine nuts and toss to coat.
11. Serve immediately.

Nutritional Information per Serving:
Calories 269; Total Fat 28.3 g; Saturated Fat 3.8 g; Cholesterol 0 mg; Sodium 50mg

Lemony Green Beans

Preparation Time: 15 minutes; Cooking Time: 12 minutes; Servings: 4
Ingredients:

- 1 lb. green beans, trimmed
- 1 tablespoon butter, melted
- 1 tablespoon fresh lemon juice
- ¼ teaspoon garlic powder
- Salt and ground black pepper, as required

- ½ teaspoon lemon zest, grated

Method:
1. In a large bowl, add all the ingredients except the lemon zest and toss to coat well.
2. Press "Power Button" of Air Fry Oven and turn the dial to select the "Air Fry" mode.
3. Press the Time button and again turn the dial to set the cooking time to 12 minutes.
4. Now push the Temp button and rotate the dial to set the temperature at 400 degrees F.
5. Press "Start/Pause" button to start.
6. When the unit beeps to show that it is preheated, open the lid.
7. Arrange the green beans in "Air Fry Basket" and insert in the oven.
8. Serve warm with the garnishing of lemon zest.

Nutritional Information per Serving:
Calories 62; Total Fat 3.1 g; Saturated Fat 1.9 g; Cholesterol 8 mg; Sodium 67 mg

Soy Sauce Green Beans

Preparation Time: 10 minutes; Cooking Time: 10 minutes; Servings: 2

Ingredients:
- 8 oz. fresh green beans, trimmed and cut in half
- 1 tablespoon soy sauce
- 1 teaspoon sesame oil
- ¼ teaspoon sesame seeds

Method:
1. In a bowl, mix together the green beans, soy sauce and sesame oil.
2. Press "Power Button" of Air Fry Oven and turn the dial to select the "Air Fry" mode.
3. Press the Time button and again turn the dial to set the cooking time to 10 minutes.
4. Now push the Temp button and rotate the dial to set the temperature at 390 degrees F.
5. Press "Start/Pause" button to start.
6. When the unit beeps to show that it is preheated, open the lid.
7. Arrange the green beans in "Air Fry Basket" and insert in the oven.
8. Serve hot with the garnishing of sesame seeds.

Nutritional Information per Serving:
Calories 62; Total Fat 2.6 g; Saturated 0.4 g; Cholesterol 0 mg; Sodium 458 mg

Green Beans with Okra

Preparation Time: 15 minutes; Cooking Time: 20 minutes; Servings: 2

Ingredients:
- ½ (10-oz.) bag frozen cut okra
- ½ (10-oz.) bag frozen cut green beans
- ¼ cup nutritional yeast
- 3 tablespoons balsamic vinegar
- Salt and ground black pepper, as required

Method:
1. In a bowl, add the okra, green beans, nutritional yeast, vinegar, salt, and black pepper and toss to coat well.
2. Press "Power Button" of Air Fry Oven and turn the dial to select the "Air Fry" mode.
3. Press the Time button and again turn the dial to set the cooking time to 20 minutes.
4. Now push the Temp button and rotate the dial to set the temperature at 400 degrees F.
5. Press "Start/Pause" button to start.
6. When the unit beeps to show that it is preheated, open the lid.
7. Arrange the okra mixture in greased "Air Fry Basket" and insert in the oven.
8. Serve hot.

Nutritional Information per Serving:
Calories 126; Total Fat 1.3 g; Saturated Fat 0.2 g; Cholesterol 0 mg; Sodium 100 mg

Green Beans & Mushroom Casserole

Preparation Time: 15 minutes; Cooking Time: 12 minutes; Servings: 6

Ingredients:

- 24 oz. fresh green beans, trimmed
- 2 cups fresh button mushrooms, sliced
- 3 tablespoons olive oil
- 2 tablespoons fresh lemon juice
- 1 teaspoon ground sage
- 1 teaspoon garlic powder
- 1 teaspoon onion powder
- Salt and ground black pepper, as required
- 1/3 cup French fried onions

Method:

1. In a bowl, add the green beans, mushrooms, oil, lemon juice, sage, and spices and toss to coat well.
2. Press "Power Button" of Air Fry Oven and turn the dial to select the "Air Fry" mode.
3. Press the Time button and again turn the dial to set the cooking time to 12 minutes.
4. Now push the Temp button and rotate the dial to set the temperature at 400 degrees F.
5. Press "Start/Pause" button to start.
6. When the unit beeps to show that it is preheated, open the lid.
7. Arrange the mushroom mixture in greased "Air Fry Basket" and insert in the oven.
8. Shake the mushroom mixture occasionally.
9. Transfer the mushroom mixture into a serving dish.
10. Top with fried onions and serve.

Nutritional Information per Serving:

Calories 125; Total Fat 8.6 g; Saturated Fat 2 g; Cholesterol 0mg; Sodium 52 mg

Wine Braised Mushrooms

Preparation Time: 15 minutes; Cooking Time: 32 minutes; Servings: 6

Ingredients:

- 1 tablespoon butter
- 2 teaspoons Herbs de Provence
- ½ teaspoon garlic powder
- 2 lbs. fresh mushrooms, quartered
- 2 tablespoons white wine

Method:

1. In a frying pan, mix together the butter, Herbs de Provence, and garlic powder over medium-low heat and stir fry for about 2 minutes.
2. Stir in the mushrooms and remove from the heat.
3. Transfer the mushroom mixture into a baking pan.
4. Press "Power Button" of Air Fry Oven and turn the dial to select the "Air Fry" mode.
5. Press the Time button and again turn the dial to set the cooking time to 30 minutes.
6. Now push the Temp button and rotate the dial to set the temperature at 320 degrees F.
7. Press "Start/Pause" button to start.
8. When the unit beeps to show that it is preheated, open the lid.
9. Arrange the pan over the "Wire Rack" and insert in the oven.
10. After 25 minutes of cooking, stir the wine into mushroom mixture.
11. Serve hot.

Nutritional Information per Serving:

Calories 54; Total Fat 2.4 g; Saturated Fat 1.2 g; Cholesterol 5 mg; Sodium 23 mg

Glazed Mushrooms

Preparation Time: 10 minutes; Cooking Time: 15 minutes; Servings: 5

Ingredients:

- ½ cup low-sodium soy sauce
- 2 teaspoons honey

- 4 tablespoons balsamic vinegar
- 4 garlic cloves, finely chopped
- 2 teaspoons Chinese five-spice powder
- ½ teaspoon ground ginger
- 20 oz. fresh cremini mushrooms, halved

Method:
1. In a bowl, add the soy sauce, honey, vinegar, garlic, five-spice powder and ground ginger and mix well. Set aside.
2. Place the mushroom into a greased baking pan in a single layer.
3. Press "Power Button" of Air Fry Oven and turn the dial to select the "Air Fry" mode.
4. Press the Time button and again turn the dial to set the cooking time to 15 minutes.
5. Now push the Temp button and rotate the dial to set the temperature at 350 degrees F.
6. Press "Start/Pause" button to start.
7. When the unit beeps to show that it is preheated, open the lid.
8. Arrange the pan over the "Wire Rack" and insert in the oven.
9. After 10 minutes of cooking, in the pan, add the vinegar mixture and stir to combine.
10. Serve hot.

Nutritional Information per Serving:
Calories 54; Total Fat 0.1 g; Saturated Fat 0 g; Cholesterol 0 mg; Sodium 1400 mg

Mushroom with Peas

Preparation Time: 15 minutes; Cooking Time: 15 minutes; Servings: 4
Ingredients:
- ½ cup soy sauce
- 4 tablespoons honey
- 4 tablespoons rice vinegar
- 2 garlic cloves, finely chopped
- 2 teaspoons Chinese five spice powder
- ½ teaspoon ground ginger
- 16 oz. cremini mushrooms, halved
- ½ cup frozen peas

Method:
1. In a bowl, mix together the soy sauce, honey, vinegar, garlic, five spice powder, and ground ginger.
2. Press "Power Button" of Air Fry Oven and turn the dial to select the "Air Fry" mode.
3. Press the Time button and again turn the dial to set the cooking time to 15 minutes.
4. Now push the Temp button and rotate the dial to set the temperature at 350 degrees F.
5. Press "Start/Pause" button to start.
6. When the unit beeps to show that it is preheated, open the lid.
7. Arrange the mushrooms in "Air Fry Basket" and insert in the oven.
8. After 10 minutes of cooking, add the peas and vinegar mixture with mushrooms and stir to combine.
9. Serve hot.

Nutritional Information per Serving:
Calories 140; Total Fat 0.2 g; Saturated Fat 0 g; Cholesterol 0 mg; Sodium 1800 mg

Herbed Bell Peppers

Preparation Time: 10 minutes; Cooking Time: 8 minutes; Servings: 4
Ingredients:
- 1½ lbs. bell peppers, seeded and cubed
- ½ teaspoon dried thyme, crushed
- ½ teaspoon dried savory, crushed
- Salt and ground black pepper, as required
- 2 teaspoons butter, melted

Method:
1. In a bowl, add the bell peppers, herbs, salt and black pepper and toss to coat well.
2. Press "Power Button" of Air Fry Oven and turn the dial to select the "Air Fry" mode.
3. Press the Time button and again turn the dial to set the cooking time to 8 minutes.

4. Now push the Temp button and rotate the dial to set the temperature at 360 degrees F.
5. Press "Start/Pause" button to start.
6. When the unit beeps to show that it is preheated, open the lid.
7. Arrange the bell peppers in "Air Fry Basket" and insert in the oven.
8. Transfer the bell peppers into a bowl and drizzle with butter.
9. Serve immediately.

Nutritional Information per Serving:
   Calories 32; Total Fat 2 g; Saturated Fat 1.2 g; Cholesterol 5 mg; Sodium 54 mg

Feta Spinach

Preparation Time: 10 minutes; Cooking Time: 15 minutes; Servings: 6
Ingredients:
- 2 lbs. fresh spinach, chopped
- 1 garlic clove, minced
- 1 jalapeño pepper, minced
- 4 tablespoons butter, melted
- Salt and ground black pepper, as required
- 1 cup feta cheese, crumbled
- 1 teaspoon fresh lemon zest, grated

Method:
1. In a bowl, add the spinach, garlic, jalapeño, butter, salt and black pepper and mix well.
2. Press "Power Button" of Air Fry Oven and turn the dial to select the "Air Fry" mode.
3. Press the Time button and again turn the dial to set the cooking time to 15 minutes.
4. Now push the Temp button and rotate the dial to set the temperature at 340 degrees F.
5. Press "Start/Pause" button to start.
6. When the unit beeps to show that it is preheated, open the lid.
7. Arrange the spinach in "Air Fry Basket" and insert in the oven.
8. Transfer the spinach into a bowl.
9. Immediately, stir in the cheese and lemon zest and serve hot.

Nutritional Information per Serving:
   Calories 170; Total Fat 13.6 g; Saturated Fat 8.7 g; Cholesterol 43 mg; Sodium 480 mg

Tarragon Yellow Squash

Preparation Time: 15 minutes; Cooking Time: 15 minutes; Servings: 6
Ingredients:
- 4 teaspoons olive oil
- 2 lbs. yellow squash, sliced
- 1 teaspoon salt
- ½ teaspoon ground white pepper
- 1 tablespoon tarragon leaves, chopped

Method:
1. In a large bowl, mix together the oil, yellow squash, salt and white pepper.
2. Press "Power Button" of Air Fry Oven and turn the dial to select the "Air Fry" mode.
3. Press the Time button and again turn the dial to set the cooking time to 15 minutes.
4. Now push the Temp button and rotate the dial to set the temperature at 390 degrees F.
5. Press "Start/Pause" button to start.
6. When the unit beeps to show that it is preheated, open the lid.
7. Arrange the yellow squash slices in "Air Fry Basket" and insert in the oven.
8. Toss the yellow squash slices 2-3 times.
9. Transfer the yellow squash into a bowl with tarragon leaves and mix until well.
10. Serve immediately.

Nutritional Information per Serving:
   Calories 53; Total Fat 3.4 g; Saturated Fat 0.5 g; Cholesterol 0 mg; Sodium 403 mg

Seasoned Zucchini & Squash

Preparation Time: 15 minutes; Cooking Time: 10 minutes; Servings: 6

Ingredients:

- 2 large yellow squash, cut into slices
- 2 large zucchinis, cut into slices
- ¼ cup olive oil
- ½ onion, sliced
- ¾ teaspoon Italian seasoning
- ½ teaspoon garlic salt
- ¼ teaspoon seasoned salt

Method:

1. In a large bowl, mix together all the ingredients.
2. Press "Power Button" of Air Fry Oven and turn the dial to select the "Air Fry" mode.
3. Press the Time button and again turn the dial to set the cooking time to 10 minutes.
4. Now push the Temp button and rotate the dial to set the temperature at 400 degrees F.
5. Press "Start/Pause" button to start.
6. When the unit beeps to show that it is preheated, open the lid.
7. Arrange the squash mixture in "Air Fry Basket" and insert in the oven.
8. Serve hot.

Nutritional Information per Serving:

Calories 113; Total Fat 9 g; Saturated Fat 1.3 g; Cholesterol 0 mg; Sodium 85 mg

Garlicky Brussels Sprout

Preparation Time: 15 minutes; Cooking Time: 12 minutes; Servings: 4

Ingredients:

- 1 lb. Brussels sprouts, cut in half
- 2 tablespoons oil
- 2 garlic cloves, minced
- ¼ teaspoon red pepper flakes, crushed
- Salt and ground black pepper, as required

Method:

1. In a bowl, add all the ingredients and toss to coat well.
2. Press "Power Button" of Air Fry Oven and turn the dial to select the "Air Fry" mode.
3. Press the Time button and again turn the dial to set the cooking time to 12 minutes.
4. Now push the Temp button and rotate the dial to set the temperature at 390 degrees F.
5. Press "Start/Pause" button to start.
6. When the unit beeps to show that it is preheated, open the lid.
7. Arrange the Brussels sprouts in "Air Fry Basket" and insert in the oven.
8. Serve hot.

Nutritional Information per Serving:

Calories 113; Total Fat 9 g; Saturated Fat 1.3 g; Cholesterol 0 mg; Sodium 185 mg

Sweet & Sour Brussels Sprout

Preparation Time: 10 minutes; Cooking Time: 10 minutes; Servings: 2

Ingredients:

- 2 cups Brussels sprouts, trimmed and halved lengthwise
- 1 tablespoon balsamic vinegar
- 1 tablespoon maple syrup
- ¼ teaspoon red pepper flakes, crushed
- Salt, as required

Method:

1. In a bowl, add all the ingredients and toss to coat well.
2. Press "Power Button" of Air Fry Oven and turn the dial to select the "Air Fry" mode.
3. Press the Time button and again turn the dial to set the cooking time to 10 minutes.
4. Now push the Temp button and rotate the dial to set the temperature at 400 degrees F.
5. Press "Start/Pause" button to start.

6. When the unit beeps to show that it is preheated, open the lid.
7. Arrange the Brussels sprouts in "Air Fry Basket" and insert in the oven.
8. Serve hot.

Nutritional Information per Serving:

Calories 66; Total Fat 0.4 g; Saturated Fat 0.1 g; Cholesterol 0 mg; Sodium 101 mg

Spiced Eggplant

Preparation Time: 15 minutes; Cooking Time: 25 minutes; Servings: 3
Ingredients:

- 2 medium eggplants, cubed
- 2 tablespoons butter, melted
- 1 tablespoon Maggi seasoning sauce
- 1 teaspoon sumac
- 1 teaspoon garlic powder
- 1 teaspoon onion powder
- Salt and ground black pepper, as required
- 1 tablespoon fresh lemon juice
- 2 tablespoons Parmesan cheese, shredded

Method:

1. In a bowl, mix together the eggplant cubes, butter, seasoning sauce and spices.
2. Press "Power Button" of Air Fry Oven and turn the dial to select the "Air Fry" mode.
3. Press the Time button and again turn the dial to set the cooking time to 15 minutes.
4. Now push the Temp button and rotate the dial to set the temperature at 320 degrees F.
5. Press "Start/Pause" button to start.
6. When the unit beeps to show that it is preheated, open the lid.
7. Arrange the eggplant cubes in "Air Fry Basket" and insert in the oven.
8. After 15 minutes of cooking, toss the eggplant cubes.
9. Now, set the temperature at 320 degrees F for 10 minutes.
10. Transfer the eggplant cubes into a bowl with the lemon juice, and Parmesan and toss to coat well.
11. Serve immediately.

Nutritional Information per Serving:

Calories 180; Total Fat 9.3 g; Saturated Fat 5.5 g; Cholesterol 23 mg; Sodium 304 mg

Herbed Eggplant

Preparation Time: 15 minutes; Cooking Time: 15 minutes; Servings: 2
Ingredients:

- ½ teaspoon dried marjoram, crushed
- ½ teaspoon dried oregano, crushed
- ½ teaspoon dried thyme, crushed
- ½ teaspoon garlic powder
- Salt and ground black pepper, as required
- 1 large eggplant, cubed
- Olive oil cooking spray

Method:

1. In a small bowl, mix together the herbs, garlic powder, salt, and black pepper.
2. Spray the eggplant cubes evenly cooking spray with and then, rub with the herbs mixture.
3. Press "Power Button" of Air Fry Oven and turn the dial to select the "Air Fry" mode.
4. Press the Time button and again turn the dial to set the cooking time to 15 minutes.
5. Now push the Temp button and rotate the dial to set the temperature at 390 degrees F.
6. Press "Start/Pause" button to start.
7. When the unit beeps to show that it is preheated, open the lid.
8. Arrange the eggplant cubes in "Air Fry Basket" and insert in the oven.
9. Spray the eggplant cubes with cooking spray 2 times.
10. Serve hot.

Nutritional Information per Serving:

Calories 62; Total Fat 0.5 g; Saturated Fat 0 g; Cholesterol 0 mg; Sodium 83 mg

Curried Eggplant

Preparation Time: 15 minutes; Cooking Time: 15 minutes; Servings: 2

Ingredients:

- 1 large eggplant, cut into ½-inch thick slices
- 1 garlic clove, minced
- ½ fresh red chili, chopped
- 1 tablespoon vegetable oil
- ¼ teaspoon curry powder
- Salt, as required

Method:

1. In a bowl, add all the ingredients and toss to coat well.
2. Press "Power Button" of Air Fry Oven and turn the dial to select the "Air Fry" mode.
3. Press the Time button and again turn the dial to set the cooking time to 15 minutes.
4. Now push the Temp button and rotate the dial to set the temperature at 300 degrees F.
5. Press "Start/Pause" button to start.
6. When the unit beeps to show that it is preheated, open the lid.
7. Arrange the eggplant cubes in "Air Fry Basket" and insert in the oven.
8. Serve hot.

Nutritional Information per Serving:

Calories 121; Total Fat 7.3 g; Saturated Fat 1.3 g; Cholesterol 0 mg; Sodium 83 mg

Stuffed Eggplants

Preparation Time: 20 minutes; Cooking Time: 8 minutes; Servings: 4

Ingredients:

- 4 small eggplants, halved lengthwise
- 1 teaspoon fresh lime juice
- 1 teaspoon vegetable oil
- 1 small onion, chopped
- ¼ teaspoon garlic, chopped
- ½ of small tomato, chopped
- Salt and ground black pepper, as required
- 1 tablespoon cottage cheese, chopped
- ¼ of green bell pepper, seeded and chopped
- 1 tablespoon tomato paste
- 1 tablespoon fresh cilantro, chopped

Method:

1. Carefully, cut a slice from one side of each eggplant lengthwise.
2. With a small spoon, scoop out the flesh from each eggplant leaving a thick shell.
3. Transfer the eggplant flesh into a bowl.
4. Drizzle the eggplants with lime juice evenly.
5. Press "Power Button" of Air Fry Oven and turn the dial to select the "Air Fry" mode.
6. Press the Time button and again turn the dial to set the cooking time to 3 minutes.
7. Now push the Temp button and rotate the dial to set the temperature at 320 degrees F.
8. Press "Start/Pause" button to start.
9. When the unit beeps to show that it is preheated, open the lid.
10. Arrange the hollowed eggplants in greased "Air Fry Basket" and insert in the oven.
11. Meanwhile, in a skillet heat the oil over medium heat and sauté the onion and garlic for about 2 minutes.
12. Add the eggplant flesh, tomato, salt, and black pepper and sauté for about 2 minutes.
13. Stir in the cheese, bell pepper, tomato paste, and cilantro and cook for about 1 minute.
14. Remove the pan of veggie mixture from heat.
15. Arrange the cooked eggplants onto a plate and stuff each with veggie mixture.
16. Close each with its cut part.
17. Press "Power Button" of Air Fry Oven and turn the dial to select the "Air Fry" mode.

18. Press the Time button and again turn the dial to set the cooking time to 8 minutes.
19. Now push the Temp button and rotate the dial to set the temperature at 55 degrees F.
20. Press "Start/Pause" button to start.
21. When the unit beeps to show that it is preheated, open the lid.
22. Arrange the eggplants shells in greased "Air Fry Basket" and insert in the oven.
23. Serve hot.

Nutritional Information per Serving:
  Calories 131; Total Fat 2 g; Saturated Fat 0.3 g; Cholesterol 0 mg; Sodium 67 mg

Herbed Potatoes

Preparation Time: 10 minutes; Cooking Time: 16 minutes; Servings: 4

Ingredients:
- 6 small potatoes, chopped
- 3 tablespoons olive oil
- 2 teaspoons mixed dried herbs
- Salt and ground black pepper, as required
- 2 tablespoons fresh parsley, chopped

Method:
1. In a large bowl, add the potatoes, oil, herbs, salt and black pepper and toss to coat well.
2. Press "Power Button" of Air Fry Oven and turn the dial to select the "Air Fry" mode.
3. Press the Time button and again turn the dial to set the cooking time to 16 minutes.
4. Now push the Temp button and rotate the dial to set the temperature at 355 degrees F.
5. Press "Start/Pause" button to start.
6. When the unit beeps to show that it is preheated, open the lid.
7. Arrange the potato pieces in "Air Fry Basket" and insert in the oven.
8. Garnish with parsley and serve.

Nutritional Information per Serving:
  Calories 268; Total Fat 10.8 g; Saturated Fat 1.6 g; Cholesterol 0 mg; Sodium 55 mg

Jacket Potatoes

Preparation Time: 15 minutes; Cooking Time: 15 minutes; Servings: 2

Ingredients:
- 2 potatoes
- 1 tablespoon mozzarella cheese, shredded
- 3 tablespoons sour cream
- 1 tablespoon butter, softened
- 1 teaspoon chives, minced
- Salt and ground black pepper, as required

Method:
1. With a fork, prick the potatoes.
2. Press "Power Button" of Air Fry Oven and turn the dial to select the "Air Fry" mode.
3. Press the Time button and again turn the dial to set the cooking time to 15 minutes.
4. Now push the Temp button and rotate the dial to set the temperature at 355 degrees F.
5. Press "Start/Pause" button to start.
6. When the unit beeps to show that it is preheated, open the lid.
7. Arrange the potatoes in greased "Air Fry Basket" and insert in the oven.
8. Meanwhile, in a bowl, add the remaining ingredients and mix until well combined.
9. Transfer the potatoes onto a platter.
10. Open potatoes from the center and stuff them with cheese mixture.
11. Serve immediately

Nutritional Information per Serving:
  Calories 277; Total Fat 12.2 g; Saturated Fat 7.6 g; Cholesterol 31 mg; Sodium 225 mg

Stuffed Potatoes

Preparation Time: 15 minutes; Cooking Time: 31 minutes; Servings: 4

Ingredients:

- 4 potatoes, peeled
- 2-3 tablespoons canola oil
- 1 tablespoon butter
- ½ of brown onion, chopped
- 2 tablespoons chives, chopped
- ½ cup Parmesan cheese, grated

Method:

1. Coat the potatoes with some oil.
2. Press "Power Button" of Air Fry Oven and turn the dial to select the "Air Fry" mode.
3. Press the Time button and again turn the dial to set the cooking time to 26 minutes.
4. Now push the Temp button and rotate the dial to set the temperature at 390 degrees F.
5. Press "Start/Pause" button to start.
6. When the unit beeps to show that it is preheated, open the lid.
7. Arrange the potatoes in greased "Air Fry Basket" and insert in the oven.
8. Coat the potatoes twice with the remaining oil.
9. Meanwhile, in a frying pan, melt the butter over medium heat and sauté the onion for about 4-5 minutes.
10. Remove from the heat and transfer the onion into a bowl.
11. In the bowl of onion, add the potato flesh, chives, and half of cheese and stir to combine.
12. After 20 minutes of cooking, press "Start/Pause" button to pause the unit and transfer the potatoes onto a platter.
13. Carefully, cut each potato in half.
14. With a small scooper, scoop out the flesh from each half.
15. Stuff the potato halves evenly with potato mixture and sprinkle with the remaining cheese.
16. Arrange the potato halves in greased "Air Fry Basket" and insert in the oven.
17. Serve immediately.

Nutritional Information per Serving:

Calories 276; Total Fat 12.5 g; Saturated Fat 3.6 g; Cholesterol 16 mg; Sodium 120 mg

Hasselback Potatoes

Preparation Time: 20 minutes; Cooking Time: 30 minutes; Servings: 4

Ingredients:

- 4 potatoes
- 2 tablespoons olive oil
- 2 tablespoons Parmesan cheese, shredded
- 1 tablespoon fresh chives, chopped

Method:

1. With a sharp knife, cut slits along each potato the short way about ¼-inch apart, making sure slices should stay connected at the bottom.
2. Gently brush each potato evenly with oil
3. Press "Power Button" of Air Fry Oven and turn the dial to select the "Air Fry" mode.
4. Press the Time button and again turn the dial to set the cooking time to 30 minutes.
5. Now push the Temp button and rotate the dial to set the temperature at 355 degrees F.
6. Press "Start/Pause" button to start.
7. When the unit beeps to show that it is preheated, open the lid.
8. Arrange the potatoes in greased "Air Fry Basket" and insert in the oven.
9. Coat the potatoes with the oil once halfway through.
10. Transfer the potatoes onto a platter and top with the cheeses, and chives.
11. Serve immediately.

Nutritional Information per Serving:

Calories 218; Total Fat 7.9 g; Saturated Fat 1.5 g; Cholesterol 2 mg; Sodium 55 mg

Potato Gratin

Preparation Time: 15 minutes; Cooking Time: 20 minutes; Servings: 4
Ingredients:

- 2 large potatoes, sliced thinly
- 5½ tablespoons cream
- 2 eggs
- 1 tablespoon plain flour
- ½ cup cheddar cheese, grated

Method:

1. Press "Power Button" of Air Fry Oven and turn the dial to select the "Air Fry" mode.
2. Press the Time button and again turn the dial to set the cooking time to 10 minutes.
3. Now push the Temp button and rotate the dial to set the temperature at 355 degrees F.
4. Press "Start/Pause" button to start.
5. When the unit beeps to show that it is preheated, open the lid.
6. Arrange the potato slices in "Air Fry Basket" and insert in the oven.
7. Meanwhile, in a bowl, add cream, eggs and flour and mix until a thick sauce forms.
8. Remove the potato slices from the basket.
9. Divide the potato slices in 4 ramekins evenly and top with the egg mixture evenly, followed by the cheese.
10. Press "Power Button" of Air Fry Oven and turn the dial to select the "Air Fry" mode.
11. Press the Time button and again turn the dial to set the cooking time to 10 minutes.
12. Now push the Temp button and rotate the dial to set the temperature at 390 degrees F.
13. Arrange the ramekins in "Air Fry Basket" and insert in the oven.
14. Press "Start/Pause" button to start.
15. Serve warm.

Nutritional Information per Serving:

Calories 233; Total Fat 8 g; Saturated Fat 4.3 g; Cholesterol 100 mg; Sodium 135 mg

Stuffed Okra

Preparation Time: 15 minutes; Cooking Time: 12 minutes; Servings: 2
Ingredients:

- 8 oz. large okra
- ¼ cup chickpea flour
- ¼ of onion, chopped
- 2 tablespoons coconut, grated freshly
- 1 teaspoon garam masala powder
- ½ teaspoon ground turmeric
- ½ teaspoon red chili powder
- ½ teaspoon ground cumin
- Salt, to taste

Method:

1. With a knife, make a slit in each okra vertically without cutting in 2 halves.
2. In a bowl, mix together the flour, onion, grated coconut, and spices.
3. Stuff each okra with the mixture.
4. Press "Power Button" of Air Fry Oven and turn the dial to select the "Air Fry" mode.
5. Press the Time button and again turn the dial to set the cooking time to 12 minutes.
6. Now push the Temp button and rotate the dial to set the temperature at 390 degrees F.
7. Press "Start/Pause" button to start.
8. When the unit beeps to show that it is preheated, open the lid.
9. Arrange the stuffed okra in "Air Fry Basket" and insert in the oven.
10. Serve hot.

Nutritional Information per Serving:

Calories 166; Total Fat 3.7 g; Saturated Fat 1.7 g; Cholesterol 0 mg; Sodium 103 mg

Stuffed Bell Peppers

Preparation Time: 15 minutes; Cooking Time: 15 minutes; Servings: 5
Ingredients:

- ½ small bell pepper, seeded and chopped
- 1 (15-oz.) can diced tomatoes with juice
- 1 (15-oz.) can red kidney beans, rinsed and drained
- 1 cup cooked rice
- 1½ teaspoons Italian seasoning
- 5 large bell peppers, tops removed and seeded
- ½ cup mozzarella cheese, shredded
- 1 tablespoon Parmesan cheese, grated

Method:

1. In a bowl, mix together the chopped bell pepper, tomatoes with juice, beans, rice, and Italian seasoning.
2. Stuff each bell pepper with the rice mixture.
3. Press "Power Button" of Air Fry Oven and turn the dial to select the "Air Fry" mode.
4. Press the Time button and again turn the dial to set the cooking time to 15 minutes.
5. Now push the Temp button and rotate the dial to set the temperature at 360 degrees F.
6. Press "Start/Pause" button to start.
7. When the unit beeps to show that it is preheated, open the lid.
8. Arrange the bell peppers in "Air Fry Basket" and insert in the oven.
9. Meanwhile, in a bowl, mix together the mozzarella and Parmesan cheese.
10. After 12 minutes of cooking, top each bell pepper with cheese mixture.
11. Serve warm.

Nutritional Information per Serving:
Calories 287; Total Fat 2.5 g; Saturated Fat 1 g; Cholesterol 5 mg; Sodium 113 mg

Stuffed Pumpkin

Preparation Time: 20 minutes; Cooking Time: 30 minutes; Servings: 5
Ingredients:

- 1 sweet potato, peeled and chopped
- 1 parsnip, peeled and chopped
- 1 carrot, peeled and chopped
- ½ cup fresh peas, shelled
- 1 onion, chopped
- 2 garlic cloves, minced
- 1 egg, beaten
- 2 teaspoons mixed dried herbs
- Salt and ground black pepper, as required
- ½ of butternut pumpkin, seeded

Method:

1. In a large bowl, mix together the vegetables, garlic, egg, herbs, salt, and black pepper.
2. Stuff the pumpkin half with vegetable mixture.
3. Press "Power Button" of Air Fry Oven and turn the dial to select the "Air Fry" mode.
4. Press the Time button and again turn the dial to set the cooking time to 30 minutes.
5. Now push the Temp button and rotate the dial to set the temperature at 355 degrees F.
6. Press "Start/Pause" button to start.
7. When the unit beeps to show that it is preheated, open the lid.
8. Arrange the pumpkin half in "Air Fry Basket" and insert in the oven.
9. Transfer the pumpkin onto a serving platter and set aside to cool slightly before serving.

Nutritional Information per Serving:
Calories 223; Total Fat 1.3 g; Saturated Fat 0.3 g; Cholesterol 27 mg; Sodium 70 mg

Veggie Ratatouille

Preparation Time: 15 minutes; Cooking Time: 15 minutes; Servings: 4

Ingredients:

- 1 green bell pepper, seeded and chopped
- 1 yellow bell pepper, seeded and chopped
- 1 eggplant, chopped
- 1 zucchini, chopped
- 3 tomatoes, chopped
- 2 small onions, chopped
- 2 garlic cloves, minced
- 2 tablespoons Herbs de Provence
- 1 tablespoon olive oil
- 1 tablespoon balsamic vinegar
- Salt and ground black pepper, as required

Method:

1. In a large bowl, add the vegetables, garlic, Herbs de Provence, oil, vinegar, salt, and black pepper and toss to coat well.
2. Transfer vegetable mixture into a greased baking pan.
3. Press "Power Button" of Air Fry Oven and turn the dial to select the "Air Fry" mode.
4. Press the Time button and again turn the dial to set the cooking time to 15 minutes.
5. Now push the Temp button and rotate the dial to set the temperature at 355 degrees F.
6. Press "Start/Pause" button to start.
7. When the unit beeps to show that it is preheated, open the lid.
8. Arrange the pan over the "Wire Rack" and insert in the oven.
9. Serve hot.

Nutritional Information per Serving:
Calories 119; Total Fat 4.2 g; Saturated Fat 0.6 g; Cholesterol 0 mg; Sodium 54 mg

Glazed Veggies

Preparation Time: 015 minutes; Cooking Time: 20 minutes; Servings: 4
Ingredients:

- 2 oz. cherry tomatoes
- 2 large zucchini, chopped
- 2 green bell peppers, seeded and chopped
- 6 tablespoons olive oil, divided
- 2 tablespoons honey
- 1 teaspoon Dijon mustard
- 1 teaspoon dried herbs
- 1 teaspoon garlic paste
- Salt, as required

Method:

1. In a parchment paper-lined baking pan, place the vegetables and drizzle with 3 tablespoons of oil.
2. Press "Power Button" of Air Fry Oven and turn the dial to select the "Air Fry" mode.
3. Press the Time button and again turn the dial to set the cooking time to 15 minutes.
4. Now push the Temp button and rotate the dial to set the temperature at 355 degrees F.
5. Press "Start/Pause" button to start.
6. When the unit beeps to show that it is preheated, open the lid.
7. Arrange the pan over the "Wire Rack" and insert in the oven.
8. Meanwhile, in a bowl, add the remaining oil, honey, mustard, herbs, garlic, salt, and black pepper and mix well.
9. After 15 minutes of cooking, add the honey mixture into vegetable mixture and mix well.
10. Now, set the temperature to 392 degrees F for 5 minutes.
11. Serve immediately.

Nutritional Information per Serving:
Calories 262; Total Fat 21.5 g; Saturated Fat 3.1 g; Cholesterol 0 mg; Sodium 72 mg

Parmesan Mixed Veggies

Preparation Time: 15 minutes; Cooking Time: 18 minutes; Servings: 5
Ingredients:

- 1 tablespoon olive oil
- 1 tablespoon garlic, minced
- 1 cup cauliflower florets
- 1 cup broccoli florets
- 1 cup zucchini, sliced
- ½ cup yellow squash, sliced
- ½ cup fresh mushrooms, sliced
- 1 small onion, sliced
- ¼ cup balsamic vinegar
- 1 teaspoon red pepper flakes
- Salt and ground black pepper, as required
- ¼ cup Parmesan cheese, grated

Method:
1. In a large bowl, add all the ingredients except cheese and toss to coat well.
2. Press "Power Button" of Air Fry Oven and turn the dial to select the "Air Fry" mode.
3. Press the Time button and again turn the dial to set the cooking time to 18 minutes.
4. Now push the Temp button and rotate the dial to set the temperature at 400 degrees F.
5. Press "Start/Pause" button to start.
6. When the unit beeps to show that it is preheated, open the lid.
7. Arrange the vegetables in greased "Air Fry Basket" and insert in the oven.
8. After 8 minutes of cooking, flip the vegetables.
9. After 16 minutes of cooking, sprinkle the vegetables with cheese evenly.
10. Serve hot.

Nutritional Information per Serving:
Calories 102; Total Fat 6.2 g; Saturated Fat 2.4 g; Cholesterol 12 mg; Sodium 352 mg

Veggie Kabobs

Preparation Time: 20 minutes; Cooking Time: 10 minutes; Servings: 6
Ingredients:
- ¼ cup carrots, peeled and chopped
- ¼ cup French beans
- ½ cup green peas
- 1 teaspoon ginger
- 3 garlic cloves, peeled
- 3 green chilies
- ¼ cup fresh mint leaves
- ½ cup cottage cheese
- 2 medium boiled potatoes, mashed
- ½ teaspoon five spice powder
- Salt, to taste
- 2 tablespoons corn flour
- Olive oil cooking spray

Method:
1. In a food processor, add the carrot, beans, peas, ginger, garlic, mint, cheese and pulse until smooth.
2. Transfer the mixture into a bowl.
3. Add the potato, five spice powder, salt and corn flour and mix until well combined.
4. Divide the mixture into equal sized small balls.
5. Press each ball around a skewer in a sausage shape.
6. Spray the skewers with cooking spray.
7. Press "Power Button" of Air Fry Oven and turn the dial to select the "Air Fry" mode.
8. Press the Time button and again turn the dial to set the cooking time to 10 minutes.
9. Now push the Temp button and rotate the dial to set the temperature at 390 degrees F.
10. Press "Start/Pause" button to start.
11. When the unit beeps to show that it is preheated, open the lid.
12. Arrange the skewers in greased "Air Fry Basket" and insert in the oven.
13. Serve warm.

Nutritional Information per Serving:
Calories 120; Total Fat 0.8 g; Saturated Fat 0.3 g; Cholesterol 2 mg; Sodium 115 mg

Beans & Veggie Burgers

Preparation Time: 20 minutes; Cooking Time: 22 minutes; Servings: 4

Ingredients:

- 1 cup cooked black beans
- 2 cups boiled potatoes, peeled and mashed
- 1 cup fresh spinach, chopped
- 1 cup fresh mushrooms, chopped
- 2 teaspoons Chile lime seasoning
- Olive oil cooking spray

Method:

1. In a large bowl, add the beans, potatoes, spinach, mushrooms, and seasoning and with your hands, mix until well combined.
2. Make 4 equal-sized patties from the mixture.
3. Spray the patties with cooking spray evenly.
4. Press "Power Button" of Air Fry Oven and turn the dial to select the "Air Fry" mode.
5. Press the Time button and again turn the dial to set the cooking time to 22 minutes.
6. Now push the Temp button and rotate the dial to set the temperature at 370 degrees F.
7. Press "Start/Pause" button to start.
8. When the unit beeps to show that it is preheated, open the lid.
9. Arrange the skewers in greased "Air Fry Basket" and insert in the oven.
10. Flip the patties once after 12 minutes.

Nutritional Information per Serving:

Calories 113; Total Fat 0.4 g; Saturated Fat 0 g; Cholesterol 0 mg; Sodium 166 mg

Marinated Tofu

Preparation Time: 15 minutes; Cooking Time: 25 minutes; Servings: 4

Ingredients:

- 2 tablespoon low-sodium soy sauce
- 2 tablespoon fish sauce
- 1 teaspoon olive oil
- 12 oz. extra-firm tofu, drained and cubed into 1-inch size
- 1 teaspoon butter, melted

Method:

1. In a large bowl, add the soy sauce, fish sauce and oil and mix until well combined.
2. Add the tofu cubes and toss to coat well.
3. Set aside to marinate for about 30 minutes, tossing occasionally.
4. Press "Power Button" of Air Fry Oven and turn the dial to select the "Air Fry" mode.
5. Press the Time button and again turn the dial to set the cooking time to 25 minutes.
6. Now push the Temp button and rotate the dial to set the temperature at 355 degrees F.
7. Press "Start/Pause" button to start.
8. When the unit beeps to show that it is preheated, open the lid.
9. Arrange the tofu cubes in greased "Air Fry Basket" and insert in the oven.
10. Flip the tofu after every 10 minutes during the cooking.
11. Serve hot.

Nutritional Information per Serving:

Calories 102; Total Fat 7.1 g; Saturated Fat 1.2 g; Cholesterol 3 mg; Sodium 1100 mg

Crusted Tofu

Preparation Time: 15 minutes; Cooking Time: 28 minutes; Servings: 3

Ingredients:

- 1 (14-oz.) block firm tofu, pressed and cubed into ½-inch size
- 2 tablespoons cornstarch
- ¼ cup rice flour
- Salt and ground black pepper, as required

- 2 tablespoons olive oil

Method:
1. In a bowl, mix together the cornstarch, rice flour, salt, and black pepper.
2. Coat the tofu with flour mixture evenly.
3. Then, drizzle the tofu with oil.
4. Press "Power Button" of Air Fry Oven and turn the dial to select the "Air Fry" mode.
5. Press the Time button and again turn the dial to set the cooking time to 28 minutes.
6. Now push the Temp button and rotate the dial to set the temperature at 360 degrees F.
7. Press "Start/Pause" button to start.
8. When the unit beeps to show that it is preheated, open the lid.
9. Arrange the tofu cubes in greased "Air Fry Basket" and insert in the oven.
10. Flip the tofu cubes once halfway through.
11. Serve hot.

Nutritional Information per Serving:
Calories 241; Total Fat 15 g; Saturated Fat 2.5 g; Cholesterol 0 mg; Sodium 67 mg

Tofu with Orange Sauce

Preparation Time: 20 minutes; Cooking Time: 10 minutes; Servings: 4
Ingredients:
For Tofu
- 1 lb. extra-firm tofu, pressed and cubed
- 1 tablespoon cornstarch
- 1 tablespoon tamari

For Sauce
- ½ cup water
- 1/3 cup fresh orange juice
- 1 tablespoon honey
- 1 teaspoon orange zest, grated
- 1 teaspoon garlic, minced
- 1 teaspoon fresh ginger, minced
- 2 teaspoons cornstarch
- ¼ teaspoon red pepper flakes, crushed

Method:
1. In a bowl, add the tofu, cornstarch, and tamari and toss to coat well.
2. Set the tofu aside to marinate for at least 15 minutes.
3. Press "Power Button" of Air Fry Oven and turn the dial to select the "Air Fry" mode.
4. Press the Time button and again turn the dial to set the cooking time to 10 minutes.
5. Now push the Temp button and rotate the dial to set the temperature at 390 degrees F.
6. Press "Start/Pause" button to start.
7. When the unit beeps to show that it is preheated, open the lid.
8. Arrange the tofu cubes in greased "Air Fry Basket" and insert in the oven.
9. Flip the tofu cubes once halfway through.
10. Meanwhile, for the sauce: in a small pan, add all the ingredients over medium-high heat and bring to a boil, stirring continuously.
11. Transfer the tofu into a serving bowl with the sauce and gently stir to combine.
12. Serve immediately.

Nutritional Information per Serving:
Calories 147; Total Fat 6.7 g; Saturated Fat 0.6 g; Cholesterol 0 mg; Sodium 262 mg

Tofu with Capers

Preparation Time: 20 minutes; Cooking Time: 20 minutes; Servings: 4
Ingredients:
For Marinade
- ¼ cup fresh lemon juice
- 2 tablespoons fresh parsley
- 1 garlic clove, peeled

- Salt and ground black pepper, as required

For Tofu
- 1 (14-oz.) block extra-firm tofu, pressed and cut into 8 rectangular cutlets
- ½ cup mayonnaise
- 1 cup panko breadcrumbs

For Sauce
- 1 cup vegetable broth
- ¼ cup lemon juice
- 1 garlic clove, peeled
- 2 tablespoons fresh parsley
- 2 teaspoons cornstarch
- Salt and ground black pepper, as required
- 2 tablespoons capers

Method:
1. For marinade: in a food processor, add all the ingredients and pulse until smooth.
2. In a bowl, mix together the marinade and tofu.
3. Set aside for about 15-30 minutes.
4. In 2 shallow bowls, place the mayonnaise and panko breadcrumbs respectively.
5. Coat the tofu pieces with mayonnaise and then, roll into the panko.
6. Press "Power Button" of Air Fry Oven and turn the dial to select the "Air Fry" mode.
7. Press the Time button and again turn the dial to set the cooking time to 20 minutes.
8. Now push the Temp button and rotate the dial to set the temperature at 375 degrees F.
9. Press "Start/Pause" button to start.
10. When the unit beeps to show that it is preheated, open the lid.
11. Arrange the tofu cubes in greased "Air Fry Basket" and insert in the oven.
12. Flip the tofu cubes once halfway through.
13. Meanwhile, for the sauce: add broth, lemon juice, garlic, parsley, cornstarch, salt and black pepper in a food processor and pulse until smooth.
14. Transfer the sauce into a small pan and stir in the capers.
15. Place the pan over medium heat and bring to a boil.
16. Reduce the heat to low and simmer for about 5-7 minutes, stirring continuously.
17. Transfer the tofu cubes onto serving plates.
18. Top with the sauce and serve.

Nutritional Information per Serving:
Calories 327; Total Fat 18 g; Saturated Fat 3 g; Cholesterol 8 mg; Sodium 540 mg

Tofu in Sweet & Sour Sauce

Preparation Time: 20 minutes; Cooking Time: 20 minutes; Servings: 4
Ingredients:
For Tofu
- 1 (14-oz.) block firm tofu, pressed and cubed
- ½ cup arrowroot flour
- ½ teaspoon sesame oil

For Sauce
- 4 tablespoons low-sodium soy sauce
- 1½ tablespoons rice vinegar
- 1½ tablespoons chili sauce
- 1 tablespoon agave nectar
- 2 large garlic cloves, minced
- 1 teaspoon fresh ginger, peeled and grated
- 2 scallions (green part), chopped

Method:
1. In a bowl, mix together the tofu, arrowroot flour, and sesame oil.
2. Press "Power Button" of Air Fry Oven and turn the dial to select the "Air Fry" mode.
3. Press the Time button and again turn the dial to set the cooking time to 20 minutes.
4. Now push the Temp button and rotate the dial to set the temperature at 360 degrees F.
5. Press "Start/Pause" button to start.

6. When the unit beeps to show that it is preheated, open the lid.
7. Arrange the tofu cubes in greased "Air Fry Basket" and insert in the oven.
8. Flip the tofu cubes once halfway through.
9. Meanwhile, for the sauce: in a bowl, add all the ingredients except scallions and beat until well combined.
10. Transfer the tofu into a skillet with sauce over medium heat and cook for about 3 minutes, stirring occasionally.
11. Garnish with scallions and serve hot.

Nutritional Information per Serving:
Calories 115; Total Fat4.8 g; Saturated Fat 1 g; Cholesterol 0 mg; Sodium 1000 mg

Tofu with Cauliflower

Preparation Time: 15 minutes; Cooking Time: 15 minutes; Servings: 2

Ingredients:
- ½ (14-oz.) block firm tofu, pressed and cubed
- ½ small head cauliflower, cut into florets
- 1 tablespoon canola oil
- 1 tablespoon nutritional yeast
- ¼ teaspoon dried parsley
- 1 teaspoon ground turmeric
- ¼ teaspoon paprika
- Salt and ground black pepper, as required

Method:
1. In a bowl, mix together the tofu, cauliflower and the remaining ingredients.
2. Press "Power Button" of Air Fry Oven and turn the dial to select the "Air Fry" mode.
3. Press the Time button and again turn the dial to set the cooking time to 15 minutes.
4. Now push the Temp button and rotate the dial to set the temperature at 390 degrees F.
5. Press "Start/Pause" button to start.
6. When the unit beeps to show that it is preheated, open the lid.
7. Arrange the tofu mixture in greased "Air Fry Basket" and insert in the oven.
8. Flip the tofu mixture once halfway through.
9. Serve hot.

Nutritional Information per Serving:
Calories 170; Total Fat 11.6 g; Saturated Fat 1.5 g; Cholesterol 0 mg; Sodium 113 mg

Chapter 9: Breads Recipes

Soda Brad

Preparation Time: 15 minutes; Cooking Time: 30 minutes; Servings: 10
Ingredients:

- 3 cups whole-wheat flour
- 1 tablespoon sugar
- 2 teaspoon caraway seeds
- 1 teaspoon baking soda
- 1 teaspoon sea salt
- ¼ cup chilled butter, cubed into small pieces
- 1 large egg, beaten
- 1½ cups buttermilk

Method:

1. In a large bowl, mix together the flour, sugar, caraway seeds, baking soda and salt and mix well.
2. With a pastry cutter, cut in the butter flour until coarse crumbs like mixture is formed.
3. Make a well in the center of flour mixture.
4. In the well, add the egg, followed by the buttermilk and with a spatula, mix until well combined.
5. With floured hand, shape the dough into a ball.
6. Place the dough onto a floured surface and lightly knead it.
7. Shape the dough into a 6-inch ball.
8. With a serrated knife, score an X on the top of the dough.
9. Press "Power Button" of Air Fry Oven and turn the dial to select the "Air Crisp" mode.
10. Press the Time button and again turn the dial to set the cooking time to 30 minutes.
11. Now push the Temp button and rotate the dial to set the temperature at 350 degrees F.
12. Press "Start/Pause" button to start.
13. When the unit beeps to show that it is preheated, open the lid.
14. Arrange the dough in lightly greased "Air Fry Basket" and insert in the oven.
15. Place the pan onto a wire rack to cool for about 10 minutes.
16. Carefully, invert the bread onto wire rack to cool completely before slicing.
17. Cut the bread into desired-sized slices and serve.

Nutritional Information per Serving:
Calories 205; Total Fat 5.9 g; Saturated Fat 3.3 g; Cholesterol 32 mg; Sodium 392 mg

Baguette Bread

Preparation Time: 15 minutes; Cooking Time: 20 minutes; Servings: 8
Ingredients:

- ¾ cup warm water
- ¾ teaspoon quick yeast
- ½ teaspoon demerara sugar
- 1 cup bread flour
- ½ cup whole-wheat flour
- ½ cup oat flour
- 1¼ teaspoons salt

Method:

1. In a large bowl, place the water and sprinkle with yeast and sugar.
2. Set aside for 5 minutes or until foamy.
3. Add the bread flour and salt mix until a stiff dough forms.
4. Put the dough onto a floured surface and with your hands, knead until smooth and elastic.
5. Now, shape the dough into a ball.
6. Place the dough into a slightly oiled bowl and turn to coat well.
7. With a plastic wrap, cover the bowl and place in a warm place for about 1 hour or until doubled in size.

8. With your hands, punch down the dough and form into a long slender loaf.
9. Place the loaf onto a lightly greased baking sheet and set aside in warm place, uncovered, for about 30 minutes.
10. Press "Power Button" of Air Fry Oven and turn the dial to select the "Air Bake" mode.
11. Press the Time button and again turn the dial to set the cooking time to 20 minutes.
12. Now push the Temp button and rotate the dial to set the temperature at 450 degrees F.
13. Press "Start/Pause" button to start.
14. When the unit beeps to show that it is preheated, open the lid.
15. Carefully, arrange the dough onto the "Wire Rack" and insert in the oven.
16. Carefully, invert the bread onto wire rack to cool completely before slicing.
17. Cut the bread into desired-sized slices and serve.

Nutritional Information per Serving:
Calories 114; Total Fat 0.8 g; Saturated Fat 0.1 g; Cholesterol 0 mg; Sodium 366 mg

Yogurt Bread

Preparation Time: 20 minutes; Cooking Time: 40 minutes; Servings: 10
Ingredients:
- 1½ cups warm water, divided
- 1½ teaspoons active dry yeast
- 1 teaspoon sugar
- 3 cups all-purpose flour
- 1 cup plain Greek yogurt
- 2 teaspoons kosher salt

Method:
1. Add ½ cup of the warm water, yeast and sugar in the bowl of a stand mixer, fitted with the dough hook attachment and mix well.
2. Set aside for about 5 minutes.
3. Add the flour, yogurt, and salt and mix on medium-low speed until the dough comes together.
4. Then, mix on medium speed for 5 minutes.
5. Place the dough into a bowl.
6. With a plastic wrap, cover the bowl and place in a warm place for about 2-3 hours or until doubled in size.
7. Transfer the dough onto a lightly floured surface and shape into a smooth ball.
8. Place the dough onto a greased parchment paper-lined rack.
9. With a kitchen towel, cover the dough and let rest for 15 minutes.
10. With a very sharp knife, cut a 4x½-inch deep cut down the center of the dough.
11. Press "Power Button" of Air Fry Oven and turn the dial to select the "Air Roast" mode.
12. Press the Time button and again turn the dial to set the cooking time to 40 minutes.
13. Now push the Temp button and rotate the dial to set the temperature at 325 degrees F.
14. Press "Start/Pause" button to start.
15. When the unit beeps to show that it is preheated, open the lid.
16. Carefully, arrange the dough onto the "Wire Rack" and insert in the oven.
17. Carefully, invert the bread onto wire rack to cool completely before slicing.
18. Cut the bread into desired-sized slices and serve.

Nutritional Information per Serving:
Calories 157; Total Fat 0.7 g; Saturated Fat 0.3 g; Cholesterol 1 mg; Sodium 484 mg

Sunflower Seed Bread

Preparation Time: 15 minutes; Cooking Time: 18 minutes; Servings: 6
Ingredients:
- 2/3 cup whole-wheat flour
- 2/3 cup plain flour
- 1/3 cup sunflower seeds
- ½ sachet instant yeast

- 1 teaspoon salt
- 2/3-1 cup lukewarm water

Method:
1. In a bowl, mix together the flours, sunflower seeds, yeast, and salt.
2. Slowly, add in the water, stirring continuously until a soft dough ball forms.
3. Now, move the dough onto a lightly floured surface and knead for about 5 minutes using your hands.
4. Make a ball from the dough and place into a bowl.
5. With a plastic wrap, cover the bowl and place at a warm place for about 30 minutes.
6. Grease a cake pan.
7. Coat the top of dough with water and place into the prepared cake pan.
8. Press "Power Button" of Air Fry Oven and turn the dial to select the "Air Crisp" mode.
9. Press the Time button and again turn the dial to set the cooking time to 18 minutes.
10. Now push the Temp button and rotate the dial to set the temperature at 390 degrees F.
11. Press "Start/Pause" button to start.
12. When the unit beeps to show that it is preheated, open the lid.
13. Arrange the pan in "Air Fry Basket" and insert in the oven.
14. Place the pan onto a wire rack to cool for about 10 minutes.
15. Carefully, invert the bread onto wire rack to cool completely before slicing.
16. Cut the bread into desired-sized slices and serve.

Nutritional Information per Serving:
Calories 132; Total Fat 1.7 g; Saturated Fat 0.1 g; Cholesterol 0 mg; Sodium 390 mg

Date Bread

Preparation Time: 15 minutes; Cooking Time: 22 minutes; Servings: 10
Ingredients:
- 2½ cup dates, pitted and chopped
- ¼ cup butter
- 1 cup hot water
- 1½ cups flour
- ½ cup brown sugar
- 1 teaspoon baking powder
- 1 teaspoon baking soda
- ½ teaspoon salt
- 1 egg

Method:
1. In a large bowl, add the dates, butter and top with the hot water.
2. Set aside for about 5 minutes.
3. In another bowl, mix together the flour, brown sugar, baking powder, baking soda, and salt.
4. In the same bowl of dates, mix well the flour mixture, and egg.
5. Grease a baking pan.
6. Place the mixture into the prepared pan.
7. Press "Power Button" of Air Fry Oven and turn the dial to select the "Air Crisp" mode.
8. Press the Time button and again turn the dial to set the cooking time to 22 minutes.
9. Now push the Temp button and rotate the dial to set the temperature at 340 degrees F.
10. Press "Start/Pause" button to start.
11. When the unit beeps to show that it is preheated, open the lid.
12. Arrange the pan in "Air Fry Basket" and insert in the oven.
13. Place the pan onto a wire rack to cool for about 10 minutes.
14. Carefully, invert the bread onto wire rack to cool completely before slicing.
15. Cut the bread into desired-sized slices and serve.

Nutritional Information per Serving:
Calories 269; Total Fat 5.4 g; Saturated Fat 3.1 g; Cholesterol 29 mg; Sodium 285 mg

Date & Walnut Bread

Preparation Time: 15 minutes; Cooking Time: 35 minutes; Servings: 5
Ingredients:

- 1 cup dates, pitted and sliced
- ¾ cup walnuts, chopped
- 1 tablespoon instant coffee powder
- 1 tablespoon hot water
- 1¼ cups plain flour
- ¼ teaspoon salt
- ½ teaspoon baking powder
- ½ teaspoon baking soda
- ½ cup condensed milk
- ½ cup butter, softened
- ½ teaspoon vanilla essence

Method:

1. In a large bowl, add the dates, butter and top with the hot water.
2. Set aside for about 30 minutes.
3. Drain well and set aside.
4. In a small bowl, add the coffee powder and hot water and mix well.
5. In a large bowl, mix together the flour, baking powder, baking soda and salt.
6. In another large bowl, add the condensed milk and butter and beat until smooth.
7. Add the flour mixture, coffee mixture and vanilla essence and mix until well combined.
8. Fold in dates and ½ cup of walnut.
9. Line a baking pan with a lightly greased parchment paper.
10. Place the mixture into the prepared pan and sprinkle with the remainng walnuts.
11. Press "Power Button" of Air Fry Oven and turn the dial to select the "Air Crisp" mode.
12. Press the Time button and again turn the dial to set the cooking time to 35 minutes.
13. Now push the Temp button and rotate the dial to set the temperature at 320 degrees F.
14. Press "Start/Pause" button to start.
15. When the unit beeps to show that it is preheated, open the lid.
16. Arrange the pan in "Air Fry Basket" and insert in the oven.
17. Place the pan onto a wire rack to cool for about 10 minutes.
18. Carefully, invert the bread onto wire rack to cool completely before slicing.
19. Cut the bread into desired-sized slices and serve.

Nutritional Information per Serving:
  Calories 593; Total Fat 32.6 g; Saturated Fat 14 g; Cholesterol 59 mg; Sodium 414 mg

Brown Sugar Banana Bread

Preparation Time: 15 minutes; Cooking Time: 30 minutes; Servings: 4
Ingredients:

- 1 egg
- 1 ripe banana, peeled and mashed
- ¼ cup milk
- 2 tablespoons canola oil
- 2 tablespoons brown sugar
- ¾ cup plain flour
- ½ teaspoon baking soda

Method:

1. Line a very small baking pan with a greased parchment paper.
2. In a small bowl, add the egg and banana and beat well.
3. Add the milk, oil and sugar and beat until well combined.
4. Add the flour and baking soda and mix until just combined.
5. Place the mixture into prepared pan.
6. Press "Power Button" of Air Fry Oven and turn the dial to select the "Air Crisp" mode.
7. Press the Time button and again turn the dial to set the cooking time to 30 minutes.
8. Now push the Temp button and rotate the dial to set the temperature at 320 degrees F.
9. Press "Start/Pause" button to start.

10. When the unit beeps to show that it is preheated, open the lid.
11. Arrange the pan in "Air Fry Basket" and insert in the oven.
12. Place the pan onto a wire rack to cool for about 10 minutes.
13. Carefully, invert the bread onto wire rack to cool completely before slicing.
14. Cut the bread into desired-sized slices and serve.

Nutritional Information per Serving:
Calories 214; Total Fat 8.7 g; Saturated Fat 1.1 g; Cholesterol 42 mg; Sodium 183 mg

Cinnamon Banana Bread

Preparation Time: 15 minutes; Cooking Time: 20 minutes; Servings: 8
Ingredients:

- 1 1/3 cups flour
- 2/3 cup sugar
- 1 teaspoon baking soda
- 1 teaspoon baking powder
- 1 teaspoon ground cinnamon
- 1 teaspoon salt
- ½ cup milk
- ½ cup olive oil
- 3 bananas, peeled and sliced

Method:
1. In the bowl of a stand mixer, add all the ingredients and mix well.
2. Grease a loaf pan.
3. Place the mixture into the prepared pan.
4. Press "Power Button" of Air Fry Oven and turn the dial to select the "Air Crisp" mode.
5. Press the Time button and again turn the dial to set the cooking time to 20 minutes.
6. Now push the Temp button and rotate the dial to set the temperature at 330 degrees F.
7. Press "Start/Pause" button to start.
8. When the unit beeps to show that it is preheated, open the lid.
9. Arrange the pan in "Air Fry Basket" and insert in the oven.
10. Place the pan onto a wire rack to cool for about 10 minutes.
11. Carefully, invert the bread onto wire rack to cool completely before slicing.
12. Cut the bread into desired-sized slices and serve.

Nutritional Information per Serving:
Calories 295; Total Fat 13.3g; Saturated Fat 2.1 g; Cholesterol 1 mg; Sodium 458 mg

Banana & Walnut Bread

Preparation Time: 15 minutes; Cooking Time: 25 minutes; Servings: 10
Ingredients:

- 1½ cups self-rising flour
- ¼ teaspoon bicarbonate of soda
- 5 tablespoons plus 1 teaspoon butter
- 2/3 cup plus ½ tablespoon caster sugar
- 2 medium eggs
- 3½ oz. walnuts, chopped
- 2 cups bananas, peeled and mashed

Method:
1. In a bowl, mix together the flour and bicarbonate of soda.
2. In another bowl, add the butter, and sugar and beat until pale and fluffy.
3. Add the eggs, one at a time along with a little flour and mix well.
4. Stir in the remaining flour and walnuts.
5. Add the bananas and mix until well combined.
6. Grease a loaf pan.
7. Place the mixture into the prepared pan.
8. Press "Power Button" of Air Fry Oven and turn the dial to select the "Air Crisp" mode.
9. Press the Time button and again turn the dial to set the cooking time to 10 minutes.

10. Now push the Temp button and rotate the dial to set the temperature at 355 degrees F.
11. Press "Start/Pause" button to start.
12. When the unit beeps to show that it is preheated, open the lid.
13. Arrange the pan in "Air Fry Basket" and insert in the oven.
14. After 10 minutes of cooking, set the temperature at 338 degrees F for 15minutes.
15. Place the pan onto a wire rack to cool for about 10 minutes.
16. Carefully, invert the bread onto wire rack to cool completely before slicing.
17. Cut the bread into desired-sized slices and serve.

Nutritional Information per Serving:
Calories 270; Total Fat 12.8 g; Saturated Fat 4.3 g; Cholesterol 48 mg; Sodium 87 mg

Banana & Raisin Bread

Preparation Time: 15 minutes; Cooking Time: 40 minutes; Servings: 6
Ingredients:
- 1½ cups cake flour
- 1 teaspoon baking soda
- ½ teaspoon ground cinnamon
- Salt, to taste
- ½ cup vegetable oil
- 2 eggs
- ½ cup sugar
- ½ teaspoon vanilla extract
- 3 medium bananas, peeled and mashed
- ½ cup raisins, chopped finely

Method:
1. In a large bowl, mix together the flour, baking soda, cinnamon, and salt.
2. In another bowl, beat well eggs and oil.
3. Add the sugar, vanilla extract, and bananas and beat until well combined.
4. Add the flour mixture and stir until just combined.
5. Place the mixture into a lightly greased baking pan and sprinkle with raisins.
6. With a piece of foil, cover the pan loosely.
7. Press "Power Button" of Air Fry Oven and turn the dial to select the "Air Bake" mode.
8. Press the Time button and again turn the dial to set the cooking time to 30 minutes.
9. Now push the Temp button and rotate the dial to set the temperature at 300 degrees F.
10. Press "Start/Pause" button to start.
11. When the unit beeps to show that it is preheated, open the lid.
12. Arrange the pan in "Air Fry Basket" and insert in the oven.
13. After 30 minutes of cooking, set the temperature to 285 degrees F for 10 minutes.
14. Place the pan onto a wire rack to cool for about 10 minutes.
15. Carefully, invert the bread onto wire rack to cool completely before slicing.
16. Cut the bread into desired-sized slices and serve.

Nutritional Information per Serving:
Calories 448; Total Fat 20.2 g; Saturated Fat 4.1 g; Cholesterol 55 mg; Sodium 261 mg

3-Ingredients Banana Bread

Preparation Time: 10 minutes; Cooking Time: 20 minutes; Servings: 6
Ingredients:
- 2 (6.4-oz.) banana muffin mix
- 1 cup water
- 1 ripe banana, peeled and mashed

Method:
1. In a bowl, add all the ingredients and with a whisk, mix until well combined.
2. Place the mixture into a lightly greased loaf pan.
3. Press "Power Button" of Air Fry Oven and turn the dial to select the "Air Bake" mode.
4. Press the Time button and again turn the dial to set the cooking time to 20 minutes.

5. Now push the Temp button and rotate the dial to set the temperature at 360 degrees F.
6. Press "Start/Pause" button to start.
7. When the unit beeps to show that it is preheated, open the lid.
8. Arrange the pan in "Air Fry Basket" and insert in the oven.
9. Place the pan onto a wire rack to cool for about 10 minutes.
10. Carefully, invert the bread onto wire rack to cool completely before slicing.
11. Cut the bread into desired-sized slices and serve.

Nutritional Information per Serving:
   Calories 144; Total Fat 3.8 g; Saturated Fat 1.7 g; Cholesterol 4 mg; Sodium 262 mg

Yogurt Banana Bread

Preparation Time: 15 minutes; Cooking Time: 28 minutes; Servings: 5

Ingredients:
- 1 medium very ripe banana, peeled and mashed
- 1 large egg
- 1 tablespoon canola oil
- 1 tablespoon plain Greek yogurt
- ¼ teaspoon pure vanilla extract
- ½ cup all-purpose flour
- ¼ cup granulated white sugar
- ¼ teaspoon ground cinnamon
- ¼ teaspoon baking soda
- 1/8 teaspoon sea salt

Method:
1. In a bowl, add the mashed banana, egg, oil, yogurt and vanilla and beat until well combined.
2. Add the flour, sugar, baking soda, cinnamon and salt and mix until just combined.
3. Place the mixture into a lightly greased mini loaf pan.
4. Press "Power Button" of Air Fry Oven and turn the dial to select the "Air Bake" mode.
5. Press the Time button and again turn the dial to set the cooking time to 28 minutes.
6. Now push the Temp button and rotate the dial to set the temperature at 350 degrees F.
7. Press "Start/Pause" button to start.
8. When the unit beeps to show that it is preheated, open the lid.
9. Arrange the pan in "Air Fry Basket" and insert in the oven.
10. Place the pan onto a wire rack to cool for about 10 minutes.
11. Carefully, invert the bread onto wire rack to cool completely before slicing.
12. Cut the bread into desired-sized slices and serve.

Nutritional Information per Serving:
   Calories 145; Total Fat 4 g; Saturated Fat 0.6 g; Cholesterol 37mg; Sodium 126 mg

Sour Cream Banana Bread

Preparation Time: 15 minutes; Cooking Time: 37 minutes; Servings: 8

Ingredients:
- ¾ cup all-purpose flour
- ¼ teaspoon baking soda
- ¼ teaspoon salt
- 2 ripe bananas, peeled and mashed
- ½ cup granulated sugar
- ¼ cup sour cream
- ¼ cup vegetable oil
- 1 large egg
- ½ teaspoon pure vanilla extract

Method:
1. In a large bowl, mix together the flour, baking soda and salt.
2. In another bowl, add the bananas, egg, sugar, sour cream, oil and vanilla and beat until well combined.
3. Add the flour mixture and mix until just combined.
4. Place the mixture into a lightly greased pan.

5. Press "Power Button" of Air Fry Oven and turn the dial to select the "Air Crisp" mode.
6. Press the Time button and again turn the dial to set the cooking time to 37 minutes.
7. Now push the Temp button and rotate the dial to set the temperature at 310 degrees F.
8. Press "Start/Pause" button to start.
9. When the unit beeps to show that it is preheated, open the lid.
10. Arrange the pan in "Air Fry Basket" and insert in the oven.
11. Place the pan onto a wire rack to cool for about 10 minutes.
12. Carefully, invert the bread onto wire rack to cool completely before slicing.
13. Cut the bread into desired-sized slices and serve.

Nutritional Information per Serving:
Calories 201; Total Fat 9.2 g; Saturated Fat 2.5 g; Cholesterol 26 mg; Sodium 125 mg

Peanut Butter Banana Bread

Preparation Time: 15 minutes; Cooking Time: 40 minutes; Servings: 6
Ingredients:

- 1 cup plus 1 tablespoon all-purpose flour
- ¼ teaspoon baking soda
- 1 teaspoon baking powder
- ¼ teaspoon salt
- 1 large egg
- 1/3 cup granulated sugar
- ¼ cup canola oil
- 2 tablespoons creamy peanut butter
- 2 tablespoons sour cream
- 1 teaspoon vanilla extract
- 2 medium ripe bananas, peeled and mashed
- ¾ cup walnuts, roughly chopped

Method:
1. In a bowl and mix together the flour, baking powder, baking soda, and salt.
2. In another large bowl, add the egg, sugar, oil, peanut butter, sour cream, and vanilla extract and beat until well combined.
3. Add the bananas and beat until well combined.
4. Add the flour mixture and mix until just combined.
5. Gently, fold in the walnuts.
6. Place the mixture into a lightly greased pan.
7. Press "Power Button" of Air Fry Oven and turn the dial to select the "Air Crisp" mode.
8. Press the Time button and again turn the dial to set the cooking time to 40 minutes.
9. Now push the Temp button and rotate the dial to set the temperature at 330 degrees F.
10. Press "Start/Pause" button to start.
11. When the unit beeps to show that it is preheated, open the lid.
12. Arrange the pan in "Air Fry Basket" and insert in the oven.
13. Place the pan onto a wire rack to cool for about 10 minutes.
14. Carefully, invert the bread onto wire rack to cool completely before slicing.
15. Cut the bread into desired-sized slices and serve.

Nutritional Information per Serving:
Calories 384; Total Fat 23 g; Saturated Fat 2.6 g; Cholesterol 33 mg; Sodium 189 mg

Chocolate Banana Bread

Preparation Time: 15 minutes; Cooking Time: 20 minutes; Servings: 8
Ingredients:

- 2 cups flour
- ½ teaspoon baking soda
- ½ teaspoon baking powder
- ½ teaspoon salt
- ¾ cup sugar
- 1/3 cup butter, softened
- 3 eggs
- 1 tablespoon vanilla extract
- 1 cup milk
- ½ cup bananas, peeled and mashed

- 1 cup chocolate chips

Method:
1. In a bowl, mix together the flour, baking soda, baking powder, and salt.
2. In another large bowl, add the butter, and sugar and beat until light and fluffy.
3. Add the eggs, and vanilla extract and whisk until well combined.
4. Add the flour mixture and mix until well combined.
5. Add the milk, and mashed bananas and mix well.
6. Gently, fold in the chocolate chips.
7. Place the mixture into a lightly greased loaf pan.
8. Press "Power Button" of Air Fry Oven and turn the dial to select the "Air Crisp" mode.
9. Press the Time button and again turn the dial to set the cooking time to 20 minutes.
10. Now push the Temp button and rotate the dial to set the temperature at 360 degrees F.
11. Press "Start/Pause" button to start.
12. When the unit beeps to show that it is preheated, open the lid.
13. Arrange the pan in "Air Fry Basket" and insert in the oven.
14. Place the pan onto a wire rack to cool for about 10 minutes.
15. Carefully, invert the bread onto wire rack to cool completely before slicing.
16. Cut the bread into desired-sized slices and serve.

Nutritional Information per Serving:
Calories 416; Total Fat 16.5 g; Saturated Fat 10.2 g; Cholesterol 89 mg; Sodium 336 mg

Walnut Zucchini Bread

Preparation Time: 15 minutes; Cooking Time: 20 minutes; Servings: 8

Ingredients:
- 1½ cups all-purpose flour
- ½ teaspoon baking soda
- ½ teaspoon baking powder
- ½ tablespoon ground cinnamon
- ½ teaspoon salt
- 2¼ cups white sugar
- ½ cup vegetable oil
- 1½ eggs
- 1½ teaspoons vanilla extract
- 1 cup zucchini, grated
- ½ cup walnuts, chopped

Method:
1. In a bowl and mix together the flour, baking powder, baking soda, cinnamon, and salt.
2. In another large bowl, add the sugar, oil, eggs, and vanilla extract and whisk until well combined.
3. Add the flour mixture and mix until just combined.
4. Gently, fold in the zucchini and walnuts.
5. Place the mixture into a lightly greased loaf pan.
6. Press "Power Button" of Air Fry Oven and turn the dial to select the "Air Crisp" mode.
7. Press the Time button and again turn the dial to set the cooking time to 20 minutes.
8. Now push the Temp button and rotate the dial to set the temperature at 320 degrees F.
9. Press "Start/Pause" button to start.
10. When the unit beeps to show that it is preheated, open the lid.
11. Arrange the pan in "Air Fry Basket" and insert in the oven.
12. Place the pan onto a wire rack to cool for about 10 minutes.
13. Carefully, invert the bread onto wire rack to cool completely before slicing.
14. Cut the bread into desired-sized slices and serve.

Nutritional Information per Serving:
Calories 483; Total Fat 19.3 g; Saturated Fat 3.2 g; Cholesterol 31mg; Sodium 241 mg

Carrot Bread

Preparation Time: 15 minutes; Cooking Time: 30 minutes; Servings: 6
Ingredients:

- 1 cup all-purpose flour
- 1 teaspoon baking soda
- ½ teaspoon ground cinnamon
- ¼ teaspoon ground cloves
- ¼ teaspoon ground nutmeg
- ½ teaspoon salt
- 2 large eggs
- ¾ cup vegetable oil
- 1/3 cup white sugar
- 1/3 cup light brown sugar
- ½ teaspoon vanilla extract
- 1½ cups carrots, peeled and grated

Method:
1. In a bowl, mix together the flour, baking soda, spices and salt.
2. In a large bowl, add the eggs, oil, sugars and vanilla extract and beat until well combined.
3. Add the flour mixture and mix until just combined.
4. Fold in the carrots.
5. Place the mixture into a lightly greased baking pan.
6. Press "Power Button" of Air Fry Oven and turn the dial to select the "Air Crisp" mode.
7. Press the Time button and again turn the dial to set the cooking time to 30 minutes.
8. Now push the Temp button and rotate the dial to set the temperature at 320 degrees F.
9. Press "Start/Pause" button to start.
10. When the unit beeps to show that it is preheated, open the lid.
11. Arrange the pan in "Air Fry Basket" and insert in the oven.
12. Place the pan onto a wire rack to cool for about 10 minutes.
13. Carefully, invert the bread onto wire rack to cool completely before slicing.
14. Cut the bread into desired-sized slices and serve.

Nutritional Information per Serving:
Calories 426; Total Fat 29.2 g; Saturated Fat 5.9 g; Cholesterol 62 mg; Sodium 450 mg

Carrot, Raisin & Walnut Bread

Preparation Time: 15 minutes; Cooking Time: 35 minutes; Servings: 8
Ingredients:

- 2 cups all-purpose flour
- 1½ teaspoons ground cinnamon
- 2 teaspoons baking soda
- ½ teaspoon salt
- 3 eggs
- ½ cup sunflower oil
- ½ cup applesauce
- ¼ cup honey
- ¼ cup plain yogurt
- 2 teaspoons vanilla essence
- 2½ cups carrots, peeled and shredded
- ½ cup raisins
- ½ cup walnuts

Method:
1. Line the bottom of a greased baking pan with parchment paper.
2. In a medium bowl, sift together the flour, baking soda, cinnamon and salt.
3. In a large bowl, add the eggs, oil, applesauce, honey and yogurt and with a hand-held mixer, mix on medium speed until well combined.
4. Add the eggs, one at a time and whisk well.
5. Add the vanilla and mix well.
6. Add the flour mixture and mix until just combined.
7. Fold in the carrots, raisins and walnuts.
8. Place the mixture into a lightly greased baking pan.
9. With a piece of foil, cover the pan loosely.
10. Press "Power Button" of Air Fry Oven and turn the dial to select the "Air Crisp" mode.

11. Press the Time button and again turn the dial to set the cooking time to 30 minutes.
12. Now push the Temp button and rotate the dial to set the temperature at 347 degrees F.
13. Press "Start/Pause" button to start.
14. When the unit beeps to show that it is preheated, open the lid.
15. Arrange the pan in "Air Fry Basket" and insert in the oven.
16. After 25 minutes of cooking, remove the foil.
17. Place the pan onto a wire rack to cool for about 10 minutes.
18. Carefully, invert the bread onto wire rack to cool completely before slicing.
19. Cut the bread into desired-sized slices and serve.

Nutritional Information per Serving:
Calories 441; Total Fat 20.3 g; Saturated Fat 2.2 g; Cholesterol 62mg; Sodium 592 mg

Pumpkin Bread

Preparation Time: 15 minutes; Cooking Time: 40 minutes; Servings: 10
Ingredients:

- 1 1/3 cups all-purpose flour
- 1 cup sugar
- ¾ teaspoon baking soda
- 1 teaspoon pumpkin pie spice
- 1/3 teaspoon ground cinnamon
- ¼ teaspoon salt
- 2 eggs
- ½ cup pumpkin puree
- 1/3 cup vegetable oil
- ¼ cup water

Method:
1. In a bowl, mix together the flour, sugar, baking soda, spices and salt
2. In another large bowl, add the eggs, pumpkin, oil and water and beat until well combined.
3. In a large mixing bowl or stand mixer.
4. Add the flour mixture and mix until just combined.
5. Place the mixture into a lightly greased loaf pan.
6. With a piece of foil, cover the pan loosely.
7. Press "Power Button" of Air Fry Oven and turn the dial to select the "Air Bake" mode.
8. Press the Time button and again turn the dial to set the cooking time to 40 minutes.
9. Now push the Temp button and rotate the dial to set the temperature at 325 degrees F.
10. Press "Start/Pause" button to start.
11. When the unit beeps to show that it is preheated, open the lid.
12. Arrange the pan in "Air Fry Basket" and insert in the oven.
13. After 25 minutes of cooking, remove the foil.
14. Place the pan onto a wire rack to cool for about 10 minutes.
15. Carefully, invert the bread onto wire rack to cool completely before slicing.
16. Cut the bread into desired-sized slices and serve.

Nutritional Information per Serving:
Calories 217; Total Fat 8.4 g; Saturated Fat 1.4 g; Cholesterol 33 mg; Sodium 167 mg

Yogurt Pumpkin Bread

Preparation Time: 10 minutes; Cooking Time: 15 minutes; Servings: 4
Ingredients:

- 2 large eggs
- 8 tablespoons pumpkin puree
- 6 tablespoons banana flour
- 4 tablespoons honey
- 4 tablespoons plain Greek yogurt
- 2 tablespoons vanilla essence
- Pinch of ground nutmeg
- 6 tablespoons oats

Method:
1. In a bowl, add in all the ingredients except oats and with a hand mixer, mix until smooth.

2. Add the oats and with a fork, mix well.
3. Grease and flour a loaf pan.
4. Place the mixture into the prepared loaf pan.
5. Press "Power Button" of Air Fry Oven and turn the dial to select the "Air Crisp" mode.
6. Press the Time button and again turn the dial to set the cooking time to 15 minutes.
7. Now push the Temp button and rotate the dial to set the temperature at 360 degrees F.
8. Press "Start/Pause" button to start.
9. When the unit beeps to show that it is preheated, open the lid.
10. Arrange the pan in "Air Fry Basket" and insert in the oven.
11. Carefully, invert the bread onto wire rack to cool completely before slicing.
12. Cut the bread into desired-sized slices and serve.

Nutritional Information per Serving:
Calories 232; Total Fat 8.33 g; Saturated Fat 1.5 g; Cholesterol 94 mg; Sodium 53 mg

Sugar-Free Pumpkin Bread

Preparation Time: 15 minutes; Cooking Time: 25 minutes; Servings: 4
Ingredients:
- ¼ cup coconut flour
- 2 tablespoons stevia blend
- 1 teaspoon baking powder
- ¾ teaspoon pumpkin pie spice
- ¼ teaspoon ground cinnamon
- 1/8 teaspoon salt
- ¼ cup canned pumpkin
- 2 large eggs
- 2 tablespoons unsweetened almond milk
- 1 teaspoon vanilla extract

Method:
1. In a bowl, add the flour, stevia blend, baking powder, spices and salt and mix well.
2. In another large bowl, add the pumpkin, eggs, almond milk, and vanilla extract and beat until well combined.
3. Add the flour mixture and mix until just combined.
4. Line a baking pan with greased parchment paper
5. Place the mixture into the prepared pan evenly.
6. Press "Power Button" of Air Fry Oven and turn the dial to select the "Air Crisp" mode.
7. Press the Time button and again turn the dial to set the cooking time to 25 minutes.
8. Now push the Temp button and rotate the dial to set the temperature at 350 degrees F.
9. Press "Start/Pause" button to start.
10. When the unit beeps to show that it is preheated, open the lid.
11. Carefully, invert the bread onto wire rack to cool completely before slicing.
12. Cut the bread into desired-sized slices and serve.

Nutritional Information per Serving:
Calories 52; Total Fat 2.8 g; Saturated Fat 1 g; Cholesterol 93 mg; Sodium 118 mg

Apple Bread

Preparation Time: 15 minutes; Cooking Time: 45 minutes; Servings: 6
Ingredients:
- 1 cup all-purpose flour
- 1/3 cup brown sugar
- 1 teaspoon ground nutmeg
- 1 teaspoon ground cinnamon
- ½ teaspoon baking soda
- Salt, to taste
- 1 egg
- 5 tablespoons plus 1 teaspoon vegetable oil
- ¾ teaspoon vanilla extract
- 2 cups apples, peeled, cored and chopped

Method:

1. In a bowl, mix together the flour, sugar, spices, baking soda, and salt.
2. In another bowl, add the egg, and oil and whisk until smooth.
3. Add the vanilla extract and whisk well.
4. Slowly, add the flour mixture, whisking continuously until well combined.
5. Fold in the chopped apples.
6. Lightly, grease a cake pan.
7. Place mixture evenly into the prepared cake pan.
8. With a piece of foil, cover the pan and poke some holes using a fork.
9. Press "Power Button" of Air Fry Oven and turn the dial to select the "Air Fry" mode.
10. Press the Time button and again turn the dial to set the cooking time to 45 minutes.
11. Now push the Temp button and rotate the dial to set the temperature at 330 degrees F.
12. Press "Start/Pause" button to start.
13. When the unit beeps to show that it is preheated, open the lid.
14. Arrange the pan in "Air Fry Basket" and insert in the oven.
15. After 40 minutes of cooking, remove the foil piece from pan.
16. Place the pan onto a wire rack for about 10-15 minutes.
17. Carefully, invert the bread onto wire rack to cool completely before slicing.
18. Cut the bread into desired-sized slices and serve.

Nutritional Information per Serving:
Calories 260; Total Fat 12.5 g; Saturated Fat 2.6 g; Cholesterol 27 mg; Sodium 145 mg

Strawberry Bread

Preparation Time: 15 minutes; Cooking Time: 30 minutes; Servings: 8
Ingredients:
- 2½ cups all-purpose flour
- 1 cup sugar
- 3 teaspoons baking powder
- 1 teaspoon salt
- 1 large egg
- 1 cup whole milk
- 3 tablespoons vegetable oil
- 1 teaspoon vanilla extract
- 1½ cups fresh strawberries, hulled and sliced

Method:
1. In a bowl, mix together the flour, sugar, baking powder and salt.
2. In another bowl, add the egg, milk, oil and vanilla and beat until well combined.
3. Add the flour mixture and mix until well combined.
4. Fold in the strawberry slices.
5. Place the mixture into a lightly greased baking pan evenly.
6. Press "Power Button" of Air Fry Oven and turn the dial to select the "Air Crisp" mode.
7. Press the Time button and again turn the dial to set the cooking time to 30 minutes.
8. Now push the Temp button and rotate the dial to set the temperature at 310 degrees F.
9. Press "Start/Pause" button to start.
10. When the unit beeps to show that it is preheated, open the lid.
11. Arrange the pan in "Air Fry Basket" and insert in the oven.
12. Place the pan onto a wire rack for about 10-15 minutes.
13. Carefully, invert the bread onto wire rack to cool completely before slicing.
14. Cut the bread into desired-sized slices and serve.

Nutritional Information per Serving:
Calories 320; Total Fat 7.2 g; Saturated Fat 1.9 g; Cholesterol 26 mg; Sodium 314 mg

Cranberry Bread

Preparation Time: 15 minutes; Cooking Time: 30 minutes; Servings: 10
Ingredients:

- 3 cups flour
- 1 2/3 cups sugar
- 2/3 cup vegetable oil
- ½ cup milk
- 1 teaspoon vanilla extract
- 4 eggs
- 3 teaspoons baking powder
- 2 cups fresh cranberries

Method:

1. In a large bowl, add all the ingredients except for cranberries and mix until well combined.
2. Gently, fold in the cranberries.
3. Place the mixture into a lightly greased baking pan evenly.
4. Press "Power Button" of Air Fry Oven and turn the dial to select the "Air Crisp" mode.
5. Press the Time button and again turn the dial to set the cooking time to 30 minutes.
6. Now push the Temp button and rotate the dial to set the temperature at 320 degrees F.
7. Press "Start/Pause" button to start.
8. When the unit beeps to show that it is preheated, open the lid.
9. Arrange the pan in "Air Fry Basket" and insert in the oven.
10. Place the pan onto a wire rack for about 10-15 minutes.
11. Carefully, invert the bread onto wire rack to cool completely before slicing.
12. Cut the bread into desired-sized slices and serve.

Nutritional Information per Serving:
Calories 436; Total Fat 16.9 g; Saturated Fat 3.6 g; Cholesterol 66 mg; Sodium 33mg

Cranberry Orange Bread

Preparation Time: 15 minutes; Cooking Time: 30 minutes; Servings: 8

Ingredients:

- 2 cups flour
- ¾ cup sugar
- 1½ teaspoons baking powder
- ½ teaspoon baking soda
- 1 teaspoon salt
- 1 large egg
- ¼ cup butter
- ¾ cup fresh orange juice
- 1 cup cranberries

Method:

1. In a large bowl, mix together the flour, sugar, baking powder, baking powder and salt.
2. Add the eggs, butter and orange juice and mix until well combined.
3. Gently, fold in the cranberries.
4. Place the mixture into a lightly greased loaf pan evenly.
5. Press "Power Button" of Air Fry Oven and turn the dial to select the "Air Crisp" mode.
6. Press the Time button and again turn the dial to set the cooking time to 30 minutes.
7. Now push the Temp button and rotate the dial to set the temperature at 310 degrees F.
8. Press "Start/Pause" button to start.
9. When the unit beeps to show that it is preheated, open the lid.
10. Arrange the pan in "Air Fry Basket" and insert in the oven.
11. Place the pan onto a wire rack for about 10-15 minutes.
12. Carefully, invert the bread onto wire rack to cool completely before slicing.
13. Cut the bread into desired-sized slices and serve.

Nutritional Information per Serving:
Calories 263; Total Fat 6.7 g; Saturated Fat 3.9 g; Cholesterol 38 mg; Sodium 421 mg

Lemon Bread

Preparation Time: 15 minutes; Cooking Time: 30 minutes; Servings: 10

Ingredients:

- 3 cups all-purpose flour
- 3 tablespoons poppy seeds

- 1½ teaspoon baking powder
- 1 teaspoon salt
- 3 eggs
- 2 cups sugar
- 1½ cups milk
- 1 cup vegetable oil
- 2 teaspoons fresh lemon juice
- 1 teaspoon pure vanilla extract
- 2 tablespoons lemon zest, grated

Method:
1. In a large bowl, mix together the flour, poppy seeds, baking powder and salt.
2. In another bowl, add the eggs, sugar, milk, oil, lemon juice, and vanilla extract and beat until well combined.
3. Add the flour mixture and mix until just combined.
4. Gently, fold in the lemon zest.
5. Place the mixture into a lightly greased baking pan evenly.
6. Press "Power Button" of Air Fry Oven and turn the dial to select the "Air Crisp" mode.
7. Press the Time button and again turn the dial to set the cooking time to 30 minutes.
8. Now push the Temp button and rotate the dial to set the temperature at 310 degrees F.
9. Press "Start/Pause" button to start.
10. When the unit beeps to show that it is preheated, open the lid.
11. Arrange the pan in "Air Fry Basket" and insert in the oven.
12. Place the pan onto a wire rack for about 10-15 minutes.
13. Carefully, invert the bread onto wire rack to cool completely before slicing.
14. Cut the bread into desired-sized slices and serve.

Nutritional Information per Serving:
Calories 533; Total Fat 25.4 g; Saturated Fat 5.3 g; Cholesterol 52 mg; Sodium 271 mg

Buttermilk Cornbread

Preparation Time: 15 minutes; Cooking Time: 25 minutes; Servings: 8
Ingredients:
- 1 cup cornmeal
- ¾ cup all-purpose flour
- 1 tablespoon sugar
- 1½ teaspoons baking powder
- ½ teaspoon baking soda
- ¼ teaspoon salt
- 1½ cups buttermilk
- 6 tablespoons unsalted butter, melted
- 2 large eggs, lightly beaten

Method:
1. In a bowl, add the flour, cornmeal, sugar, baking soda, baking powder, and salt.
2. In another bowl, add the buttermilk, butter, and eggs and mix well.
3. Add the flour mixture and mix until just combined.
4. Place the mixture into a greased baking pan evenly.
5. Press "Power Button" of Air Fry Oven and turn the dial to select the "Air Crisp" mode.
6. Press the Time button and again turn the dial to set the cooking time to 25 minutes.
7. Now push the Temp button and rotate the dial to set the temperature at 360 degrees F.
8. Press "Start/Pause" button to start.
9. When the unit beeps to show that it is preheated, open the lid.
10. Arrange the pan in "Air Fry Basket" and insert in the oven.
11. Place the pan onto a wire rack for about 10-15 minutes.
12. Carefully, invert the bread onto wire rack to cool completely before serving.
13. Cut the bread into desired-sized pieces and serve.

Nutritional Information per Serving:
Calories 217; Total Fat 10.9 g; Saturated Fat 6.12 g; Cholesterol 171 mg; Sodium 286 mg

Oatmeal Cornbread

Preparation Time: 15 minutes; Cooking Time: 20 minutes; Servings: 10

Ingredients:

- 1½ cups old-fashioned oatmeal
- 1 cup yellow cornmeal
- ¼ cup granulated sugar
- 2 teaspoons baking powder
- ¼ teaspoon salt
- 1 large egg
- 1 cup soy milk
- ½ cup unsweetened applesauce

Method:

1. In a food processor, add the oatmeal and pulse until powdered.
2. Transfer the oatmeal powder into a bowl with the cornmeal, sugar, baking powder and salt and mix well.
3. Add the egg, soy milk and applesauce and mix until well combined.
4. Place the mixture into a greased baking pan evenly.
5. Press "Power Button" of Air Fry Oven and turn the dial to select the "Air Bake" mode.
6. Press the Time button and again turn the dial to set the cooking time to 20 minutes.
7. Now push the Temp button and rotate the dial to set the temperature at 400 degrees F.
8. Press "Start/Pause" button to start.
9. When the unit beeps to show that it is preheated, open the lid.
10. Arrange the pan in "Air Fry Basket" and insert in the oven.
11. Place the pan onto a wire rack for about 10-15 minutes.
12. Carefully, invert the bread onto wire rack to cool completely before serving.
13. Cut the bread into desired-sized pieces and serve.

Nutritional Information per Serving:

Calories 136; Total Fat 2.2 g; Saturated Fat 0.4 g; Cholesterol 19 mg; Sodium 84 mg

Pineapple Cornbread

Preparation Time: 10 minutes; Cooking Time: 15 minutes; Servings: 5

Ingredients:

- 1 (8½-oz.) package Jiffy corn muffin
- 7 oz. canned crushed pineapple
- 1/3 cup canned pineapple juice
- 1 egg

Method:

1. In a bowl, mix together all the ingredients.
2. Place the mixture into the round cake pan.
3. Press "Power Button" of Air Fry Oven and turn the dial to select the "Air Fry" mode.
4. Press the Time button and again turn the dial to set the cooking time to 15 minutes.
5. Now push the Temp button and rotate the dial to set the temperature at 330 degrees F.
6. Press "Start/Pause" button to start.
7. When the unit beeps to show that it is preheated, open the lid.
8. Arrange the pan in "Air Fry Basket" and insert in the oven.
9. Place the pan onto a wire rack for about 10-15 minutes.
10. Carefully, invert the bread onto a wire rack to cool completely before serving.
11. Cut the bread into desired-sized pieces and serve.

Nutritional Information per Serving:

Calories 222; Total Fat 6.4 g; Saturated Fat 2.7 g; Cholesterol 39 mg; Sodium 424 mg

Mini Rosemary Cornbread

Preparation Time: 15 minutes; Cooking Time: 25 minutes; Servings: 6

Ingredients:

- ¾ cup fine yellow cornmeal
- ½ cup sorghum flour

- ¼ cup tapioca starch
- ½ teaspoon xanthan gum
- 2 teaspoons baking powder
- ¼ cup granulated sugar
- ¼ teaspoon salt
- 1 cup plain almond milk
- 3 tablespoons olive oil
- 2 teaspoons fresh rosemary, minced

Method:
1. In a large bowl, mix together the flour, cornmeal, starch, sugar, xanthan gum, baking powder, and salt.
2. Add the almond milk, oil, and rosemary. Mix until well combined.
3. Put the mixture into 4 greased ramekins evenly.
4. Press "Power Button" of Air Fry Oven and turn the dial to select the "Air Fry" mode.
5. Press the Time button and again turn the dial to set the cooking time to 25 minutes.
6. Now push the Temp button and rotate the dial to set the temperature at 400 degrees F.
7. Press "Start/Pause" button to start.
8. When the unit beeps to show that it is preheated, open the lid.
9. Arrange the pan in "Air Fry Basket" and insert in the oven.
10. Place the ramekins onto a wire rack for about 10-15 minutes.
11. Carefully, invert the breads onto a wire rack to cool completely before serving.

Nutritional Information per Serving:
Calories 220; Total Fat 8.5 g; Saturated Fat 1.1 g; Cholesterol 0 mg; Sodium 135 mg

Monkey Bread

Preparation Time: 15 minutes; Cooking Time: 7 minutes; Servings: 8

Ingredients:
- 1 cup fat-free Greek yogurt
- 1 cup self-rising flour
- 1 teaspoon of sugar
- ½ teaspoon ground cinnamon
- 2 tablespoons butter, melted

Method:
1. In a bowl, add the yogurt and flour and mix until a dough comes together.
2. Shape the dough into a ball.
3. Shape the dough ball into a flattened circle.
4. Cut the dough circle into 8 wedges and then, roll each into a ball.
5. In a plastic Ziploc bag, add the sugar, cinnamon and dough balls.
6. Seal the bag and shake well to coat evenly.
7. Arrange the dough balls in a greased loaf an.
8. Drizzle the dough balls with butter.
9. Press "Power Button" of Air Fry Oven and turn the dial to select the "Air Fry" mode.
10. Press the Time button and again turn the dial to set the cooking time to 7 minutes.
11. Now push the Temp button and rotate the dial to set the temperature at 375 degrees F.
12. Press "Start/Pause" button to start.
13. When the unit beeps to show that it is preheated, open the lid.
14. Arrange the pan in "Air Fry Basket" and insert in the oven.
15. Place the pan onto a wire rack for about 5 minutes before serving.

Nutritional Information per Serving:
Calories 106; Total Fat 3.4 g; Saturated Fat 2.2 g; Cholesterol 9 mg; Sodium 42 mg

Apple Pull Apart bread

Preparation Time: 25 minutes; Cooking Time: 15 minutes; Servings: 4
Ingredients:

- 2 frozen dinner rolls, thawed overnight like Rhodes White Yeast Dinner Rolls
- 1 large Granny Smith apple, cored, peeled and chopped
- ¼ cup brown sugar
- ¼ cup granulated white sugar
- 4 teaspoons ground cinnamon, divided
- ¼ cup of unsalted butter, melted

Method:
1. Cut the dinner rolls in half and then, flatten each into a 2-inch circle.
2. In a large bowl, add the apples, brown sugar and 2 teaspoons of cinnamon and mix well.
3. Place about 1 teaspoon of apple mixture filling in center of each circle.
4. Pinch the edges together to form a smooth ball.
5. Arrange the dough balls in the greased "Air Fry Basket" and insert in the oven. (Do not turn the oven on).
6. Let the dough rise for about 1 hour.
7. In a bowl, mix together the white sugar and remaining cinnamon.
8. Remove the basket from oven and brush the stuffed rolls with butter mixture generously.
9. Sprinkle with the cinnamon sugar on top.
10. Press "Power Button" of Air Fry Oven and turn the dial to select the "Air Fry" mode.
11. Press the Time button and again turn the dial to set the cooking time to 15 minutes.
12. Now push the Temp button and rotate the dial to set the temperature at 330 degrees F.
13. Press "Start/Pause" button to start.
14. When the unit beeps to show that it is preheated, open the lid.
15. Arrange the pan in "Air Fry Basket" and insert in the oven.
16. Place the pan onto a wire rack for about 5 minutes before serving.

Nutritional Information per Serving:
Calories 349; Total Fat 14.4 g; Saturated Fat 7.9 g; Cholesterol 32 mg; Sodium 315 mg

Cream Bread Rolls

Preparation Time: 20 minutes; Cooking Time: 55 minutes; Servings: 10
Ingredients:
- 1 cup milk
- ¾ cup whipping cream
- 1 large egg
- 4½ cups bread flour
- ½ cup all-purpose flour
- 2 tablespoons milk powder
- 1 teaspoon salt
- ¼ cup fine sugar
- 3 teaspoons dry yeast

Method:
1. In the baking pan of a bread machine, place all the ingredients in the order recommended by the manufacturer.
2. Place the baking pan in bread machine and close with the lid.
3. Select the "Dough" cycle and press Start button.
4. Once the cycle is completed, remove the paddles from bread machine but keep the dough inside for about 45-50 minutes to proof.
5. Grease 2 small loaf pans.
6. Remove the dough from pan and place onto a lightly floured surface.
7. Divide the dough into four equal-sized balls and then, roll each into a rectangle.
8. Tightly, roll each rectangle like a Swiss roll.
9. Place two rolls into each prepared loaf pan.
10. Set aside for about 1 hour.
11. Press "Power Button" of Air Fry Oven and turn the dial to select the "Air Bake" mode.
12. Press the Time button and again turn the dial to set the cooking time to 55 minutes.
13. Now push the Temp button and rotate the dial to set the temperature at 375 degrees F.

14. Press "Start/Pause" button to start.
15. When the unit beeps to show that it is preheated, open the lid.
16. Arrange the pans in "Air Fry Basket" and insert in the oven.
17. Place the pans onto a wire rack to cool for about 10 minutes.
18. Carefully, invert the bread onto wire rack to cool completely before slicing.
19. Cut the bread into desired-sized slices and serve.

Nutritional Information per Serving:
Calories 305; Total Fat 4.5 g; Saturated Fat 2.3 g; Cholesterol 31 mg; Sodium 265 mg

Buttered Dinner Rolls

Preparation Time: 15 minutes; Cooking Time: 30 minutes; Servings: 12

Ingredients:

- 1 cup milk
- 1 tablespoon coconut oil
- 1 tablespoon olive oil
- 3 cups plain flour
- 7½ tablespoons unsalted butter
- 1 teaspoon yeast
- Salt and ground black pepper, as required

Method:

1. In a pan, add the milk, coconut oil, and olive oil and cook until lukewarm.
2. Remove from the heat and stir well.
3. In a large bowl, add the flour, butter, yeast, salt, black pepper, and milk mixture and mix until a dough forms.
4. With your hands, knead for about 4-5 minutes
5. With a damp cloth, cover the dough and set aside in a warm place for about 5 minutes.
6. Again, with your hands, knead the dough for about 4-5 minutes
7. With a damp cloth, cover the dough and set aside in a warm place for about 30 minutes.
8. Place the dough onto a lightly floured surface.
9. Divide the dough into 12 equal pieces and form each into a ball.
10. Press "Power Button" of Air Fry Oven and turn the dial to select the "Air Fry" mode.
11. Press the Time button and again turn the dial to set the cooking time to 15 minutes.
12. Now push the Temp button and rotate the dial to set the temperature at 360 degrees F.
13. Press "Start/Pause" button to start.
14. When the unit beeps to show that it is preheated, open the lid.
15. Arrange half of the rolls in "Air Fry Basket" and insert in the oven.
16. Repeat with the remaining buns.
17. Place the pan onto a wire rack for about 5 minutes before serving.

Nutritional Information per Serving:
Calories 208; Total Fat 10.3 g; Saturated Fat 6 g; Cholesterol 121 mg; Sodium 72 mg

Milky Buns

Preparation Time: 15 minutes; Cooking Time: 10 minutes; Servings: 15

Ingredients:

For Buns:

- 1 1/3 cups plus 1½ tablespoons all-purpose flour
- 1½ tablespoons sugar
- 5 tablespoons milk
- 1/3 of egg
- 1 teaspoon instant yeast
- ½ teaspoon salt
- 1 oz. butter, melted

For Egg Wash:

- 1 egg yolk
- 1 tablespoon milk

Method:

1. In a large bowl, add all ingredients, except the butter and mix until a smooth and elastic dough forms.
2. Add the butter and mix until well combined.
3. With a mixer on low setting, mix the dough for at least 30 seconds.
4. With cling wrap, cover the dough and keep in warm place for about 2¾ hours.
5. Divide the dough into 15 equal sized buns.
6. For egg wash in a small bowl, mix together egg yolk and milk.
7. Brush the top of buns with egg wash.
8. With cling wrap, cover the buns and keep in warm place for about 45 minutes.
9. Arrange half of the buns into a greased baking pan.
10. Press "Power Button" of Air Fry Oven and turn the dial to select the "Air Fry" mode.
11. Press the Time button and again turn the dial to set the cooking time to 5 minutes.
12. Now push the Temp button and rotate the dial to set the temperature at 320 degrees F.
13. Press "Start/Pause" button to start.
14. When the unit beeps to show that it is preheated, open the lid.
15. Arrange the pan in "Air Fry Basket" and insert in the oven.
16. Repeat with the remaining buns.
17. Place the pan onto a wire rack for about 5 minutes before serving.

Nutritional Information per Serving:
Calories 67; Total Fat 2.2 g; Saturated Fat 1.2 g; Cholesterol 22 mg; Sodium 94 mg

Lemony Buns

Preparation Time: 20 minutes; Cooking Time: 16 minutes; Servings: 12
Ingredients:
For Buns:
- 3½ oz. butter
- 5 tablespoons caster sugar
- ½ teaspoon vanilla essence
- 2 medium eggs
- 2/3 cup self-rising flour

For Topping:
- 3½ tablespoons butter
- 1 cup icing sugar
- 1 tablespoon fresh lemon juice
- 1 teaspoon fresh lemon rind, grated finely

Method:
1. In a bowl, add butter and sugar and beat until light and fluffy.
2. Add the vanilla essence and ix well.
3. Add the eggs, one at a time with a little flour and eat until well combined.
4. Gently fold in remaining flour.
5. Fill the little bun cases with the mixture evenly.
6. Preheat the Airfryer to 340 degrees F.
7. Press "Power Button" of Air Fry Oven and turn the dial to select the "Air Fry" mode.
8. Press the Time button and again turn the dial to set the cooking time to 8 minutes.
9. Now push the Temp button and rotate the dial to set the temperature at 340 degrees F.
10. Press "Start/Pause" button to start.
11. When the unit beeps to show that it is preheated, open the lid.
12. Arrange 1 bun case in "Air Fry Basket" and insert in the oven.
13. Repeat with the remaining bun case.
14. Place the bun case onto a wire rack for about 5 minutes before serving.
15. For topping in a bowl, add the butter and beat until creamy.
16. Slowly, add the icing sugar, beating continuously.
17. Stir in lemon juice and rind.

18. Cut the buns in half.
19. Spread the lemon mixture over each half and serve.

Nutritional Information per Serving:
Calories 213; Total Fat 14.2 g; Saturated Fat 8.8g; Cholesterol 63 mg; Sodium 106 mg

Stilton Buns

Preparation Time: 15 minutes; Cooking Time: 15 minutes; Servings: 4
Ingredients:

- 3½ tablespoons butter, cubed
- 1/3 cup plain flour
- 1/3 cup stilton
- ¼ cup walnuts, chopped

Method:
1. In a food processor, add all ingredients and pulse until a dough forms.
2. Place the dough onto a lightly floured surface and roll into a log.
3. Wrap the log in a Clingfilm and freeze for about 30 minutes.
4. Cut the dough into about 1/3-inch rounds.
5. Press "Power Button" of Air Fry Oven and turn the dial to select the "Air Fry" mode.
6. Press the Time button and again turn the dial to set the cooking time to 15 minutes.
7. Now push the Temp button and rotate the dial to set the temperature at 355 degrees F.
8. Press "Start/Pause" button to start.
9. When the unit beeps to show that it is preheated, open the lid.
10. Arrange the dough rounds in greased "Air Fry Basket" and insert in the oven.
11. Place the buns onto a wire rack for about 5 minutes before serving.

Nutritional Information per Serving:
Calories 224; Total Fat 18.8 g; Saturated Fat 0.3 g; Cholesterol 40 mg; Sodium 263 mg

Parmesan Garlic Bread

Preparation Time: 15 minutes; Cooking Time: 5 minutes; Servings: 2
Ingredients:

- 2 dinner rolls
- ½ cup Parmesan cheese, grated
- 2 tablespoons butter, melted
- 2 tablespoons garlic and herb seasoning

Method:
1. With a knife, make a crisscross cut, almost all the way down into each roll, leaving the bottom crusts intact.
2. Then, stuff all the slits with Parmesan cheese.
3. Brush the tops of the rolls with melted butter and then, sprinkle with garlic seasoning.
4. Press "Power Button" of Air Fry Oven and turn the dial to select the "Air Fry" mode.
5. Press the Time button and again turn the dial to set the cooking time to 5 minutes.
6. Now push the Temp button and rotate the dial to set the temperature at 350 degrees F.
7. Press "Start/Pause" button to start.
8. When the unit beeps to show that it is preheated, open the lid.
9. Arrange the rolls in greased "Air Fry Basket" and insert in the oven.
10. Place the rolls onto a wire rack for about 5 minutes before serving.

Nutritional Information per Serving:
Calories 440; Total Fat 21.9 g; Saturated Fat 10.9 g; Cholesterol 50 mg; Sodium 815 mg

Chili Garlic Bread

Preparation Time: 10 minutes; Cooking Time: 2 minutes; Servings: 4
Ingredients:

- 4 bread slices, edges removed and halved
- 2 tablespoons butter, melted
- 6-8 garlic cloves, minced
- 2 tablespoons red pepper flakes, crushed

Method:
1. Coat each bread slice with butter and top with garlic evenly.
2. Press "Power Button" of Air Fry Oven and turn the dial to select the "Air Fry" mode.
3. Press the Time button and again turn the dial to set the cooking time to 2 minutes.
4. Now push the Temp button and rotate the dial to set the temperature at 360 degrees F.
5. Press "Start/Pause" button to start.
6. When the unit beeps to show that it is preheated, open the lid.
7. Arrange the bread slices into greased "Air Fry Basket" and insert in the oven.
8. Serve hot.

Nutritional Information per Serving:
Calories 90; Total Fat 6.5 g; Saturated Fat 3.8 g; Cholesterol 15 mg; Sodium 104 mg

Mozzarella Flatbread

Preparation Time: q5 minutes; Cooking Time: 5 minutes; Servings: 10
Ingredients:
- 1 tube prepared pizza dough
- ½ cup butter
- 1 teaspoon garlic
- Pinch of dried parsley
- 2 cups mozzarella cheese, shredded

Method:
1. Open and unroll the pizza dough.
2. From the long side, reroll the dough.
3. Cut 1-inch rolls from dough and then flatten each roll.
4. In a bowl, add the butter, garlic, and parsley and mix well.
5. Brush the top of dough with butter mixture.
6. Press "Power Button" of Air Fry Oven and turn the dial to select the "Air Fry" mode.
7. Press the Time button and again turn the dial to set the cooking time to 5 minutes.
8. Now push the Temp button and rotate the dial to set the temperature at 350 degrees F.
9. Press "Start/Pause" button to start.
10. When the unit beeps to show that it is preheated, open the lid.
11. Arrange the rolls in greased "Air Fry Basket" and insert in the oven.
12. Place the rolls onto a wire rack for about 5 minutes before serving.

Nutritional Information per Serving:
Calories1 26; Total Fat 12.1 g; Saturated Fat 6.9 g; Cholesterol 27 mg; Sodium 128 mg

Chapter 10: Dessert Recipes

Banana Split

Preparation Time: 15 minutes; Cooking Time: 14 minutes; Servings: 8
Ingredients:

- 3 tablespoons coconut oil
- 1 cup panko breadcrumbs
- ½ cup corn flour
- 2 eggs
- 4 bananas, peeled and halved lengthwise
- 3 tablespoons sugar
- ¼ teaspoon ground cinnamon
- 2 tablespoons walnuts, chopped

Method:
1. In a medium skillet, melt the coconut oil over medium heat and cook breadcrumbs for about 3-4 minutes or until golden browned and crumbled, stirring continuously.
2. Transfer the breadcrumbs into a shallow bowl and set aside to cool.
3. In a second bowl, place the corn flour.
4. In a third bowl, whisk the eggs.
5. Coat the banana slices with flour and then, dip into eggs and finally, coat evenly with the breadcrumbs.
6. In a small bowl, mix together the sugar and cinnamon.
7. Press "Power Button" of Air Fry Oven and turn the dial to select the "Air Fry" mode.
8. Press the Time button and again turn the dial to set the cooking time to 10 minutes.
9. Now push the Temp button and rotate the dial to set the temperature at 280 degrees F.
10. Press "Start/Pause" button to start.
11. When the unit beeps to show that it is preheated, open the lid.
12. Arrange the banana slices in "Air Fry Basket" and sprinkle with cinnamon sugar.
13. Insert the basket in the oven.
14. Transfer the banana slices onto plates to cool slightly
15. Sprinkle with chopped walnuts and serve.

Nutritional Information per Serving:
Calories 216; Total Fat 8.8g; Saturated Fat 5.3 g; Cholesterol 41 mg; Sodium 16 mg

Crispy Banana Slices

Preparation Time: 15 minutes; Cooking Time: 15 minutes; Servings: 8
Ingredients:

- 4 medium ripe bananas, peeled
- 1/3 cup rice flour, divided
- 2 tablespoons all-purpose flour
- 2 tablespoons corn flour
- 2 tablespoons desiccated coconut
- ½ teaspoon baking powder
- ½ teaspoon ground cardamom
- Pinch of salt
- Water, as required
- ¼ cup sesame seeds

Method:
1. In a shallow bowl, mix together 2 tablespoons of rice flour, all-purpose flour, corn flour, coconut, baking powder, cardamom, and salt.
2. Gradually, add the water and mix until a thick and smooth mixture forms.
3. In a second bowl, place the remaining rice flour.
4. In a third bowl, add the sesame seeds.
5. Cut each banana into half and then, cut each half in 2 pieces lengthwise.
6. Dip the banana slices into coconut mixture and then, coat with the remaining rice flour, followed by the sesame seeds.
7. Press "Power Button" of Air Fry Oven and turn the dial to select the "Air Fry" mode.
8. Press the Time button and again turn the dial to set the cooking time to 15 minutes.

9. Now push the Temp button and rotate the dial to set the temperature at 390 degrees F.
10. Press "Start/Pause" button to start.
11. When the unit beeps to show that it is preheated, open the lid.
12. Arrange the banana slices in "Air Fry Basket" and insert in the oven.
13. Transfer the banana slices onto plates to cool slightly
14. Transfer the banana slices onto plates to cool slightly before serving.

Nutritional Information per Serving:
Calories 121; Total Fat 3 g; Saturated Fat 0.8g; Cholesterol 0 mg; Sodium 21 mg

Pineapple Bites

Preparation Time: 10 minutes; Cooking Time: 10 minutes; Servings: 4
Ingredients:
For Pineapple Sticks:
- ½ of pineapple
- ¼ cup desiccated coconut

For Yogurt Dip:
- 1 tablespoon fresh mint leaves, minced
- 1 cup vanilla yogurt

Method:
1. Remove the outer skin of the pineapple and cut into long 1-2 inch thick sticks.
2. In a shallow dish place the coconut.
3. Coat the pineapple sticks with coconut evenly.
4. Press "Power Button" of Air Fry Oven and turn the dial to select the "Air Fry" mode.
5. Press the Time button and again turn the dial to set the cooking time to 10 minutes.
6. Now push the Temp button and rotate the dial to set the temperature at 390 degrees F.
7. Press "Start/Pause" button to start.
8. When the unit beeps to show that it is preheated, open the lid.
9. Arrange the pineapple sticks in lightly greased "Air Fry Basket" and insert in the oven.
10. Meanwhile, for dip in a bowl, mix together mint and yogurt.
11. Serve pineapple sticks with yogurt dip.

Nutritional Information per Serving:
Calories 124; Total Fat 2.6 g; Saturated Fat 21 g; Cholesterol 4 mg; Sodium 46 mg

Cheesecake Bites

Preparation Time: 20 minutes; Cooking Time: 2 minutes; Servings: 12
Ingredients:
- 8 oz. cream cheese, softened
- ½ cup plus 2 tablespoons sugar, divided
- 4 tablespoons heavy cream, divided
- ½ teaspoon vanilla extract
- ½ cup almond flour

Method:
1. In a bowl of a stand mixer, fitted with paddle attachment, add the cream cheese, ½ cup of sugar, 2 tablespoons of heavy cream and vanilla extract and beat until smooth.
2. With a scooper, scoop the mixture onto a parchment paper-lined baking pan.
3. Freeze for about 30 minutes or until firm.
4. In a small bowl, place the remaining cream.
5. In another small bowl, add the almond flour and remaining sugar and mix well.
6. Dip each cheesecake bite in cream and then coat with the flour mixture.
7. Press "Power Button" of Air Fry Oven and turn the dial to select the "Air Fry" mode.
8. Press the Time button and again turn the dial to set the cooking time to 2 minutes.
9. Now push the Temp button and rotate the dial to set the temperature at 300 degrees F.
10. Press "Start/Pause" button to start.
11. When the unit beeps to show that it is preheated, open the lid.

12. Arrange the pan in "Air Fry Basket" and insert in the oven.
13. Serve warm.

Nutritional Information per Serving:

Calories 149; Total Fat 10.7 g; Saturated Fat 5.5 g; Cholesterol 28 mg; Sodium 60 mg

Chocolate Bites

Preparation Time: 15 minutes; Cooking Time: 13 minutes; Servings: 8

Ingredients:

- 2 cups plain flour
- 2 tablespoons cocoa powder
- ½ cup icing sugar
- Pinch of ground cinnamon
- 1 teaspoon vanilla extract
- ¾ cup chilled butter
- ¼ cup chocolate, chopped into 8 chunks

Method:

1. In a bowl, mix together the flour, icing sugar, cocoa powder, cinnamon and vanilla extract.
2. With a pastry cutter, cut the butter and mix till a smooth dough forms.
3. Divide the dough into 8 equal-sized balls.
4. Press 1 chocolate chunk in the center of each ball and cover with the dough completely.
5. Place the balls into the baking pan.
6. Press "Power Button" of Air Fry Oven and turn the dial to select the "Air Fry" mode.
7. Press the Time button and again turn the dial to set the cooking time to 8 minutes.
8. Now push the Temp button and rotate the dial to set the temperature at 355 degrees F.
9. Press "Start/Pause" button to start.
10. When the unit beeps to show that it is preheated, open the lid.
11. Arrange the pan in "Air Fry Basket" and insert in the oven.
12. After 8 minutes of cooking, set the temperature at 320 degrees F for 5 minutes.
13. Place the baking pan onto the wire rack to cool completely before serving.

Nutritional Information per Serving:

Calories 328; Total Fat 19.3 g; Saturated Fat 12.2 g; Cholesterol 47 mg; Sodium 128 mg

Shortbread Fingers

Preparation Time: 15 minutes; Cooking Time: 12 minutes; Servings: 10

Ingredients:

- 1/3 cup caster sugar
- 1 2/3 cups plain flour
- ¾ cup butter

Method:

1. In a large bowl, mix together the sugar and flour.
2. Add the butter and mix until a smooth dough forms.
3. Cut the dough into 10 equal-sized fingers.
4. With a fork, lightly prick the fingers.
5. Place the fingers into the lightly greased baking pan.
6. Press "Power Button" of Air Fry Oven and turn the dial to select the "Air Fry" mode.
7. Press the Time button and again turn the dial to set the cooking time to 12 minutes.
8. Now push the Temp button and rotate the dial to set the temperature at 355 degrees F.
9. Press "Start/Pause" button to start.
10. When the unit beeps to show that it is preheated, open the lid.
11. Arrange the pan in "Air Fry Basket" and insert in the oven.
12. Place the baking pan onto a wire rack to cool for about 5-10 minutes.
13. Now, invert the short bread fingers onto wire rack to completely cool before serving.

Nutritional Information per Serving:

Calories 223; Total Fat 14 g; Saturated Fat 8.8 g; Cholesterol 37 mg; Sodium 99 mg

Berry Tacos

Preparation Time: 15 minutes; Cooking Time: 5 minutes; Servings: 2
Ingredients:
- 2 soft shell tortillas
- 4 tablespoons strawberry jelly
- ¼ cup fresh blueberries
- ¼ cup fresh raspberries
- 2 tablespoons powdered sugar

Method:
1. Spread 2 tablespoons of strawberry jelly over each tortilla
2. Top each with berries evenly and sprinkle with powdered sugar.
3. Press "Power Button" of Air Fry Oven and turn the dial to select the "Air Fry" mode.
4. Press the Time button and again turn the dial to set the cooking time to 5 minutes.
5. Now push the Temp button and rotate the dial to set the temperature at 300 degrees F.
6. Press "Start/Pause" button to start.
7. When the unit beeps to show that it is preheated, open the lid.
8. Arrange the tortillas in "Air Fry Basket" and insert in the oven.
9. Serve warm.

Nutritional Information per Serving:
Calories 216; Total Fat 0.8 g; Saturated Fat 0.1 g; Cholesterol 0mg; Sodium 11 mg

Apple Pastries

Preparation Time: 15 minutes; Cooking Time: 10 minutes; Servings: 6
Ingredients:
- ½ of large apple, peeled, cored and chopped
- 1 teaspoon fresh orange zest, grated finely
- ½ tablespoon white sugar
- ½ teaspoon ground cinnamon
- 7.05 oz. prepared frozen puff pastry

Method:
1. In a bowl, mix together all ingredients except puff pastry.
2. Cut the pastry in 16 squares.
3. Place about a teaspoon of the apple mixture in the center of each square.
4. Fold each square into a triangle and press the edges slightly with wet fingers.
5. Then with a fork, press the edges firmly.
6. Press "Power Button" of Air Fry Oven and turn the dial to select the "Air Fry" mode.
7. Press the Time button and again turn the dial to set the cooking time to 10 minutes.
8. Now push the Temp button and rotate the dial to set the temperature at 390 degrees F.
9. Press "Start/Pause" button to start.
10. When the unit beeps to show that it is preheated, open the lid.
11. Arrange the pastries in greased "Air Fry Basket" and insert in the oven.
12. Serve warm.

Nutritional Information per Serving:
Calories 198; Total Fat 12.7 g; Saturated Fat 3.2 g; Cholesterol 0 mg; Sodium 83 mg

Marshmallow Pastries

Preparation Time: 10 minutes; Cooking Time: 5 minutes; Servings: 4
Ingredients:
- 4 phyllo pastry sheets, thawed
- 2 oz. butter, melted
- ¼ cup chunky peanut butter
- 4 teaspoons marshmallow fluff
- Pinch of salt

Method:
1. Brush 1 sheet of phyllo with butter.
2. Place a second sheet of phyllo on top of first one and brush it with butter.
3. Repeat until all 4 sheets are used.
4. Cut the phyllo layers in 4 (3x12-inch) strips.
5. Place 1 tablespoon of peanut butter and 1 teaspoon of marshmallow fluff on the underside of a strip of phyllo.
6. Carefully, fold the tip of sheet over the filling to make a triangle.
7. Fold repeatedly in a zigzag manner until the filling is fully covered.
8. Press "Power Button" of Air Fry Oven and turn the dial to select the "Air Fry" mode.
9. Press the Time button and again turn the dial to set the cooking time to 5 minutes.
10. Now push the Temp button and rotate the dial to set the temperature at 360 degrees F.
11. Press "Start/Pause" button to start.
12. When the unit beeps to show that it is preheated, open the lid.
13. Arrange the pastries in greased "Air Fry Basket" and insert in the oven.
14. Sprinkle with a pinch of salt and serve warm.

Nutritional Information per Serving:
Calories 248; Total Fat 20.5 g; Saturated Fat 9.2 g; Cholesterol 30 mg; Sodium 268 mg

Nutella Banana Pastries

Preparation Time: 15 minutes; Cooking Time: 12 minutes; Servings: 4
Ingredients:
- 1 puff pastry sheet
- ½ cup Nutella
- 2 bananas, peeled and sliced

Method:
1. Cut the pastry sheet into 4 equal-sized squares.
2. Spread the Nutella on each square of pastry evenly.
3. Divide the banana slices over Nutella.
4. Fold each square into a triangle and with wet fingers, slightly press the edges.
5. Then with a fork, press the edges firmly.
6. Press "Power Button" of Air Fry Oven and turn the dial to select the "Air Fry" mode.
7. Press the Time button and again turn the dial to set the cooking time to 12 minutes.
8. Now push the Temp button and rotate the dial to set the temperature at 375 degrees F.
9. Press "Start/Pause" button to start.
10. When the unit beeps to show that it is preheated, open the lid.
11. Arrange the pastries in greased "Air Fry Basket" and insert in the oven.
12. Serve warm.

Nutritional Information per Serving:
Calories 221; Total Fat 10 g; Saturated Fat 2.7 g; Cholesterol 26 mg; Sodium 103 mg

Lemon Mousse

Preparation Time: 15 minutes; Cooking Time: 12 minutes; Servings: 2
Ingredients:
- 4 oz. cream cheese, softened
- ½ cup heavy cream
- 2 tablespoon fresh lemon juice
- 4-6 drops liquid stevia
- 2 pinches salt

Method:
1. In a bowl, add all the ingredients and mix until well combined.
2. Transfer the mixture into 2 ramekins.
3. Press "Power Button" of Air Fry Oven and turn the dial to select the "Air Bake" mode.

4. Press the Time button and again turn the dial to set the cooking time to 12 minutes.
5. Now push the Temp button and rotate the dial to set the temperature at 350 degrees F.
6. Press "Start/Pause" button to start.
7. When the unit beeps to show that it is preheated, open the lid.
8. Arrange the ramekins over the "Wire Rack" and insert in the oven.
9. Place the ramekins onto a wire rack to cool.
10. Refrigerate for at least 3 hours before serving.

Nutritional Information per Serving:
Calories 305; Total Fat 31 g; Saturated Fat 19.5 g; Cholesterol 103 mg; Sodium 337 mg

Chocolate Pudding

Preparation Time: 20 minutes; Cooking Time: 12 minutes; Servings: 4
Ingredients:
- ½ cup butter
- 2/3 cup dark chocolate, chopped
- ¼ cup caster sugar
- 2 medium eggs
- 2 teaspoons fresh orange rind, finely grated
- ¼ cup fresh orange juice
- 2 tablespoons self-rising flour

Method:
1. In a microwave-safe bowl, add the butter, and chocolate and microwave on high heat for about 2 minutes or until melted completely, stirring after every 30 seconds.
2. Remove from microwave and stir the mixture until smooth.
3. Add the sugar, and eggs and whisk until frothy.
4. Add the orange rind and juice, followed by flour and mix until well combined.
5. Divide mixture into 4 greased ramekins about ¾ full.
6. Press "Power Button" of Air Fry Oven and turn the dial to select the "Air Fry" mode.
7. Press the Time button and again turn the dial to set the cooking time to 12 minutes.
8. Now push the Temp button and rotate the dial to set the temperature at 355 degrees F.
9. Press "Start/Pause" button to start.
10. When the unit beeps to show that it is preheated, open the lid.
11. Arrange the ramekins in "Air Fry Basket" and insert in the oven.
12. Place the ramekins set aside to cool completely before serving.

Nutritional Information per Serving:
Calories 454; Total Fat 33.6 g; Saturated Fat 21.1 g; Cholesterol 149 mg; Sodium 217 mg

Vanilla Soufflé

Preparation Time: 15 minutes; Cooking Time: 23 minutes; Servings: 6
Ingredients:
- ¼ cup butter, softened
- ¼ cup all-purpose flour
- ½ cup plus 2 tablespoons sugar, divided
- 1 cup milk
- 3 teaspoons vanilla extract, divided
- 4 egg yolks
- 5 egg whites
- 1 teaspoon cream of tartar
- 2 tablespoons powdered sugar plus extra for dusting

Method:
1. In a bowl, add the butter, and flour and mix until a smooth paste forms.
2. In a medium pan, mix together ½ cup of sugar and milk over medium-low heat and cook for about 3 minutes or until the sugar is dissolved, stirring continuously.
3. Add the flour mixture, whisking continuously and simmer for about 3-4 minutes or until mixture becomes thick.
4. Remove from the heat and stir in 1 teaspoon of vanilla extract.

5. Set aside for about 10 minutes to cool.
6. In a bowl, add the egg yolks and 1 teaspoon of vanilla extract and mix well.
7. Add the egg yolk mixture into milk mixture and mix until well combined.
8. In another bowl, add the egg whites, cream of tartar, remaining sugar, and vanilla extract and with a wire whisk, beat until stiff peaks form.
9. Fold the egg whites mixture into milk mixture.
10. Grease 6 ramekins and sprinkle each with a pinch of sugar.
11. Place mixture into the prepared ramekins and with the back of a spoon, smooth the top surface.
12. Press "Power Button" of Air Fry Oven and turn the dial to select the "Air Fry" mode.
13. Press the Time button and again turn the dial to set the cooking time to 16 minutes.
14. Now push the Temp button and rotate the dial to set the temperature at 330 degrees F.
15. Press "Start/Pause" button to start.
16. When the unit beeps to show that it is preheated, open the lid.
17. Arrange the ramekins in "Air Fry Basket" and insert in the oven.
18. Place the ramekins onto a wire rack to cool slightly.
19. Sprinkle with the powdered sugar and serve warm.

Nutritional Information per Serving:
Calories 250; Total Fat 11.6 g; Saturated Fat 6.5 g; Cholesterol 163 mg; Sodium 107 mg

Chocolate Soufflé

Preparation Time: 15 minutes; Cooking Time: 16 minutes; Servings: 2
Ingredients:
- 3 oz. semi-sweet chocolate, chopped
- ¼ cup butter
- 2 eggs, yolks and whites separated
- 3 tablespoons sugar
- ½ teaspoon pure vanilla extract
- 2 tablespoons all-purpose flour
- 1 teaspoon powdered sugar plus extra for dusting

Method:
1. In a microwave-safe bowl, place the butter, and chocolate. Microwave on high heat for about 2 minutes or until melted completely, stirring after every 30 seconds.
2. Remove from microwave and stir the mixture until smooth.
3. In another bowl, add the egg yolks and whisk well.
4. Add the sugar, and vanilla extract and whisk well.
5. Add the chocolate mixture and mix until well combined.
6. Add the flour and mix well.
7. In a clean glass bowl, add the egg whites and whisk until soft peaks form.
8. Fold the whipped egg whites in 3 portions into the chocolate mixture.
9. Grease 2 ramekins and sprinkle each with a pinch of sugar.
10. Place mixture into the prepared ramekins and with the back of a spoon, smooth the top surface.
11. Press "Power Button" of Air Fry Oven and turn the dial to select the "Air Fry" mode.
12. Press the Time button and again turn the dial to set the cooking time to 14 minutes.
13. Now push the Temp button and rotate the dial to set the temperature at 330 degrees F.
14. Press "Start/Pause" button to start.
15. When the unit beeps to show that it is preheated, open the lid.
16. Arrange the ramekins in "Air Fry Basket" and insert in the oven.
17. Place the ramekins onto a wire rack to cool slightly.
18. Sprinkle with the powdered sugar and serve warm.

Nutritional Information per Serving:
Calories 591; Total Fat 38.7 g; Saturated Fat 23 g; Cholesterol 225 mg; Sodium 225 mg

Fudge Brownies

Preparation Time: 15 minutes; Cooking Time: 20 minutes; Servings: 8

Ingredients:

- 1 cup sugar
- ½ cup butter, melted
- ½ cup flour
- 1/3 cup cocoa powder
- 1 teaspoon baking powder
- 2 eggs
- 1 teaspoon vanilla extract

Method:

1. Grease a baking pan.
2. In a large bowl, add the sugar, and butter and whisk until light and fluffy.
3. Add the remaining ingredients and mix until well combined.
4. Place mixture into the prepared pan and with the back of spatula, smooth the top surface.
5. Press "Power Button" of Air Fry Oven and turn the dial to select the "Air Fry" mode.
6. Press the Time button and again turn the dial to set the cooking time to 20 minutes.
7. Now push the Temp button and rotate the dial to set the temperature at 350 degrees F.
8. Press "Start/Pause" button to start.
9. When the unit beeps to show that it is preheated, open the lid.
10. Arrange the pan in "Air Fry Basket" and insert in the oven.
11. Place the baking pan onto a wire rack to cool completely.
12. Cut into 8 equal-sized squares and serve.

Nutritional Information per Serving:

Calories 250; Total Fat 13.2 g; Saturated Fat 7.9 g; Cholesterol 71 mg; Sodium 99 mg

Walnut Brownies

Preparation Time: 15 minutes; Cooking Time: 22 minutes; Servings: 4

Ingredients:

- ½ cup chocolate, roughly chopped
- 1/3 cup butter
- 5 tablespoons sugar
- 1 egg, beaten
- 1 teaspoon vanilla extract
- Pinch of salt
- 5 tablespoons self-rising flour
- ¼ cup walnuts, chopped

Method:

1. In a microwave-safe bowl, add the chocolate and butter. Microwave on high heat for about 2 minutes, stirring after every 30 seconds.
2. Remove from microwave and set aside to cool.
3. In another bowl, add the sugar, egg, vanilla extract, and salt and whisk until creamy and light.
4. Add the chocolate mixture and whisk until well combined.
5. Add the flour, and walnuts and mix until well combined.
6. Line a baking pan with a greased parchment paper.
7. Place mixture evenly into the prepared pan and with the back of spatula, smooth the top surface.
8. Press "Power Button" of Air Fry Oven and turn the dial to select the "Air Fry" mode.
9. Press the Time button and again turn the dial to set the cooking time to 20 minutes.
10. Now push the Temp button and rotate the dial to set the temperature at 355 degrees F.
11. Press "Start/Pause" button to start.
12. When the unit beeps to show that it is preheated, open the lid.
13. Arrange the pan in "Air Fry Basket" and insert in the oven.
14. Place the baking pan onto a wire rack to cool completely.
15. Cut into 4 equal-sized squares and serve.

Nutritional Information per Serving:
Calories 407; Total Fat 27.4g; Saturated Fat 14.7 g; Cholesterol 86 mg; Sodium 180 mg

Nutella Banana Muffins

Preparation Time: 15 minutes; Cooking Time: 25 minutes; Servings: 12

Ingredients:

- 1 2/3 cups plain flour
- 1 teaspoon baking soda
- 1 teaspoon baking powder
- 1 teaspoon ground cinnamon
- ¼ teaspoon salt
- 4 ripe bananas, peeled and mashed
- 2 eggs
- ½ cup brown sugar
- 1 teaspoon vanilla essence
- 3 tablespoons milk
- 1 tablespoon Nutella
- ¼ cup walnuts

Method:

1. Grease 12 muffin molds. Set aside.
2. In a large bowl, sift together the flour, baking soda, baking powder, cinnamon, and salt.
3. In another bowl, mix together the remaining ingredients except walnuts.
4. Add the banana mixture into flour mixture and mix until just combined.
5. Fold in the walnuts.
6. Place the mixture into the prepared muffin molds.
7. Press "Power Button" of Air Fry Oven and turn the dial to select the "Air Fry" mode.
8. Press the Time button and again turn the dial to set the cooking time to 25 minutes.
9. Now push the Temp button and rotate the dial to set the temperature at 250 degrees F.
10. Press "Start/Pause" button to start.
11. When the unit beeps to show that it is preheated, open the lid.
12. Arrange the muffin molds in "Air Fry Basket" and insert in the oven.
13. Place the muffin molds onto a wire rack to cool for about 10 minutes.
14. Carefully, invert the muffins onto the wire rack to completely cool before serving.

Nutritional Information per Serving:
Calories 227; Total Fat 6.6 g; Saturated Fat 1.5 g; Cholesterol 45 mg; Sodium 221 mg

Blueberry Muffins

Preparation Time: 15 minutes; Cooking Time: 12 minutes; Servings: 12

Ingredients:

- 2 cups plus 2 tablespoons self-rising flour
- 5 tablespoons white sugar
- ½ cup milk
- 2 oz. butter, melted
- 2 eggs
- 2 teaspoons fresh orange zest, finely grated
- 2 tablespoons fresh orange juice
- ½ teaspoon vanilla extract
- ½ cup fresh blueberries

Method:

1. Grease 12 muffin molds. Set aside.
2. In a bowl, mix together the flour, and white sugar.
3. In another large bowl, mix well the remaining ingredients except blueberries.
4. Add the flour mixture and mix until just combined.
5. Fold in the blueberries.
6. Place the mixture into the prepared muffin molds.
7. Press "Power Button" of Air Fry Oven and turn the dial to select the "Air Fry" mode.
8. Press the Time button and again turn the dial to set the cooking time to 12 minutes.
9. Now push the Temp button and rotate the dial to set the temperature at 355 degrees F.
10. Press "Start/Pause" button to start.

11. When the unit beeps to show that it is preheated, open the lid.
12. Arrange the muffin molds in "Air Fry Basket" and insert in the oven.
13. Place the muffin molds onto a wire rack to cool for about 10 minutes.
14. Carefully, invert the muffins onto the wire rack to completely cool before serving.

Nutritional Information per Serving:
Calories 149; Total Fat 5 g; Saturated Fat 2.8 g; Cholesterol 38 mg; Sodium 43 mg

Cranberry Muffins

Preparation Time: 15 minutes; Cooking Time: 15 minutes; Servings: 8

Ingredients:
- ¼ cup unsweetened almond milk
- 2 large eggs
- ½ teaspoon vanilla extract
- 1½ cups almond flour
- ¼ cup Erythritol
- 1 teaspoon baking powder
- ¼ teaspoon ground cinnamon
- 1/8 teaspoon salt
- ½ cup fresh cranberries
- ¼ cup walnuts, chopped

Method:
1. In a blender, add the almond milk, eggs and vanilla extract and pulse for about 20-30 seconds.
2. Add the almond flour, Erythritol, baking powder, cinnamon and salt and pulse for about 30-45 seconds until well blended.
3. Transfer the mixture into a bowl.
4. Gently, fold in half of the cranberries and walnuts.
5. Place the mixture into 8 silicone muffin cups and top each with remaining cranberries.
6. Press "Power Button" of Air Fry Oven and turn the dial to select the "Air Fry" mode.
7. Press the Time button and again turn the dial to set the cooking time to 15 minutes.
8. Now push the Temp button and rotate the dial to set the temperature at 325 degrees F.
9. Press "Start/Pause" button to start.
10. When the unit beeps to show that it is preheated, open the lid.
11. Arrange the muffin cups in "Air Fry Basket" and insert in the oven.
12. Place the muffin molds onto a wire rack to cool for about 10 minutes.
13. Carefully, invert the muffins onto the wire rack to completely cool before serving.

Nutritional Information per Serving:
Calories 175; Total Fat 13.6 g; Saturated Fat 1.3 g; Cholesterol 47 mg; Sodium 66 mg

Brownie Muffins

Preparation Time: 10 minutes; Cooking Time: 10 minutes; Servings: 12

Ingredients:
- 1 package Betty Crocker fudge brownie mix
- ¼ cup walnuts, chopped
- 1 egg
- 1/3 cup vegetable oil
- 2 teaspoons water

Method:
1. Grease 12 muffin molds. Set aside.
2. In a bowl, mix together all the ingredients.
3. Place the mixture into the prepared muffin molds.
4. Press "Power Button" of Air Fry Oven and turn the dial to select the "Air Fry" mode.
5. Press the Time button and again turn the dial to set the cooking time to 10 minutes.
6. Now push the Temp button and rotate the dial to set the temperature at 300 degrees F.
7. Press "Start/Pause" button to start.
8. When the unit beeps to show that it is preheated, open the lid.
9. Arrange the muffin molds in "Air Fry Basket" and insert in the oven.

10. Place the muffin molds onto a wire rack to cool for about 10 minutes.
11. Carefully, invert the muffins onto the wire rack to completely cool before serving.

Nutritional Information per Serving:
Calories 168; Total Fat 8.9 g; Saturated Fat 1.4 g; Cholesterol 14 mg; Sodium 89 mg

Double Chocolate Muffins

Preparation Time: 15 minutes; Cooking Time: 15 minutes; Servings: 12

Ingredients:

- 1 1/3 cups self-rising flour
- 2/3 cup plus 3 tablespoons caster sugar
- 2½ tablespoons cocoa powder
- 3½ oz. butter
- 5 tablespoons milk
- 2 medium eggs
- ½ teaspoon vanilla extract
- Water, as required
- 2½ oz. milk chocolate, finely chopped

Method:

1. In a bowl, mix together the flour, sugar, and cocoa powder.
2. With a pastry cutter, cut in the butter until a breadcrumb like mixture forms.
3. In another bowl, mix together the milk, and eggs.
4. Add the egg mixture into flour mixture and mix until well combined.
5. Add the vanilla extract and a little water and mix until well combined.
6. Fold in the chopped chocolate.
7. Place the mixture into the prepared muffin molds.
8. Press "Power Button" of Air Fry Oven and turn the dial to select the "Air Fry" mode.
9. Press the Time button and again turn the dial to set the cooking time to 9 minutes.
10. Now push the Temp button and rotate the dial to set the temperature at 355 degrees F.
11. Press "Start/Pause" button to start.
12. When the unit beeps to show that it is preheated, open the lid.
13. Arrange the muffin molds in "Air Fry Basket" and insert in the oven.
14. After 9 minutes of cooking, set the temperature at 320 degrees F for 6 minutes.
15. Place the muffin molds onto a wire rack to cool for about 10 minutes.
16. Carefully, invert the muffins onto the wire rack to completely cool before serving.

Nutritional Information per Serving:
Calories 200; Total Fat 9.6 g; Saturated Fat 5.9 g; Cholesterol 47 mg; Sodium 66 mg

Strawberry Cupcakes

Preparation Time: 20 minutes; Cooking Time: 8 minutes; Servings: 10

Ingredients:

For Cupcakes

- ½ cup caster sugar
- 7 tablespoons butter
- 2 eggs
- ½ teaspoon vanilla essence
- 7/8 cup self-rising flour

For Frosting

- 1 cup icing sugar
- 3½ tablespoons butter
- 1 tablespoon whipped cream
- ¼ cup fresh strawberries, pureed
- ½ teaspoon pink food color

Method:

1. In a bowl, add the butter, and sugar and beat until fluffy and light.
2. Add the eggs, one at a time and beat until well combined.
3. Stir in the vanilla extract.
4. Gradually, add the flour beating continuously until well combined.
5. Place the mixture into 10 silicon cups.

6. Press "Power Button" of Air Fry Oven and turn the dial to select the "Air Fry" mode.
7. Press the Time button and again turn the dial to set the cooking time to 8 minutes.
8. Now push the Temp button and rotate the dial to set the temperature at 340 degrees F.
9. Press "Start/Pause" button to start.
10. When the unit beeps to show that it is preheated, open the lid.
11. Arrange the silicon cups in "Air Fry Basket" and insert in the oven.
12. Place the silicon cups onto a wire rack to cool for about 10 minutes.
13. Carefully, invert the muffins onto the wire rack to completely cool before frosting.
14. For frosting: in a bowl, add the icing sugar, and butter and whisk until fluffy and light.
15. Add the whipped cream, strawberry puree, and color. Mix until well combined.
16. Fill the pastry bag with frosting and decorate the cupcakes.

Nutritional Information per Serving:
Calories 250; Total Fat 13.6 g; Saturated Fat 8.2 g; Cholesterol 66 mg; Sodium 99 mg

Raspberry Cupcakes

Preparation Time: 15 minutes; Cooking Time: 15 minutes; Servings: 10
Ingredients:

- 4½ oz. self-rising flour
- ½ teaspoon baking powder
- Pinch of salt
- ½ oz. cream cheese, softened
- 4¾ oz. butter, softened
- 4¼ oz. caster sugar
- 2 eggs
- 2 teaspoons fresh lemon juice
- ½ cup fresh raspberries

Method:
1. In a bowl, mix together the flour, baking powder, and salt.
2. In another bowl, mix together the cream cheese, and butter.
3. Add the sugar and beat until fluffy and light.
4. Add the eggs, one at a time and whisk until just combined.
5. Add the flour mixture and stir until well combined.
6. Stir in the lemon juice.
7. Place the mixture into silicon cups and top each with 2 raspberries.
8. Press "Power Button" of Air Fry Oven and turn the dial to select the "Air Fry" mode.
9. Press the Time button and again turn the dial to set the cooking time to 15 minutes.
10. Now push the Temp button and rotate the dial to set the temperature at 365 degrees F.
11. Press "Start/Pause" button to start.
12. When the unit beeps to show that it is preheated, open the lid.
13. Arrange the silicon cups in "Air Fry Basket" and insert in the oven.
14. Place the silicon cups onto a wire rack to cool for about 10 minutes.
15. Carefully, invert the cupcakes onto the wire rack to completely cool before serving.

Nutritional Information per Serving:
Calories 209; Total Fat 12.5 g; Saturated Fat 7.5 g; Cholesterol 63 mg; Sodium 110 mg

Red Velvet Cupcakes

Preparation Time: 20 minutes; Cooking Time: 12 minutes; Servings: 12
Ingredients:
For Cupcakes

- 2 cups refined flour
- ¾ cup icing sugar
- 2 teaspoons beet powder
- 1 teaspoon cocoa powder
- ¾ cup peanut butter
- 3 eggs

For Frosting
- 1 cup butter

- 1 (8-oz.) package cream cheese, softened
- 2 teaspoons vanilla extract
- ¼ teaspoon salt
- 4½ cups powdered sugar

For Garnishing
- ½ cup fresh raspberries

Method:
1. For cupcakes: in a bowl, add all the ingredients and with an electric whisker, whisk until well combined.
2. Place the mixture into silicon cups.
3. Press "Power Button" of Air Fry Oven and turn the dial to select the "Air Fry" mode.
4. Press the Time button and again turn the dial to set the cooking time to 12 minutes.
5. Now push the Temp button and rotate the dial to set the temperature at 340 degrees F.
6. Press "Start/Pause" button to start.
7. When the unit beeps to show that it is preheated, open the lid.
8. Arrange the silicon cups in "Air Fry Basket" and insert in the oven.
9. Place the silicon cups onto a wire rack to cool for about 10 minutes.
10. Carefully, invert the cupcakes onto the wire rack to completely cool before frosting.
11. For frosting: in a large bowl, mix well butter, cream cheese, vanilla extract, and salt.
12. Add the powdered sugar, one cup at a time, whisking well after each addition.
13. Spread frosting evenly over each cupcake.
14. Garnish with raspberries and serve.

Nutritional Information per Serving:
Calories 599; Total Fat 31.5 g; Saturated Fat 16 g; Cholesterol 102 mg; Sodium 308 mg

Banana Mug Cake

Preparation Time: 15 minutes; Cooking Time: 30 minutes; Serving: 1

Ingredients:
- ¼ cup all-purpose flour
- 1/8 teaspoon ground cinnamon
- ¼ teaspoon baking soda
- 1/8 teaspoon salt
- ½ cup banana, peeled and mashed
- 2 tablespoons sugar
- 1 tablespoon butter, melted
- 1 egg yolk
- ¼ teaspoon vanilla extract

Method:
1. In a bowl, mix together the flour, baking soda, cinnamon and salt.
2. In another bowl, add the mashed banana and sugar and beat well.
3. Add the butter, the egg yolk, and the vanilla and mix well.
4. Add the flour mixture and mix until just combined.
5. Place the mixture into a lightly greased ramekin.
6. Press "Power Button" of Air Fry Oven and turn the dial to select the "Air Bake" mode.
7. Press the Time button and again turn the dial to set the cooking time to 30 minutes.
8. Now push the Temp button and rotate the dial to set the temperature at 350 degrees F.
9. Press "Start/Pause" button to start.
10. When the unit beeps to show that it is preheated, open the lid.
11. Arrange the ramekin over the "Wire Rack" and insert in the oven.
12. Place the ramekin onto a wire rack to cool slightly before serving.

Nutritional Information per Serving:
Calories 430; Total Fat 16.6 g; Saturated Fat 9 g; Cholesterol 240 mg; Sodium 697 mg

Carrot Mug Cake

Preparation Time: 15 minutes; Cooking Time: 20 minutes; Serving: 1

Ingredients:
- ¼ cup whole-wheat pastry flour
- 1 tablespoon coconut sugar
- ¼ teaspoon baking powder
- 1/8 teaspoon ground cinnamon
- 1/8 teaspoon ground ginger
- Pinch of ground cloves
- Pinch of ground allspice
- Pinch of salt
- 2 tablespoons plus 2 teaspoons unsweetened almond milk
- 2 tablespoons carrot, peeled and grated
- 2 tablespoons walnuts, chopped
- 1 tablespoon raisins
- 2 teaspoons applesauce

Method:
1. In a bowl, mix together the flour, sugar, baking powder, spices and salt.
2. Add the remaining ingredients and mix until well combined.
3. Place the mixture into a lightly greased ramekin.
4. Press "Power Button" of Air Fry Oven and turn the dial to select the "Air Bake" mode.
5. Press the Time button and again turn the dial to set the cooking time to 20 minutes.
6. Now push the Temp button and rotate the dial to set the temperature at 350 degrees F.
7. Press "Start/Pause" button to start.
8. When the unit beeps to show that it is preheated, open the lid.
9. Arrange the ramekin over the "Wire Rack" and insert in the oven.
10. Place the ramekin onto a wire rack to cool slightly before serving.

Nutritional Information per Serving:
Calories 301; Total Fat 10.1 g; Saturated Fat 0.7 g; Cholesterol 0 mg; Sodium 191 mg

Chocolate Mug Cake

Preparation Time: 15 minutes; Cooking Time: 13 minutes; Serving: 1
Ingredients:
- ¼ cup self-rising flour
- 5 tablespoons caster sugar
- 1 tablespoon cocoa powder
- 3 tablespoons coconut oil
- 3 tablespoons whole milk

Method:
1. In a shallow mug, add all the ingredients and mix until well combined.
2. Press "Power Button" of Air Fry Oven and turn the dial to select the "Air Fry" mode.
3. Press the Time button and again turn the dial to set the cooking time to 13 minutes.
4. Now push the Temp button and rotate the dial to set the temperature at 392 degrees F.
5. Press "Start/Pause" button to start.
6. When the unit beeps to show that it is preheated, open the lid.
7. Arrange the mug in "Air Fry Basket" and insert in the oven.
8. Place the mug onto a wire rack to cool slightly before serving.

Nutritional Information per Serving:
Calories 729; Total Fat 43.3 g; Saturated Fat 36.6 g; Cholesterol 5 mg; Sodium 20 mg

Chocolate Lava Cake

Preparation Time: 10 minutes; Cooking Time: 9 minutes; Servings: 4
Ingredients:
- 2/3 cup chocolate chips
- ½ cup unsalted butter, softened
- 2 large eggs
- 2 large egg yolks
- 1 cup confectioners' sugar
- 1 teaspoon peppermint extract
- 1/3 cup all-purpose flour plus more for dusting
- 2 tablespoons powdered sugar
- 1/3 cup fresh raspberries

Method:

1. Grease 4 ramekins and dust each with a little flour.
2. In a microwave-safe bowl, add the chocolate chips and butter. Microwave on high heat for about 30 seconds.
3. Remove the bowl from microwave and stir the mixture well.
4. Add the eggs, egg yolks and confectioners' sugar and whisk until well combined.
5. Add the flour and gently, stir to combine.
6. Place mixture into the prepared ramekins evenly.
7. Press "Power Button" of Air Fry Oven and turn the dial to select the "Air Fry" mode.
8. Press the Time button and again turn the dial to set the cooking time to 12 minutes.
9. Now push the Temp button and rotate the dial to set the temperature at 375 degrees F.
10. Press "Start/Pause" button to start.
11. When the unit beeps to show that it is preheated, open the lid.
12. Arrange the ramekins in "Air Fry Basket" and insert in the oven.
13. Place the ramekins onto a wire rack to cool for about 5 minutes.
14. Carefully run a knife around sides of each ramekin several times to loosen the cake.
15. Carefully, invert each cake onto a dessert plate and dust with powdered sugar.
16. Garnish with raspberries and serve immediately.

Nutritional Information per Serving:
Calories 598; Total Fat 36.2 g; Saturated Fat 22 g; Cholesterol 265 mg; Sodium 225 mg

Butter Cake

Preparation Time: 15 minutes; Cooking Time: 15 minutes; Servings: 6
Ingredients:
- 3 oz. butter, softened
- ½ cup caster sugar
- 1 egg
- 1 1/3 cups plain flour, sifted
- Pinch of salt
- ½ cup milk
- 1 tablespoon icing sugar

Method:
1. In a bowl, add the butter, and sugar and whisk until light and creamy.
2. Add the egg and whisk until smooth and fluffy.
3. Add the flour, and salt and mix well alternately with the milk.
4. Grease a small Bundt cake pan.
5. Place mixture evenly into the prepared cake pan.
6. Press "Power Button" of Air Fry Oven and turn the dial to select the "Air Fry" mode.
7. Press the Time button and again turn the dial to set the cooking time to 15 minutes.
8. Now push the Temp button and rotate the dial to set the temperature at 350 degrees F.
9. Press "Start/Pause" button to start.
10. When the unit beeps to show that it is preheated, open the lid.
11. Arrange the pan in "Air Fry Basket" and insert in the oven.
12. Place the cake pan onto a wire rack to cool for about 10 minutes.
13. Carefully, invert the cake onto wire rack to completely cool before slicing.
14. Dust the cake with icing sugar and cut into desired size slices.

Nutritional Information per Serving:
Calories 291; Total Fat 12.9 g; Saturated Fat 7.8 g; Cholesterol 59 mg; Sodium 129 mg

Semolina Cake

Preparation Time: 15 minutes; Cooking Time: 15 minutes; Servings: 6
Ingredients:
- 2½ cups semolina
- ½ cup vegetable oil
- 1 cup milk
- 1 cup plain Greek yogurt

- 1 cup sugar
- ½ teaspoon baking soda
- 1½ teaspoons baking powder
- Pinch of salt
- ¼ cup raisins
- ¼ cup walnuts, chopped

Method:
1. In a bowl, mix together the semolina, oil, milk, yogurt, and sugar.
2. Cover and set aside for about 15 minutes.
3. In the bowl f semolina mixture, add the baking soda, baking powder, and salt in the bowl of semolina mixture and mix until well combined.
4. Fold in the raisins and walnuts.
5. Place the mixture evenly into a lightly greased cake pan.
6. Press "Power Button" of Air Fry Oven and turn the dial to select the "Air Fry" mode.
7. Press the Time button and again turn the dial to set the cooking time to 15 minutes.
8. Now push the Temp button and rotate the dial to set the temperature at 320 degrees F.
9. Press "Start/Pause" button to start.
10. When the unit beeps to show that it is preheated, open the lid.
11. Arrange the pan in "Air Fry Basket" and insert in the oven.
12. Place the cake pan onto a wire rack to cool for about 10 minutes.
13. Carefully, invert the cake onto wire rack to completely cool before slicing.
14. Cut the cake into desired-sized slices and serve.

Nutritional Information per Serving:
Calories 637; Total Fat 23.3 g; Saturated Fat 4.8 g; Cholesterol 6 mg; Sodium 181 mg

Chocolate Cream Cake

Preparation Time: 15 minutes; Cooking Time: 25 minutes; Servings: 6
Ingredients:
- 1 cup flour
- 1/3 cup cocoa powder
- 1 teaspoon baking powder
- ½ teaspoon baking soda
- 1/8 teaspoon salt
- 3 eggs
- 2/3 cup sugar
- ½ cup sour cream
- ½ cup butter, softened
- 2 teaspoons vanilla extract

Method:
1. In a large bowl, mix together the flour, cocoa powder, baking powder, baking soda, and salt.
2. Add the remaining ingredients and with an electric whisker, whisk on low speed until well combined.
3. Lightly, grease a cake pan.
4. Place the mixture evenly into a lightly greased cake pan.
5. Press "Power Button" of Air Fry Oven and turn the dial to select the "Air Fry" mode.
6. Press the Time button and again turn the dial to set the cooking time to 25 minutes.
7. Now push the Temp button and rotate the dial to set the temperature at 320 degrees F.
8. Press "Start/Pause" button to start.
9. When the unit beeps to show that it is preheated, open the lid.
10. Arrange the pan in "Air Fry Basket" and insert in the oven.
11. Place the cake pan onto a wire rack to cool for about 10 minutes.
12. Carefully, invert the cake onto wire rack to completely cool before slicing.
13. Cut the cake into desired-sized slices and serve.

Nutritional Information per Serving:
Calories 383; Total Fat 22.4 g; Saturated Fat 13.3 g; Cholesterol 131 mg; Sodium 307 mg

Mini Cheesecakes

Preparation Time: 15 minutes; Cooking Time: 10 minutes; Servings: 2
Ingredients:
- ¾ cup Erythritol
- 2 eggs
- 1 teaspoon vanilla extract
- ½ teaspoon fresh lemon juice
- 16 oz. cream cheese, softened
- 2 tablespoon sour cream

Method:
1. In a blender, add the Erythritol, eggs, vanilla extract and lemon juice and pulse until smooth.
2. Add the cream cheese and sour cream and pulse until smooth.
3. Place the mixture into 2 (4-inch) springform pans evenly.
4. Press "Power Button" of Air Fry Oven and turn the dial to select the "Air Fry" mode.
5. Press the Time button and again turn the dial to set the cooking time to 10 minutes.
6. Now push the Temp button and rotate the dial to set the temperature at 350 degrees F.
7. Press "Start/Pause" button to start.
8. When the unit beeps to show that it is preheated, open the lid.
9. Arrange the pans in "Air Fry Basket" and insert in the oven.
10. Place the pans onto a wire rack to cool completely.
11. Refrigerate overnight before serving.

Nutritional Information per Serving:
Calories 886; Total Fat 86 g; Saturated Fat 52.8 g; Cholesterol 418 mg; Sodium 740 mg

Vanilla Cheesecake

Preparation Time: 15 minutes; Cooking Time: 14 minutes; Servings: 6
Ingredients:
- 1 cup honey graham cracker crumbs
- 2 tablespoons unsalted butter, softened
- 1 lb. cream cheese, softened
- ½ cup sugar
- 2 large eggs
- ½ teaspoon vanilla extract

Method:
1. Line a round baking pan with parchment paper.
2. For crust: in a bowl, add the graham cracker crumbs, and butter.
3. Place the crust into baking dish and press to smooth.
4. Press "Power Button" of Air Fry Oven and turn the dial to select the "Air Fry" mode.
5. Press the Time button and again turn the dial to set the cooking time to 4 minutes.
6. Now push the Temp button and rotate the dial to set the temperature at 350 degrees F.
7. Press "Start/Pause" button to start.
8. When the unit beeps to show that it is preheated, open the lid.
9. Arrange the baking pan of crust in "Air Fry Basket" and insert in the oven.
10. Place the crust aside to cool for about 10 minutes.
11. Meanwhile, in a bowl, add the cream cheese, and sugar and whisk until smooth.
12. Now, place the eggs, one at a time and whisk until mixture becomes creamy.
13. Add the vanilla extract and mix well.
14. Place the cream cheese mixture evenly over the crust.
15. Press "Power Button" of Air Fry Oven and turn the dial to select the "Air Fry" mode.
16. Press the Time button and again turn the dial to set the cooking time to 10 minutes.
17. Now push the Temp button and rotate the dial to set the temperature at 350 degrees F.
18. Press "Start/Pause" button to start.
19. When the unit beeps to show that it is preheated, open the lid.

20. Arrange the baking pan of crust in "Air Fry Basket" and insert in the oven.
21. Place the pan onto a wire rack to cool completely.
22. Refrigerate overnight before serving.

Nutritional Information per Serving:

Calories 470; Total Fat 33.9 g; Saturated Fat 20.6 g; Cholesterol 155 mg; Sodium 42 mg

Ricotta Cheesecake

Preparation Time: 15 minutes; Cooking Time: 25 minutes; Servings: 8

Ingredients:

- 17.6 oz. ricotta cheese
- 3 eggs
- ¾ cup sugar
- 3 tablespoons corn starch
- 1 tablespoon fresh lemon juice
- 2 teaspoons vanilla extract
- 1 teaspoon fresh lemon zest, finely grated

Method:

1. In a large bowl, place all ingredients and mix until well combined.
2. Place the mixture into a baking pan.
3. Press "Power Button" of Air Fry Oven and turn the dial to select the "Air Fry" mode.
4. Press the Time button and again turn the dial to set the cooking time to 25 minutes.
5. Now push the Temp button and rotate the dial to set the temperature at 320 degrees F.
6. Press "Start/Pause" button to start.
7. When the unit beeps to show that it is preheated, open the lid.
8. Arrange the pan in "Air Fry Basket" and insert in the oven.
9. Place the cake pan onto a wire rack to cool completely.
10. Refrigerate overnight before serving.

Nutritional Information per Serving:

Calories 197; Total Fat 6.6 g; Saturated Fat 3.6 g; Cholesterol 81 mg; Sodium 102 mg

Pecan Pie

Preparation Time: 15 minutes; Cooking Time: 35 minutes; Servings: 5

Ingredients:

- ¾ cup brown sugar
- ¼ cup caster sugar
- 1/3 cup butter, melted
- 2 large eggs
- 1¾ tablespoons flour
- 1 tablespoon milk
- 1 teaspoon vanilla extract
- 1 cup pecan halves
- 1 frozen pie crust, thawed

Method:

1. In a large bowl, mix together the sugars, and butter.
2. Add the eggs and whisk until foamy.
3. Add the flour, milk, and vanilla extract and whisk until well combined.
4. Fold in the pecan halves.
5. Grease a pie pan.
6. Arrange the crust in the bottom of prepared pie pan.
7. Place the pecan mixture over the crust evenly.
8. Press "Power Button" of Air Fry Oven and turn the dial to select the "Air Fry" mode.
9. Press the Time button and again turn the dial to set the cooking time to 22 minutes.
10. Now push the Temp button and rotate the dial to set the temperature at 300 degrees F.
11. Press "Start/Pause" button to start.
12. When the unit beeps to show that it is preheated, open the lid.
13. Arrange the pan in "Air Fry Basket" and insert in the oven.
14. After 22 minutes of cooking, to set the temperature at w85 degrees F for 13 minutes.

15. Place the pie pan onto a wire rack to cool for about 10-15 minutes before serving.

Nutritional Information per Serving:

Calories 501; Total Fat 35 g; Saturated Fat 10.8 g; Cholesterol 107 mg; Sodium 187 mg

Fruity Crumble

Preparation Time: 15 minutes; Cooking Time: 20 minutes; Servings: 4

Ingredients:

- ½ lb. fresh apricots, pitted and cubed
- 1 cup fresh blackberries
- 1/3 cup sugar, divided
- 1 tablespoon fresh lemon juice
- 7/8 cup flour
- Pinch of salt
- 1 tablespoon cold water
- ¼ cup chilled butter, cubed

Method:

1. Grease a baking pan.
2. In a large bowl, mix well apricots, blackberries, 2 tablespoons of sugar, and lemon juice.
3. Spread apricot mixture into the prepared baking pan.
4. In another bowl, add the flour, remaining sugar, salt, water, and butter and mix until a crumbly mixture forms.
5. Spread the flour mixture over apricot mixture evenly.
6. Press "Power Button" of Air Fry Oven and turn the dial to select the "Air Fry" mode.
7. Press the Time button and again turn the dial to set the cooking time to 20 minutes.
8. Now push the Temp button and rotate the dial to set the temperature at 390 degrees F.
9. Press "Start/Pause" button to start.
10. When the unit beeps to show that it is preheated, open the lid.
11. Arrange the pan in "Air Fry Basket" and insert in the oven.
12. Place the pan onto a wire rack to cool for about 10-15 minutes before serving.

Nutritional Information per Serving:

Calories 307; Total Fat 12.4 g; Saturated Fat 7.4 g; Cholesterol 31 mg; Sodium 123 mg

Cherry Clafoutis

Preparation Time: 15 minutes; Cooking Time: 25 minutes; Servings: 4

Ingredients:

- 1½ cups fresh cherries, pitted
- 3 tablespoons vodka
- ¼ cup flour
- 2 tablespoons sugar
- Pinch of salt
- ½ cup sour cream
- 1 egg
- 1 tablespoon butter
- ¼ cup powdered sugar

Method:

1. In a bowl, mix together the cherries and vodka.
2. In another bowl, mix together the flour, sugar, and salt.
3. Add the sour cream, and egg and mix until a smooth dough forms.
4. Grease a cake pan.
5. Place flour mixture evenly into the prepared cake pan.
6. Spread cherry mixture over the dough.
7. Place butter on top in the form of dots.
8. Press "Power Button" of Air Fry Oven and turn the dial to select the "Air Fry" mode.
9. Press the Time button and again turn the dial to set the cooking time to 25 minutes.
10. Now push the Temp button and rotate the dial to set the temperature at 355 degrees F.
11. Press "Start/Pause" button to start.
12. When the unit beeps to show that it is preheated, open the lid.
13. Arrange the pan in "Air Fry Basket" and insert in the oven.

14. Place the pan onto a wire rack to cool for about 10-15 minutes before serving.
15. Now, invert the Clafoutis onto a platter and sprinkle with powdered sugar.
16. Cut the Clafoutis into desired size slices and serve warm.

Nutritional Information per Serving:
Calories 241; Total Fat 10.1 g; Saturated Fat 5.9 g; Cholesterol 61 mg; Sodium 90 mg

Apple Bread Pudding

Preparation Time: 15 minutes; Cooking Time: 44 minutes; Servings: 8
Ingredients:
For Bread Pudding:
- 10½ oz. bread, cubed
- ½ cup apple, peeled, cored and chopped
- ½ cup raisins
- ¼ cup walnuts, chopped
- 1½ cups milk
- ¾ cup water
- 5 tablespoons honey
- 2 teaspoons ground cinnamon
- 2 teaspoons cornstarch
- 1 teaspoon vanilla extract

For Topping:
- 1 1/3 cups plain flour
- 3/5 cup brown sugar
- 7 tablespoons butter

Method:
1. In a large bowl, mix together the bread, apple, raisins, and walnuts.
2. In another bowl, add the remaining pudding ingredients and mix until well combined.
3. Add the milk mixture into bread mixture and mix until well combined.
4. Refrigerate for about 15 minutes, tossing occasionally.
5. For topping: in a bowl, mix together the flour and sugar.
6. With a pastry cutter, cut in the butter until a crumbly mixture forms.
7. Place the mixture into 2 baking pans and spread the topping mixture on top of each.
8. Press "Power Button" of Air Fry Oven and turn the dial to select the "Air Fry" mode.
9. Press the Time button and again turn the dial to set the cooking time to 22 minutes.
10. Now push the Temp button and rotate the dial to set the temperature at 355 degrees F.
11. Press "Start/Pause" button to start.
12. When the unit beeps to show that it is preheated, open the lid.
13. Arrange 1 pan in "Air Fry Basket" and insert in the oven.
14. Place the pan onto a wire rack to cool slightly before serving.
15. Repeat with the remaining pan.
16. Serve warm.

Nutritional Information per Serving:
Calories 432; Total Fat 14.8 g; Saturated Fat 7.4 g; Cholesterol 30 mg; Sodium 353mg

Raisin Bread Pudding

Preparation Time: 15 minutes; Cooking Time: 12 minutes; Servings: 3
Ingredients:
- 1 cup milk
- 1 egg
- 1 tablespoon brown sugar
- ½ teaspoon ground cinnamon
- ¼ teaspoon vanilla extract
- 2 tablespoons raisins, soaked in hot water for about 15 minutes
- 2 bread slices, cut into small cubes
- 1 tablespoon chocolate chips
- 1 tablespoon sugar

Method:
1. In a bowl, mix together the milk, egg, brown sugar, cinnamon, and vanilla extract.
2. Stir in the raisins.

3. In a baking pan, spread the bread cubes and top evenly with the milk mixture.
4. Refrigerate for about 15-20 minutes.
5. Press "Power Button" of Air Fry Oven and turn the dial to select the "Air Fry" mode.
6. Press the Time button and again turn the dial to set the cooking time to 12 minutes.
7. Now push the Temp button and rotate the dial to set the temperature at 375 degrees F.
8. Press "Start/Pause" button to start.
9. When the unit beeps to show that it is preheated, open the lid.
10. Arrange the pan over the "Wire Rack" and insert in the oven.
11. Serve warm.

Nutritional Information per Serving:
Calories 143; Total Fat 4.4 g; Saturated Fat 2.2 g; Cholesterol 628 mg; Sodium 104 mg

Donuts Pudding

Preparation Time: 15 minutes; Cooking Time: 1 hour; Servings: 6

Ingredients:
- 6 glazed donuts, cut into small pieces
- ¾ cup frozen sweet cherries
- ½ cup raisins
- ½ cup semi-sweet chocolate baking chips
- ¼ cup sugar
- 1 teaspoon ground cinnamon
- 4 egg yolks
- 1½ cups whipping cream

Method:
1. In a large bowl, mix together the donut pieces, cherries, raisins, chocolate chips, sugar, and cinnamon.
2. In another bowl, add the egg yolks, and whipping cream and whisk until well combined.
3. Add the egg yolk mixture into doughnut mixture and mix well.
4. Line a baking dish with a piece of foil.
5. Place donuts mixture into the prepared baking pan.
6. Press "Power Button" of Air Fry Oven and turn the dial to select the "Air Fry" mode.
7. Press the Time button and again turn the dial to set the cooking time to 60 minutes.
8. Now push the Temp button and rotate the dial to set the temperature at 360 degrees F.
9. Press "Start/Pause" button to start.
10. When the unit beeps to show that it is preheated, open the lid.
11. Arrange the pan in "Air Fry Basket" and insert in the oven.
12. Place the pan onto a wire rack to cool for about 10-15 minutes before serving.
13. Serve warm.

Nutritional Information per Serving:
Calories 537; Total Fat 28.7 g; Saturated Fat 12.2 g; Cholesterol 173 mg; Sodium 194 mg

Buttery Scallops

Prep Time: 10 minutes; Cooking Time: 25 minutes; Serving: 8

Ingredients
- 2 lb. scallops
- 6 tablespoons butter, melted
- 2 tablespoons dry white wine
- 1 tablespoon lemon juice
- 1/2 cup Parmesan cheese, grated
- 1 teaspoon salt
- 1/2 teaspoon black pepper
- 1 teaspoon garlic powder
- 1 teaspoon dried parsley
- 1/8 teaspoon cayenne pepper
- 1/4 teaspoon sweet paprika
- 2 tablespoons parsley chopped

Method:
1. Mix everything in a bowl except scallops.
2. Toss in scallops and mix well to coat them.

3. Spread the scallops with the sauce in a baking tray.
4. Press "Power Button" of Air Fry Oven and turn the dial to select the "Bake" mode.
5. Press the Time button and again turn the dial to set the cooking time to 25 minutes.
6. Now push the Temp button and rotate the dial to set the temperature at 350 degrees F.
7. Once preheated, place the scallop's baking tray in the oven and close its lid.
8. Serve warm.

Nutritional Information per Serving:
Calories 227; Total Fat 10.1g; Saturated Fat 5.7g; Cholesterol 89mg; Sodium 388mg

Crusted Scallops

Prep Time: 10 minutes; Cooking Time: 20 minutes; Serving: 4
Ingredients
- 1 1/2 lbs. bay scallops, rinsed
- 3 garlic cloves, minced
- 1/2 cup panko crumbs
- 1 teaspoon onion powder
- 4 tablespoons butter, melted
- 1/2 teaspoon cayenne pepper
- 1 teaspoon garlic powder
- 1/4 cup Parmesan cheese, shredded

Method:
1. Mix everything in a bowl except scallops.
2. Toss in scallops and mix well to coat them.
3. Spread the scallops with the sauce in a baking tray.
4. Press "Power Button" of Air Fry Oven and turn the dial to select the "Bake" mode.
5. Press the Time button and again turn the dial to set the cooking time to 20 minutes.
6. Now push the Temp button and rotate the dial to set the temperature at 400 degrees F.
7. Once preheated, place the scallop's baking tray in the oven and close its lid.

Nutritional Information per Serving:
Calories 242; Total Fat 11.1g; Saturated Fat 6.4g; Cholesterol 65mg; Sodium 500mg

Lobster Tails with White Wine Sauce

Prep Time: 10 minutes; Cooking Time: 14 minutes; Serving: 4
Ingredients
- 4 lobster tails, shell cut from the top
- 1/2 onion, quartered
- 1/2 cup butter
- 1/3 cup wine
- 1/4 cup honey
- 6 garlic cloves crushed
- 1 tablespoon lemon juice
- 1 teaspoon salt or to taste
- Cracked pepper to taste
- Lemon slices to serve
- 2 tablespoons fresh chopped parsley

Method:
1. Place the lobster tails in the oven's baking tray.
2. Whisk rest of the ingredients in a bowl and pour over the lobster tails.
3. Press "Power Button" of Air Fry Oven and turn the dial to select the "Broil" mode.
4. Press the Time button and again turn the dial to set the cooking time to 14 minutes.
5. Now push the Temp button and rotate the dial to set the temperature at 350 degrees F.
6. Once preheated, place the lobster's baking tray in the oven and close its lid.
7. Serve warm.

Nutritional Information per Serving:
Calories 340; Total Fat 23.1g; Saturated Fat 14.6g; Cholesterol 61mg; Sodium 1249mg

Broiled Lobster Tails

Prep Time: 10 minutes; Cooking Time: 6 minutes; Serving: 4
Ingredients

- 2 lobster tails, shell cut from the top
- 1/2 cup butter, melted
- 1/2 teaspoon ground paprika
- Salt to taste
- White pepper, to taste
- 1 lemon, juiced

Method:
1. Place the lobster tails in the oven's baking tray.
2. Whisk rest of the ingredients in a bowl and pour over the lobster tails.
3. Press "Power Button" of Air Fry Oven and turn the dial to select the "Broil" mode.
4. Press the Time button and again turn the dial to set the cooking time to 6 minutes.
5. Now push the Temp button and rotate the dial to set the temperature at 350 degrees F.
6. Once preheated, place the lobster's baking tray in the oven and close its lid.
7. Serve warm.

Nutritional Information per Serving:
   Calories 227; Total Fat 23.1g; Saturated Fat 14.6g; Cholesterol 61mg; Sodium 414mg

Paprika Lobster Tail

Prep Time: 10 minutes; Cooking Time: 10 minutes; Serving: 4
Ingredients
- 2 (4 to 6 oz) Lobster Tails, shell cut from the top
- 1/8 teaspoon salt
- 1/8 teaspoon black pepper
- 1/8 teaspoon paprika
- 2 tablespoon butter
- 1/2 lemon, cut into wedges
- Chopped parsley for garnish

Method:
1. Place the lobster tails in the oven's baking tray.
2. Whisk rest of the ingredients in a bowl and pour over the lobster tails.
3. Press "Power Button" of Air Fry Oven and turn the dial to select the "Broil" mode.
4. Press the Time button and again turn the dial to set the cooking time to 10 minutes.
5. Now push the Temp button and rotate the dial to set the temperature at 350 degrees F.
6. Once preheated, place the lobster's baking tray in the oven and close its lid.
7. Serve warm.

Nutritional Information per Serving:
   Calories 204; Total Fat 12.5g; Saturated Fat 7.5g; Cholesterol 196mg; Sodium 780mg

Lobster Tails with Lemon Butter

Prep Time: 10 minutes; Cooking Time: 8 minutes; Serving: 4
Ingredients
- 4 lobster tails, shell cut from the top
- 1 tablespoon fresh parsley, chopped
- 2 garlic cloves, pressed
- 1 teaspoon Dijon mustard
- 1/4 teaspoon salt
- 1/8 teaspoon black pepper
- 1 1/2 tablespoon olive oil
- 1 1/2 tablespoon fresh lemon juice
- 4 tablespoon butter, divided

Method:
1. Place the lobster tails in the oven's baking tray.
2. Whisk rest of the ingredients in a bowl and pour over the lobster tails.
3. Press "Power Button" of Air Fry Oven and turn the dial to select the "Broil" mode.
4. Press the Time button and again turn the dial to set the cooking time to 8 minutes.
5. Now push the Temp button and rotate the dial to set the temperature at 350 degrees F.
6. Once preheated, place the lobster's baking tray in the oven and close its lid.
7. Serve warm.

Nutritional Information per Serving:
   Calories 281; Total Fat 18.1g; Saturated Fat 8.4g; Cholesterol 242mg; Sodium 950mg

Sheet Pan Seafood bake

Prep Time: 10 minutes; Cooking Time: 14 minutes; Serving: 4

Ingredients

- 2 corn ears, husked and diced
- 1 lb. red potatoes, boiled, diced
- 2 lbs. clams, scrubbed
- 1 lb. shrimp, peeled and de-veined
- 12 oz. sausage, sliced
- 1/2 red onion, sliced
- 4 lobster tails, peeled
- black pepper to taste
- 1 lemon, cut into wedges
- 1 cup butter
- 3 teaspoons minced garlic
- 1 tablespoon Old Bay seasoning
- fresh parsley for garnish

Method:

1. Toss all the veggies, corn, seafood, oil, and seasoning in a baking tray.
2. Press "Power Button" of Air Fry Oven and turn the dial to select the "Broil" mode.
3. Press the Time button and again turn the dial to set the cooking time to 14 minutes.
4. Now push the Temp button and rotate the dial to set the temperature at 425 degrees F.
5. Once preheated, place the seafood's baking tray in the oven and close its lid.
6. Serve warm.

Nutritional Information per Serving:

Calories 532; Total Fat 35.6g; Saturated Fat 18.8g; Cholesterol 219mg; Sodium 1379mg

Chapter 11: Meal Plan for 30 Days

Day 1

Breakfast: Cheddar Omelet

Lunch: Lemony Green Beans

Dinner: Chicken Drumsticks

Day 2

Breakfast: Cinnamon French Toast

Lunch: Tofu with Cauliflower

Dinner: Honey Glazed Salmon

Day 3

Breakfast: Savory Carrot Muffins

Lunch: Seasoned Zucchini & Squash

Dinner: Garlic Braised Ribs

Day 4

Breakfast: Sweet Potato Rosti

Lunch: Feta Spinach

Dinner: Seasoned Catfish

Day 5

Breakfast: Eggs with Turkey & Spinach

Lunch: Mushroom with Peas

Dinner: Pork Sirloin Steak

Day 6

Breakfast: Yogurt Bread

Lunch: Prawn Burgers

Dinner: Pork Au Gratin

Day 7

Breakfast: Chicken & Broccoli Quiche

Lunch: Curried Eggplant

Dinner: Lamb Shanks with Garlic

Day 8

Breakfast: Eggs in Bread & Bacon Cups

Lunch: Carrot with Spinach

Dinner: Cod Parcel

Day 9

Breakfast: Potato & Bell Pepper Hash

Lunch: Spicy Butternut Squash

Dinner: Basic Meatloaf

Day 10

Breakfast: Chicken Omelet

Lunch: Veggie Ratatouille

Dinner: Lamb with Pea Couscous

Day 11

Breakfast: Mini Mushroom Frittatas

Lunch: Tofu with Capers

Dinner: Braised Pork Shanks

Day 12

Breakfast: Sausage & Bell Pepper Casserole

Lunch: Stuffed Okra

Dinner: Maple Chicken Thighs

Day 13

Breakfast: Eggs, Tofu & Mushroom Omelet

Lunch: Glazed Veggies

Dinner: BBQ Beef Roast

Day 14

Breakfast: Mini Macaroni Quiches

Lunch: Garlic Shrimp

Dinner: Pork Chops with Cashew Sauce

Day 15

Breakfast: Ricotta Toasts with Salmon

Lunch: Broccoli with Olives

Dinner: Beef Short Ribs

Day 15

Breakfast: Ham & Hash Brown Casserole

Lunch: Stuffed Bell Peppers

Dinner: Braised Pork Shanks

Day 16

Breakfast: Spinach Muffins

Lunch: Chicken Mushroom Kebabs

Dinner: Ranch Tilapia

Day 17

Breakfast: Cheddar Mustard Toasts

Lunch: Potato Gratin

Dinner: Roasted Turkey Breast

Day 18

Breakfast: Trout Frittata

Lunch: Glazed Veggies

Dinner: Tarragon Beef Shanks

Day 19

Breakfast: Strawberry Bread

Lunch: Chicken Fajita Skewers

Dinner: Lamb Rack with Lemon Crust

Day 20

Breakfast: Pumpkin Pancakes

Lunch: Garlic Mussels

Dinner: Potato Pork Satay

Day 21

Breakfast: Eggs in Avocado Cups

Lunch: Beans & Veggie Burgers

Dinner: Oregano Chicken Breast

Day 22

Breakfast: Apple Bread

Lunch: Italian Shrimp Skewers

Dinner: Roasted Pork Shoulder

Day 23

Breakfast: Tomato Quiche

Lunch: Wine Braised Mushrooms

Dinner: Blackened Chicken Bake

Day 24

Breakfast: Ham Muffins

Lunch: Parmesan Mixed Veggies

Dinner: Glazed Halibut

Day 25

Breakfast: Sweet Spiced French Toast

Lunch: Tofu in Sweet & Sour Sauce

Dinner: Garlicky Lamb Chops

Day 26

Breakfast: Eggs in Bread & Tomato Cups

Lunch: Tahini Pork Kebabs

Dinner: Chicken Alfredo Bake

Day 27

Breakfast: Pancetta & Spinach Frittata

Lunch: Broccoli with Sweet Potatoes

Dinner: Rosemary Beef Roast

Day 28

Breakfast: Eggs with Ham

Lunch: Stuffed Tomatoes

Dinner: Sauce Glazed Meatloaf

Day 29

Breakfast: Zucchini Fritters

Lunch: Onion Lamb Kebabs

Dinner: Thyme Turkey Breast

Day 30

Breakfast: Blueberry Muffins

Lunch: Tarragon Yellow Squash

Dinner: Buttered Salmon

Conclusion

Now you know that Air fryer ovens are no less than a kitchen miracle, which have significantly brought ease and convenience with their user-friendly control systems, time and energy-efficient heating mechanism, and multiplicity of the cooking options. In this cookbook, the author has managed to share as many as different recipes, to provide an extensive guideline to all the frequent oven users. With its latest technology, you can bake, air fry, broil, dehydrate, toast, and roast all sorts of the meal, whether it is your morning breakfast or range of seafood, poultry, pork, beef, lamb, and vegetables. Give it a full read and find out tons of new ways to add more colors and flavors to your dinner table using the latest Air fryer ovens.

Made in the USA
Middletown, DE
12 August 2020